ENGLISH LITERATURE

FROM THE 19th CENTURY THROUGH TODAY

ENGLISH LITERATURE

FROM THE 19th CENTURY THROUGH TODAY

EDITED BY J.E. LUEBERING, MANAGER AND
SENIOR EDITOR, LITERATURE

Britannica®
Educational Publishing

IN ASSOCIATION WITH

ROSEN
EDUCATIONAL SERVICES

Published in 2011 by Britannica Educational Publishing
(a trademark of Encyclopædia Britannica, Inc.)
in association with Rosen Educational Services, LLC
29 East 21st Street, New York, NY 10010.

For a listing of additional Britannica Educational Publishing titles, call toll free (800) 237-9932.

First Edition

Britannica Educational Publishing
Michael I. Levy: Executive Editor
J.E. Luebering: Senior Manager
Marilyn L. Barton: Senior Coordinator, Production Control
Steven Bosco: Director, Editorial Technologies
Lisa S. Braucher: Senior Producer and Data Editor
Yvette Charboneau: Senior Copy Editor
Kathy Nakamura: Manager, Media Acquisition
J.E. Luebering: Senior Editor, Literature

Rosen Educational Services
Jeanne Nagle: Senior Editor
Nelson Sá: Art Director, Designer
Cindy Reiman: Photography Manager
Matthew Cauli: Designer, Cover Design
Introduction by Richard Barrington

Library of Congress Cataloging-in-Publication Data

English literature from the 19th century through today / edited by J.E. Luebering.
p. cm. — (The Britannica guide to world literature)
In association with Britannica Educational Publishing, Rosen Educational Services.
Includes bibliographical references and index.
ISBN 978-1-61530-117-1 (library binding)
1. English literature—19th century—History and criticism. 2. English literature—20th
century—History and criticism. I. Luebering, J.E.
PR451.E555 2010
820.9—dc22

2010014261

Manufactured in the United States of America

On the cover: George Eliot (right) helped popularize the novel and Tom Stoppard
continues to energize the stage and screen. *London Stereoscopic Company/Hulton Archive/Getty
Images (Eliot); Hal Horowitz/WireImage/Getty Images (Stoppard).*

On page 8: An illustration from an early edition of Robert Louis Stevenson's *Treasure Island.*
Mansell/Time & Life Pictures/Getty Images

Pages 16 (map), 280, 282, 284, 287 © www.istockphoto.com / Nicholas Belton; pp. 16 (books),
17, 141, 233 © www.istockphoto.com

CONTENTS

**Chapter 2: The 20th Century:
From 1900 to 1945**   **141**

148

160

188

222

235

243

251

271

INTRODUCTION

The history of English literature is itself like a well-written novel or drama. Events build on one another, as each new wave of writers impacts both the overall body of work and the subsequent efforts of other writers. There are unexpected twists and turns, as the styles and subject matter of English literature have sometimes rebelled against existing conventions or simply moved in unprecedented directions. Finally, as with any good story, the pace of action in English literature has seemed to accelerate over time, with the most recent two centuries representing an era of prolific productivity and creativity.

This volume explores representative authors and movements of the 19th and 20th centuries. Many beloved works of English literature have been produced in this period. Because this flowering of poetry, prose, and drama continues to the present day, readers of this book will come away with not just a sense of this literature's history, but an appreciation for the ongoing literary environment in which they live.

The modern era of English literature can be traced to the emergence of the novel as an all-conquering force in the literary marketplace during the reign of Queen Victoria (1837–1901). There is an image of Victorian times as dignified to the point of repression, but the mid-to-late 19th century actually represented a tumultuous era in British history. Great Britain's rise to the stature of leading world power was juxtaposed with deepening urban poverty at home. During Victoria's reign, an economic crisis in the 1840s, democratic reforms in the 1860s and 1880s, and growing demands for women's suffrage were all elements of a period marked by rapid, and sometimes wrenching, changes.

The emergence of Charles Dickens onto this scene roughly coincided with the beginning of Queen Victoria's reign. For the next four decades, he was to capture the public's imagination with a wide range of works, including his first published novel, the comic *Pickwick Papers*; works with serious themes such as *David Copperfield*, *Bleak House*, and *Hard Times*; and a masterpiece from late in his career, *Great Expectations*.

Part of Dickens' popularity stemmed from the then-new practice of serializing novels, which meant they were published in weekly or monthly installments. This approach lent itself to Dickens' gift for creating a rich gallery of intricately crafted character studies. Most of all, his ability to combine humour with an unflinching look at some of life's hardships and injustices made Dickens popular in his day, and also marked him as an enduring and important novelist.

While Dickens stands out in particular, there were other noteworthy novelists in this period. The late 1840s, for example, saw the publication of major novels by William Makepeace Thackeray, Elizabeth Gaskell, and Benjamin Disraeli (who would later become prime minister). This same period also saw first novels published by Charles Kingsley, Anthony Trollope, and the Brontë sisters, Charlotte, Emily, and Anne.

In some ways, it was as if a torch had been passed. A generation earlier, the prime years of the Romantic poets had put poetry in the centre of the literary stage. Now, in the mid-1800s, it seemed that the finest literary talents of the age were expressing themselves in prose fiction. The Brontës had actually started out as poets, and their sensibilities represent a translation of the Romantic tradition into the novel. In turn, this longer form allowed the sisters to break new ground in presenting a woman's point of view, both emotionally and intellectually. They did this to great effect. For all their Gothic atmosphere, the best works of the Brontë sisters, including *Jane Eyre* by Charlotte and *Wuthering Heights* by Emily, combine precise detail of place and dialect with strong psychological elements.

Even with the novel attracting so much talent, some writers kept the English poetic tradition alive after the end of the Romantic period, including Alfred Tennyson, Robert Browning, and Elizabeth Barrett Browning. Still, as the 19th century moved into its latter half, it was the novel that continued to show the steepest trajectory of popular and artistic growth.

A prime contributor to late Victorian fiction was Mary Ann Evans, who published under the name George Eliot. From early works such as *The Mill on the Floss* to her later masterpiece *Middlemarch*, Eliot brings to bear some of the observational wit of Jane Austen. Rather than dealing with the relatively simple dilemmas of society and romance, however, Eliot uses her impeccably crafted fiction to analyze the deep internal ethical and existential dilemmas of her characters. With this complex subject matter being juxtaposed against highly realistic depictions of provincial settings, the effect is especially striking.

Eliot stands out, but she was far from alone in producing distinguished work in the latter half of the 1800s. Part of the richness of this period is that it embraced so many different styles; realism battled with a revival of Gothic and Romantic themes, not to mention with early examples of science fiction. Writers as diverse as George Meredith, Robert Louis Stevenson, Oscar Wilde, and H.G. Wells thrived during these years.

One of the greatest lights of the late 19th century was Thomas Hardy. His books dealt with tragic themes that were highly personal, but on a larger scale, his rural settings embodied a simplicity and tranquility that was being lost to the modern world. Whatever ambivalence Hardy may have felt toward the passage of time, with novels such as *The Mayor of Casterbridge*, *Tess of the D'Urbervilles*, and *Jude the Obscure*, he helped bring the century, and the Victorian era, to a close with English prose fiction in top form.

It is natural for the turning of any century to bring feelings of a new beginning and a break from the past, but when the 19th century gave way to the 20th, change on the calendar was accompanied by genuinely radical changes in society and politics, as well as science and technology. This conflict was natural material for some novelists. Wells, along with Joseph Conrad and E.M. Forster, examined the toll taken by progress and commerce on cultures and individual lives.

Other writers reacted to encroaching modernity by looking backward, reviving traditional forms and themes. Hardy, who turned to poetry in the new century and equaled his earlier standard of success as a novelist, was an example of this wistful traditionalism, along with Rudyard Kipling, G.K. Chesterton, and A.E. Housman.

By the beginning of the 20th century, some poets and novelists were eager to rebel against the traditions of the past. These writers came to be known as the Modernists. They used free verse, unconventional language, and experimental forms not simply to liberate forms of expression from traditional boundaries, but to emphasize individual perception rather than a uniform, linear account of events. Their sentiment was that traditional literature had become tiresome, and that more insightful modes of expression were needed.

Here, the history of English literature intertwines significantly with that of American and Irish literature, as some of the most prominent figures of the Modernist movement were American or Irish writers who at times lived and worked in England. They were to have a tremendous influence on the development of poetry and the novel in English. These writers included the poets Ezra

Pound, T.S. Eliot, and William Butler Yeats, and the novelist James Joyce.

In his novel *Ulysses*, Joyce used stream of consciousness to relate the inner observations and fantasies of various characters. In the process, he suggested that there were certain universal sentiments buried beneath the restrictions and conventions of society. He echoed this theme later in the even more experimental *Finnegans Wake*.

Yeats, on the other hand, presented a somewhat more curious example of Modernism. While he explored the structural and linguistic freedoms of the movement, his themes often centred on an idealized vision of his native Ireland that could be traced as far back as the Romanticism of the early 19th century. Yeats wrote in sympathy with Irish nationalism, but his works are more in touch with the historic ideals of an independent Ireland than with the violence of the nationalist movement. Part of Yeats's maturity as a poet stems from his recognition that his version of Ireland was something of a myth, and this self-awareness adds poignancy to his work.

Another noteworthy Modernist was Virginia Woolf. Writing primarily in the period between World Wars I and II, Woolf was part of a community of writers and artists known as the Bloomsbury group. Part of the ethic of this group was that the pursuit of artistic honesty represented an antidote to what they viewed as the stifling hypocrisy of their parents' generation. While class tensions had long been a theme of English literature, the post-World War I period brought to the fore expressions of the generational tensions that would come to be so heavily associated with 20th century literature. To Woolf and her contemporaries, not only were traditional morals outdated, but so were established forms of fiction. In such works as *To the Lighthouse*, Woolf demonstrated how the internal arc of a character could be more important to a novel than the outward flow of events.

As the period between the wars progressed, the tone of English literature reflected the deepening pessimism of a world that found itself in an economic depression and heading toward a second global conflict. Themes of class injustice, sexual repression, and the decline of England's vitality were explored with increasing frankness and starkness. The novelist George Orwell and the poet W.H. Auden were among the writers who found their voices during this period. Ultimately, though, during World War II it was the more established T.S. Eliot who best summed up the challenges of the times. His *Four Quartets* is a search for a response in the midst of the destruction of war that is more constructive than despair, more thoughtful than nationalism.

Religion influenced the post-war works of artists such as Eliot, Auden, and Evelyn Waugh. At the same time, the shadow of totalitarianism loomed over the works of Orwell, as well as William Golding's *Lord of the Flies* and Muriel Spark's *The Prime of Miss Jean Brodie*. These novels are notable for being concise and compact, with symbols and allegory becoming almost a form of shorthand to expedite storytelling.

A counterpoint to the parables of Golding and Spark were the highly personal and sometimes brutally detailed and direct works of the Angry Young Men, a group of writers in the 1950s and 1960s that included Alan Sillitoe, John Osborne, and Kingsley Amis. As art often does, though, English literature subsequently swung in the opposite direction, with the last decades of the 20th century marked by novels of a more epic scale, often looking back on Great Britain's colonial past and examining the dismantling of its empire.

Twentieth-century English poetry also saw some swings of the stylistic pendulum. At mid-century, poetry was characterized by the New Apocalypse movement. Writers of this school, such as Dylan Thomas, favoured grand statements in flamboyant language. In contrast, poetry of the latter part of the century typically exhibited a more understated style, like that of Philip Larkin. The autobiographical approach of Ted Hughes and Seamus Heaney also became common.

As for the theatre, English drama broke out of its comfortable, conventional mold with such plays as Osborne's *Look Back in Anger*, which simmered with raw emotion. Another revolt against conventional theatre came in the form of the Theatre of the Absurd. These plays represented a deconstruction of traditional storytelling. Examples were as varied as Samuel Beckett's sparsely populated *Waiting for Godot* and Tom Stoppard's witty *Rosencrantz and Guildenstern Are Dead*, a retelling of *Hamlet* from the point of view of two minor characters. Effectively, this reinvention of the theatre led to the late 20th century becoming, arguably, the most productive period for top-quality drama in English since at least the Restoration period.

The 21st century has begun with the major aspects of English literature—the novel, the short story, poetry, and drama—all in fine form. As a result, the examination of English literature found in the pages that follow is not so much a study of the past as a look at a story in progress. That makes this subject all the more rewarding. After all, the joy of reading is not in finishing a book, but in experiencing a story that has reached its fullest momentum. The story told in this book shows that English literature is at just such a sweet spot. It is well established, yet new developments continue to come every year. The story is far from over.

CHAPTER 1

THE POST-ROMANTIC AND VICTORIAN ERAS

S elf-consciousness was the quality that John Stuart Mill identified, in 1838, as "the daemon of the men of genius of our time." Introspection was inevitable in the literature of an immediately Post-Romantic period, and the age itself was as prone to self-analysis as were its individual authors. Hazlitt's essays in *The Spirit of the Age* (1825) were echoed by Mill's articles of the same title in 1831, by Thomas Carlyle's essays "Signs of the Times" (1829) and "Characteristics" (1831), and by Richard Henry Horne's *New Spirit of the Age* in 1844.

This persistent scrutiny was the product of an acute sense of change. Britain had emerged from the long war with France (1793–1815) as a great power and as the world's predominant economy. Visiting England in 1847, the American writer Ralph Waldo Emerson observed of the English that "the modern world is theirs. They have made and make it day by day."

This new status as the world's first urban and industrialized society was responsible for the extraordinary wealth, vitality, and self-confidence of the period. Abroad these energies expressed themselves in the growth of the British Empire. At home they were accompanied by rapid social change and fierce intellectual controversy.

The juxtaposition of this new industrial wealth with a new kind of urban poverty is only one of the paradoxes that characterize this long and diverse period. In religion the climax of the Evangelical revival coincided with an unprecedentedly severe set of challenges to faith. The idealism and transcendentalism of Romantic thought were challenged by the growing prestige of empirical science and utilitarian moral philosophy, a process that encouraged more-objective modes in literature. Realism would be one of the great artistic movements of the era. In politics a widespread commitment to economic and personal freedom was, nonetheless, accompanied by a steady growth in the power of the state. The prudery for which the Victorian Age is notorious in fact went hand in hand with an equally violent immoralism, seen, for example, in Algernon Charles Swinburne's poetry or the writings of the Decadents. Most fundamentally of all, the rapid change that many writers interpreted as progress inspired in others a fierce nostalgia. Enthusiastic rediscoveries of ancient Greece, Elizabethan England, and, especially, the Middle Ages by writers, artists, architects, and designers made this age of change simultaneously an age of active and determined historicism.

John Stuart Mill caught this contradictory quality, with characteristic acuteness, in his essays on Jeremy Bentham (1838) and Samuel Taylor Coleridge (1840). Every contemporary thinker, he argued, was indebted to these two "seminal minds." Yet Bentham, as the enduring voice of the Enlightenment, and Coleridge, as the chief English example of the Romantic reaction against it, held diametrically opposed views.

A similar sense of sharp controversy is given by Carlyle in *Sartor Resartus* (1833–34). An eccentric philosophical fiction in the tradition of Swift and Sterne, the book argues for a new mode of spirituality in an age that Carlyle himself suggests to be one of mechanism. Carlyle's choice of the novel form and the book's humour, generic flexibility, and political engagement point forward to distinctive characteristics of Victorian literature.

EARLY VICTORIAN LITERATURE: THE AGE OF THE NOVEL

Several major figures of English Romanticism lived on into this period. Coleridge died in 1834, De Quincey in 1859. Wordsworth succeeded Southey as poet laureate in 1843 and held the post until his own death seven years later. Posthumous publication caused some striking chronological anomalies. Percy Bysshe Shelley's "A Defence of Poetry" was not published until 1840. Keats's letters appeared in 1848 and Wordsworth's *Prelude* in 1850.

Despite this persistence, critics of the 1830s felt that there had been a break in the English literary tradition, which they identified with the death of Byron in 1824. The deaths of Austen in 1817 and Scott in 1832 should perhaps have been seen as even more significant, for the new literary era has, with justification, been seen as the age of the novel. More than 60,000 works of prose fiction were published in Victorian Britain by as many as 7,000 novelists. The three-volume format (or "three-decker") was the standard mode of first publication; it was a form created for sale to and circulation by lending libraries. It was challenged in the 1830s by the advent of serialization in magazines and by the publication of novels in 32-page monthly parts. But only in the 1890s did the three-decker finally yield to the modern single-volume format.

CHARLES DICKENS

Charles Dickens first attracted attention with descriptive essays and tales originally written for newspapers, beginning in 1833, when he was 21. These writings were subsequently collected as *Sketches by "Boz"* (February 1836). The same month, he was invited to provide a comic serial narrative to accompany engravings by a well-known artist; seven weeks later the first installment of *Pickwick Papers* appeared. Within a few months *Pickwick* was the rage and Dickens the most popular author of the day. During 1836 he also wrote two plays and a pamphlet on a topical issue (how the poor should be allowed to enjoy the Sabbath) and, resigning from his newspaper job, undertook to edit a monthly magazine, *Bentley's Miscellany*, in which he serialized *Oliver Twist* (1837–39). Thus, he had two serial installments to write every month. Already the first of his nine surviving children had been born; he had married (in April 1836) Catherine, eldest daughter of a respected Scottish journalist and man of letters, George Hogarth.

For several years his life continued at this intensity. Finding serialization congenial and profitable, he repeated the *Pickwick* pattern of 20 monthly parts in *Nicholas Nickleby* (1838–39); then he experimented with shorter weekly installments for *The Old Curiosity Shop* (1840–41) and *Barnaby Rudge* (1841). Exhausted at last, he then took a five-month vacation in America, touring strenuously and receiving quasi-royal honours as a literary celebrity but offending national sensibilities by protesting against the absence of copyright protection. A radical critic of British institutions, he had expected more from "the republic of my imagination," but he found more vulgarity and sharp practice to detest than social arrangements to admire. Some of these feelings appear in *American Notes* (1842) and *Martin Chuzzlewit* (1843–44).

His writing during these prolific years was remarkably various and, except for his plays, resourceful. *Pickwick* began as high-spirited farce and contained many conventional comic butts and traditional jokes; like other early

Charles Dickens, portrayed about the time he was writing under the pseudonym "Boz"; engraved by R. Graves after D. Maclise. Hulton Archive/Getty Images

works, it was manifestly indebted to the contemporary theatre, the 18th-century English novelists, and a few foreign classics, notably *Don Quixote*. But, besides giving new life to old stereotypes, *Pickwick* displayed, if sometimes in embryo, many of the features that were to be blended in varying proportions throughout his fiction: attacks, satirical or denunciatory, on social evils and inadequate institutions; topical references; an encyclopaedic knowledge of London (always his predominant fictional locale); pathos; a vein of the macabre; a delight in the demotic joys of Christmas; a pervasive spirit of benevolence and geniality; inexhaustible powers of character creation; a wonderful ear for characteristic speech, often imaginatively heightened; a strong narrative impulse; and a prose style that, if here overdependent on a few comic mannerisms, was highly individual and inventive. Rapidly improvised and written only weeks or days ahead of its serial publication, *Pickwick* contains weak and jejune passages and is an unsatisfactory whole—partly because Dickens was rapidly developing his craft as a novelist while writing and publishing it. What is remarkable is that a first novel, written in such circumstances, not only established him overnight and created a new tradition of popular literature but also survived, despite its crudities, as one of the best known novels in the world.

EARLIEST NOVELS

His self-assurance and artistic ambitiousness had appeared in *Oliver Twist*, where he rejected the temptation to repeat the successful *Pickwick* formula. Though containing much comedy still, *Oliver Twist* is more centrally concerned with social and moral evil (the workhouse and the criminal world); it culminates in Bill Sikes's murdering Nancy and Fagin's last night in the condemned cell at Newgate. The latter episode was memorably depicted in George Cruikshank's engraving. The imaginative potency of Dickens' characters and settings owes much, indeed, to his original illustrators — Cruikshank for *Sketches by "Boz"* and *Oliver Twist*, "Phiz," a.k.a. Hablot K. Browne, for most of the other novels until the 1860s.

The currency of his fiction also owed much to its being so easy to adapt into effective stage versions. Sometimes 20 London theatres simultaneously were producing adaptations of his latest story. Even nonreaders became acquainted with simplified versions of his works. The theatre was often a subject of his fiction, too, as in the Crummles troupe in *Nicholas Nickleby*. This novel reverted to the *Pickwick* shape and atmosphere, though the indictment of the brutal Yorkshire schools (Dotheboys Hall) continued the important innovation in English fiction seen in *Oliver Twist* — the spectacle of the lost or oppressed child as an occasion for pathos and social criticism. This was amplified in *The Old Curiosity Shop*, where the death of Little Nell was found overwhelmingly powerful at the time, though a few decades later it became a byword for "Victorian sentimentality." In *Barnaby Rudge* he attempted another genre, the historical novel. Like his later attempt in this kind, *A Tale of Two Cities*, it was set in the late 18th century and presented with great vigour and understanding (and some ambivalence of attitude) the spectacle of large-scale mob violence.

To create an artistic unity out of the wide range of moods and materials included in every novel, with often several complicated plots involving scores of characters, was made even more difficult by Dickens' writing and publishing them serially. In *Martin Chuzzlewit* he tried "to resist the temptation of the current Monthly Number, and to keep a steadier eye upon the general purpose and design" (1844 Preface). Its American episodes had, however, been unpremeditated (he suddenly decided to boost the disappointing sales by some America-baiting and to revenge himself against insults and injuries from the American press). A concentration on "the general purpose and design" was more effective in the next novel, *Dombey and Son* (1846–48), though the experience of writing the shorter, and unserialized, Christmas books had helped him obtain greater coherence.

A Christmas Carol, suddenly conceived and written in a few weeks, was the first of these Christmas books, a new literary genre thus created incidentally. Tossed off while he was amply engaged in writing *Chuzzlewit*, it was an extraordinary achievement—the one great Christmas myth of modern literature. His view of life was later to be described or dismissed as "Christmas philosophy," and he himself spoke of "*Carol* philosophy" as the basis of a projected work. His "philosophy," never very elaborated, involved more than wanting the Christmas spirit to prevail throughout the year, but his great attachment to Christmas (in his family life as well as his writings) is indeed significant and has contributed to his popularity. "Dickens dead?" exclaimed a London costermonger's girl in 1870. "Then will Father Christmas die too?"—a tribute both to his association with Christmas and to the mythological status of the man as well as of his work. The *Carol* immediately entered the general consciousness. In a review, Thackeray called it "a national benefit, and to every man and woman who reads it a personal kindness." Further Christmas books, essays, and stories followed annually (except in 1847) through 1867. None equalled the *Carol* in potency, though some achieved great immediate popularity. Cumulatively they represent a celebration of Christmas attempted by no other great author.

How he struck his contemporaries in these early years appears in R.H. Horne's *New Spirit of the Age* (1844). Dickens occupied the first and longest chapter, as:

> . . . *manifestly the product of his age . . . a genuine emanation from its aggregate and entire spirit . . . He mixes extensively in society, and continually. Few public meetings in a benevolent cause are without him. He speaks effectively . . . His influence upon his age is extensive—pleasurable, instructive, healthy, reformatory . . . Mr. Dickens is, in private, very much what might be expected from his works . . . His conversation is genial . . . [He] has singular personal activity, and is fond of games of practical skill. He is also a great walker, and very much given to dancing Sir Roger de Coverley. In private, the general impression of him is that of a first-rate practical intellect, with "no nonsense" about him.*

He was indeed very much a public figure, actively and centrally involved in his world, and a man of confident presence. He was reckoned the best after-dinner speaker of the age; other superlatives he attracted included his having been the best shorthand reporter on the London press and his being the best amateur actor on the stage. Later he became one of the most successful periodical editors and the finest dramatic recitalist of the day. He was splendidly endowed with many skills. "Even irrespective of his literary genius," wrote an obituarist, "he was an able and strong-minded man, who would have succeeded in almost any profession to which he devoted himself" (*Times*, June 10, 1870). Few of his extraliterary skills and interests were irrelevant to the range and mode of his fiction.

Privately in these early years, he was both domestic and social. He loved home and family life and was a proud and efficient householder; he once contemplated writing a cookbook. To his many children, he was a devoted and delightful father, at least while they were young; relations with them proved less happy during their adolescence. Apart from periods in Italy (1844–45) and Switzerland and France (1846–47), he still lived in London, moving from an apartment in Furnival's Inn to larger houses as his income and family grew. Here he entertained his many friends, most of them popular authors, journalists, actors, or artists, though some came from the law and other professions or from commerce and a few from the aristocracy. Some friendships dating from his youth endured to the end, and, though often exasperated by the financial demands of his parents and other relatives, he was very fond of some of his family and loyal to most of the rest.

Some literary squabbles came later, but he was on friendly terms with most of his fellow authors, of the older generation as well as his own. Necessarily solitary while writing and during the long walks (especially through the streets at night) that became essential to his creative processes, he was generally social at other times. He enjoyed society that was unpretentious and conversation that was genial and sensible but not too intellectualized or exclusively literary. High society he generally avoided, after a few early incursions into the great houses; he hated to be lionized or patronized.

He had about him "a sort of swell and overflow as of a prodigality of life," an American journalist said. Everyone was struck by the brilliance of his eyes and his smart, even dandyish, appearance ("I have the fondness of a savage for finery," he confessed). John Forster, his intimate friend and future biographer, recalled him at the *Pickwick* period:

> *the quickness, keenness, and practical power, the eager, restless,*
> *energetic outlook on each several feature [of his face] seemed to*

*tell so little of a student or writer of books, and so much of a
man of action and business in the world. Light and motion
flashed from every part of it.*

He was proud of his art and devoted to improving it
and using it to good ends (his works would show, he wrote,
that "Cheap Literature is not behind-hand with the Age,
but holds its place, and strives to do its duty"), but his art
never engaged all his formidable energies. He had no
desire to be narrowly literary.

A notable, though unsuccessful, demonstration of this
was his being founder-editor in 1846 of the *Daily News*
(soon to become the leading Liberal newspaper). His journalistic origins, his political convictions and readiness to
act as a leader of opinion, and his wish to secure a steady
income independent of his literary creativity and of any
shifts in novel readers' tastes made him attempt or plan
several periodical ventures in the 1840s. The return to
daily journalism soon proved a mistake—the biggest fiasco
in a career that included few such misdirections or fail-
ures. A more limited but happier exercise of his practical
talents began soon afterward: for more than a decade he
directed, energetically and with great insight and compassion, a reformatory home for young female delinquents,
financed by his wealthy friend Angela Burdett-Coutts.
The benevolent spirit apparent in his writings often found
practical expression in his public speeches, fund-raising
activities, and private acts of charity.

Dombey and Son (1846–48) was a crucial novel in his
development, a product of more thorough planning and
maturer thought and the first in which "a pervasive uneas-
iness about contemporary society takes the place of an
intermittent concern with specific social wrongs"
(Kathleen Tillotson). Using railways prominently and
effectively, it was very up-to-date, though the questions

An illustration from an early edition of David Copperfield, *a personal favourite of Dickens.* Hulton Archive/Getty Images

posed included such perennial moral and religious challenges as are suggested by the child Paul's first words in
the story: "Papa, what's money?" Some of the corruptions
of money and pride of place and the limitations of "respectable" values are explored, virtue and human decency being
discovered most often (as elsewhere in Dickens) among
the poor, humble, and simple. In Paul's early death
Dickens offered another famous pathetic episode; in Mr.
Dombey he made a more ambitious attempt than before
at serious and internal characterization.

David Copperfield (1849–50) has been described as a
"holiday" from these larger social concerns and most
notable for its childhood chapters, "an enchanting vein
which he had never quite found before and which he was
never to find again" (Edmund Wilson). Largely for this
reason and for its autobiographical interest, it has always
been among his most popular novels and was Dickens'
own "favourite child." It incorporates material from the
autobiography he had recently begun but soon abandoned
and is written in the first person, a new technique for him.
David differs from his creator in many ways, however,
though Dickens uses many early experiences that had
meant much to him—his period of work in the factory
while his father was jailed, his schooling and reading, his
passion for Maria Beadnell, and (more cursorily) his emergence from parliamentary reporting into successful novel
writing. In Micawber the novel presents one of the
"Dickens characters" whose imaginative potency extends
far beyond the narratives in which they figure; Pickwick
and Sam Weller, Mrs. Gamp and Mr. Pecksniff, and
Scrooge are some others.

MIDDLE YEARS

Dickens' journalistic ambitions at last found a permanent
form in *Household Words* (1850–59) and its successor, *All the*

Year Round (1859–88). Popular weekly miscellanies of fiction, poetry, and essays on a wide range of topics, these had substantial and increasing circulations, reaching 300,000 for some of the Christmas numbers. Dickens contributed some serials—the lamentable *Child's History of England* (1851–53), *Hard Times* (1854), *A Tale of Two Cities* (1859), and *Great Expectations* (1860–61)—and essays, some of which were collected in *Reprinted Pieces* (1858) and *The Uncommercial Traveller* (1861, later amplified). Particularly in 1850–52 and during the Crimean War, he contributed many items on current political and social affairs. In later years he wrote less—much less on politics—and the magazine was less political, too.

Other distinguished novelists contributed serials, including Mrs. Gaskell, Wilkie Collins, Charles Reade, and Bulwer Lytton. The poetry was uniformly feeble; Dickens was imperceptive here. The reportage, often solidly based, was bright (sometimes painfully so) in manner. His conduct of these weeklies shows his many skills as editor and journalist but also some limitations in his tastes and intellectual ambitions. The contents are revealing in relation to his novels. He took responsibility for all the opinions expressed (for articles were anonymous) and selected and amended contributions accordingly. Thus comments on topical events and so on may generally be taken as representing his opinions, whether or not he wrote them. No English author of comparable status has devoted 20 years of his maturity to such unremitting editorial work, and the weeklies' success was due not only to his illustrious name but also to his practical sagacity and sustained industry. Even in his creative work, as his eldest son said:

No city clerk was ever more methodical or orderly than he; no humdrum, monotonous, conventional task could ever have been discharged with more punctuality, or with more businesslike regularity.

The novels of these years, *Bleak House* (1852–53), *Hard Times* (1854), and *Little Dorrit* (1855–57), were much "darker" than their predecessors. Presenting a remarkably inclusive and increasingly sombre picture of contemporary society, they were inevitably often seen at the time as fictionalized propaganda about ephemeral issues. They are much more than this, though it is never easy to state how Dickens' imagination transforms their many topicalities into an artistically coherent vision that transcends their immediate historical context. Similar questions are raised by his often basing fictional characters, places, and institutions on actual originals. He once spoke of his mind's taking "a fanciful photograph" of a scene, and there is a continual interplay between photographic realism and "fancy" (or imagination). "He describes London like a special correspondent for posterity" (Walter Bagehot, 1858), and posterity has certainly found in his fiction the response of an acute, knowledgeable, and concerned observer to the social and political developments of "the moving age."

In the novels of the 1850s, Dickens is politically more despondent, emotionally more tragic. The satire is harsher, the humour less genial and abundant, the "happy endings" more subdued than in the early fiction. Technically, the later novels are more coherent, plots being more fully related to themes, and themes being often expressed through a more insistent use of imagery and symbols (grim symbols, too, such as the fog in *Bleak House* or the prison in *Little Dorrit*). His art here is more akin to poetry than to what is suggested by the photographic or journalistic comparisons. "Dickensian" characterization continues in the sharply defined and simplified grotesque or comic figures, such as Chadband in *Bleak House* or Mrs. Sparsit in *Hard Times*, but large-scale figures of this type are less frequent (the Gamps and Micawbers belong to the first half of his career). Characterization also has become more subordinate to "the general purpose and design." Moreover, Dickens is presenting characters of greater complexity, who provoke more complex responses in the reader (William Dorrit, for instance). Even the juvenile leads, who had usually been thinly conceived conventional figures, are now often more complicated in their make-up and less easily rewarded by good fortune.

With his secular hopes diminishing, Dickens becomes more concerned with "the great final secret of all life"—a phrase from *Little Dorrit*, where the spiritual dimension of his work is most overt. Critics disagree as to how far so worldly a novelist succeeds artistically in enlarging his view to include the religious. These novels, too, being manifestly an ambitious attempt to explore the prospects of humanity at this time, raise questions, still much debated, about the intelligence and profundity of his understanding of society.

Dickens' spirits and confidence in the future had indeed declined; 1855 was "a year of much unsettled discontent for him," his friend Forster recalled. Thus was the case partly for political reasons or, as Forster hints, Dickens's political indignation was exacerbated by a "discontent" that had personal origins. The Crimean War, besides exposing governmental inefficiency, was distracting attention from the "poverty, hunger, and ignorant desperation" at home. In *Little Dorrit*, "I have been blowing off a little of indignant steam which would otherwise blow me up . . . ," he wrote, "but I have no present political faith or hope—not a grain." Not only were the present government and Parliament contemptible but "representative government is become altogether a failure with us, . . . the whole thing has broken down . . . and has no hope in it." Nor had he a coherent alternative to suggest.

This desperation coincided with an acute state of personal unhappiness. The brief tragicomedy of Maria

Beadnell's reentry into his life, in 1855, finally destroyed one nostalgic illusion and also betrayed a perilous emotional immaturity and hunger. He now openly identified himself with some of the sorrows dramatized in the adult David Copperfield:

Why is it, that as with poor David, a sense comes always crushing on me, now, when I fall into low spirits, as of one happiness I have missed in life, and one friend and companion I have never made?

This comes from the correspondence with Forster in 1854–55, which contains the first admissions of his marital unhappiness. By 1856 he is writing, "I find the skeleton in my domestic closet is becoming a pretty big one." By 1857–58, as Forster remarks, an "unsettled feeling" had become almost habitual with him, "and the satisfactions which home should have supplied, and which indeed were essential requirements of his nature, he had failed to find in his home." From May 1858, Catherine Dickens lived apart from him. A painful scandal arose, and Dickens did not act at this time with tact, patience, or consideration. The affair disrupted some of his friendships and narrowed his social circle, but surprisingly it seems not to have damaged his popularity with the public.

Catherine Dickens maintained a dignified silence, and most of Dickens' family and friends, including his official biographer, Forster, were discreetly reticent about the separation. Not until 1939 did one of his children (Katey), speaking posthumously through conversations recorded by a friend, offer a candid inside account. It was discreditable to him, and his self-justifying letters must be viewed with caution. He there dated the unhappiness of his marriage back to 1838, attributed to his wife various "peculiarities" of temperament (including her sometimes labouring under "a mental disorder"), emphatically agreed with her (alleged) statement that "she felt herself unfit for the life she had to lead as my wife," and maintained that she never cared for the children nor they for her. In more temperate letters, where he acknowledged her "amiable and complying" qualities, he simply and more acceptably asserted that their temperaments were utterly incompatible. She was, apparently, pleasant but rather limited. Such faults as she had were rather negative than positive, though family tradition from a household that knew the Dickenses well speaks of her as "a whiney woman" and as having little understanding of, or patience with, the artistic temperament.

Dickens' self-justifying letters lack candour in omitting to mention Ellen Ternan, an actress 27 years his junior, his passion for whom had precipitated the separation. Two months earlier he had written more frankly to an intimate friend:

> *The domestic unhappiness remains so strong upon me that I can't write, and (waking) can't rest, one minute. I have never known a moment's peace or content, since the last night of The Frozen Deep.*

The Frozen Deep was a play in which he and Nelly (as Ellen was called) had performed together in August 1857. She was an intelligent girl, of an old theatrical family; reports speak of her as having "a pretty face and well-developed figure"—or "passably pretty and not much of an actress." She left the stage in 1860; after Dickens' death she married a clergyman and helped him run a school. The affair was hushed up until the 1930s, and evidence about it remains scanty, but every addition confirms that Dickens was deeply attached to her and that their relationship lasted until his death. It seems likely that she became his mistress, though probably not until the 1860s; assertions that a child, or children, resulted remain unproved. Similarly, suggestions that the anguish experienced by some of the lovers in the later novels may reflect Dickens' own feelings remain speculative. It is tempting, indeed, to associate Nelly with some of their heroines (who are more spirited and complex, less of the "legless angel," than most of their predecessors), especially as her given names, Ellen Lawless, seem to be echoed by those of heroines in the three final novels—Estella, Bella, and Helena Landless—but nothing definite is known about how she responded to Dickens, what she felt for him at the time, or how close any of these later love stories were to aspects or phases of their relationship.

"There is nothing very remarkable in the story," commented one early transmitter of it, and this seems just. Many middle-aged men feel an itch to renew their emotional lives with a pretty young girl, even if, unlike Dickens, they cannot plead indulgence for "the wayward and unsettled feeling which is part (I suppose) of the tenure on which one holds an imaginative life." But the eventual disclosure of this episode caused surprise, shock, or piquant satisfaction, being related of a man whose rebelliousness against his society had seemed to take only impeccably reformist shapes. A critic in 1851, listing the reasons for his unique popularity, had cited "above all, his deep reverence for the household sanctities, his enthusiastic worship of the household gods." After these disclosures he was, disconcertingly or intriguingly, a more complex man, and, partly as a consequence, Dickens the novelist also began to be seen as more complex, less conventional, than had been realized. The stimulus was important, though Nelly's significance, biographically and critically, has proved far from inexhaustible.

In the longer term, Kathleen Tillotson's remark is more suggestive: "His lifelong love-affair with his reading public, when all is said, is by far the most interesting love-affair of his life." This took a new form, about the time of Dickens' separation from his wife, in his giving public readings from his works, and it is significant that, when trying to justify this enterprise as certain to succeed, he referred to "that particular relation (personally affectionate and like no other man's) which subsists between me and the public." The remark suggests how much Dickens valued his public's affection, not only as a stimulus to his creativity and a condition for his commercial success but also as a substitute for the love he could not find at home. He had been toying with the idea of turning paid reader since 1853, when he began giving occasional readings in aid of charity. The paid series began in April 1858, the immediate impulse being to find some energetic distraction from his marital unhappiness. But the readings drew on more permanent elements in him and his art: his remarkable histrionic talents, his love of theatricals and of seeing and delighting an audience, and the eminently performable nature of his fiction. Moreover, he could earn more by reading than by writing, and more certainly; it was easier to force himself to repeat a performance than create a book.

His initial repertoire consisted entirely of Christmas books but was soon amplified by episodes from the novels and magazine Christmas stories. A performance usually consisted of two items; of the 16 eventually performed, the most popular were "The Trial from *Pickwick*" and the *Carol*. Comedy predominated, though pathos was important in the repertoire, and horrifics were startlingly introduced in the last reading he devised, "Sikes and Nancy," with which he petrified his audiences and half killed himself. Intermittently, until shortly before his

Dickens depicted as preparing to read from his works. Public readings were not just a way for Dickens to make money. He enjoyed the give-and-take with audiences. Hulton Archive/Getty Images

death, he gave seasons of readings in London and embarked upon hardworking tours through the provinces and (in 1867–68) the United States. Altogether he performed about 471 times. He was a magnificent performer, and important elements in his art—the oral and dramatic qualities—were demonstrated in these renderings. His insight and skill revealed nuances in the narration and characterization that few readers had noticed.

Necessarily, such extracts or short stories, suitable for a two-hour entertainment, excluded some of his larger and deeper effects—notably, his social criticism and analysis—and his later novels were underrepresented. Dickens never mentions these inadequacies. He manifestly enjoyed the experience until, near the end, he was becoming ill and exhausted. He was writing much less in the 1860s. It is debatable how far this was because the readings exhausted his energies, while providing the income, creative satisfaction, and continuous contact with an audience that he had formerly obtained through the novels. He gloried in his audiences' admiration and love. Some friends thought this too crude a gratification, too easy a triumph, and a sad declension into a lesser and ephemeral art. In whatever way the episode is judged, it was characteristic of him—of his relationship with his public, his business sense, his stamina, his ostentatious display of supplementary skills, and also of his originality. No important author (at least, according to reviewers, since Homer) and no English author since who has had anything like his stature has devoted so much time and energy to this activity. The only comparable figure is his contemporary, Mark Twain, who acknowledged Dickens as the pioneer.

LAST YEARS

Tired and ailing though he was, he remained inventive and adventurous in his final novels. *A Tale of Two Cities* (1859) was an experiment, relying less than before on character-ization, dialogue, and humour. An exciting and compact narrative, it lacks too many of his strengths to count among his major works. Sydney Carton's self-sacrifice was found deeply moving by Dickens and by many readers; Dr. Manette now seems a more impressive achievement in serious characterization. The French Revolution scenes are vivid, if superficial in historical understanding.

Great Expectations (1860–61) resembles *Copperfield* in being a first-person narration and in drawing on parts of Dickens' personality and experience. Compact like its predecessor, it lacks the panoramic inclusiveness of *Bleak House*, *Little Dorrit*, and *Our Mutual Friend*, but, though not his most ambitious, it is his most finely achieved novel. The hero Pip's mind is explored with great subtlety, and his development through a childhood and youth beset with hard tests of character is traced critically but sympa-thetically. Various "great expectations" in the book proved ill founded—a comment as much on the values of the age as on the characters' weaknesses and misfortunes. *Our Mutual Friend* (1864–65), a large inclusive novel, continues this critique of monetary and class values. London is now grimmer than ever before, and the corruption, compla-cency, and superficiality of "respectable" society are fiercely attacked.

Many new elements are introduced into Dickens' fic-tional world, but his handling of the old comic-eccentrics (such as Boffin, Wegg, and Venus) is sometimes tiresomely mechanical. How the unfinished *Edwin Drood* (1870) would have developed is uncertain. Here again Dickens left panoramic fiction to concentrate on a limited private action. The central figure was evidently to be John Jasper, whose eminent respectability as a cathedral organist was in extreme contrast to his haunting low opium dens and, out of violent sexual jealousy, murdering his nephew.

The novel would have been his most elaborate treatment of the themes of crime, evil, and psychological abnormality that had recurred throughout his novels; a great celebrator of life, he was also obsessed with death. Part dramatist, part journalist, part mythmaker, and part wit, Dickens took the picaresque tradition of Smollett and Fielding and gave it a Shakespearean vigour and variety.

THACKERAY, GASKELL, AND OTHERS

Unlike Dickens, William Makepeace Thackeray came from a wealthy and educated background. The loss of his fortune at age 22, however, meant that he too learned his trade in the field of sketch writing and occasional journalism. His early fictions were published as serials in *Fraser's Magazine* or as contributions to the great Victorian comic magazine *Punch* (founded 1841). For his masterpiece, *Vanity Fair* (1847–48), however, he adopted Dickens's procedure of publication in monthly parts. Thackeray's satirical acerbity is here combined with a broad narrative sweep, a sophisticated self-consciousness about the conventions of fiction, and an ambitious historical survey of the transformation of English life in the years between the Regency and the mid-Victorian period. His later novels never match this sharpness. *Vanity Fair* was subtitled "A Novel Without a Hero." Subsequently, it has been suggested, a more sentimental Thackeray wrote novels without villains.

Elizabeth Gaskell began her career as one of the "Condition of England" novelists of the 1840s, responding like Frances Trollope, Benjamin Disraeli, and Charles Kingsley to the economic crisis of that troubled decade. *Mary Barton* (1848) and *Ruth* (1853) are both novels about social problems, as is *North and South* (1854–55), although, like her later work—*Sylvia's Lovers* (1863), *Wives and Daughters* (1864–66), and the remarkable novella *Cousin Phyllis* (1864)—this book also has a psychological complexity that anticipates George Eliot's novels of provincial life.

Political novels, religious novels, historical novels, sporting novels, Irish novels, crime novels, and comic novels all flourished in this period. The years 1847–48, indeed, represent a pinnacle of simultaneous achievement in English fiction. In addition to *Vanity Fair*, *Dombey and Son*, and *Mary Barton*, they saw the completion of Disraeli's trilogy of political novels—*Coningsby* (1844), *Sybil* (1845), and *Tancred* (1847)—and the publication of first novels by Kingsley, Anne Brontë, Charlotte Brontë, Emily Brontë, and Anthony Trollope. For the first time, literary genius appeared to be finding its most natural expression in prose fiction, rather than in poetry or drama. By 1853 the poet Arthur Hugh Clough would concede that "the modern novel is preferred to the modern poem."

THE BRONTËS

In many ways, however, the qualities of Romantic verse could be absorbed, rather than simply superseded, by the Victorian novel. This is suggested clearly by the work of the Brontë sisters. Growing up in a remote but cultivated vicarage in Yorkshire, they, as children, invented the imaginary kingdoms of Angria and Gondal. These inventions supplied the context for many of the poems in their first, and pseudonymous, publication, *Poems by Currer, Ellis, and Acton Bell* (1846). Their Gothic plots and Byronic passions also informed the novels that began to be published in the following year.

Anne Brontë wrote of the painful reality of disagreeable experience, although both her novels have cheerful romantic endings. *Agnes Grey* (1847) is a stark account of the working life of a governess, and *The Tenant of Wildfell Hall* (1848) paints a grim picture of the heroine's marriage to an abusive husband. Charlotte Brontë, like her sisters, appears at first sight to have been writing a literal fiction of provincial life. In her first novel, *Jane Eyre* (1847), for example, the heroine's choice between sexual need and ethical duty belongs very firmly to the mode of moral realism. But her hair's-breadth escape from a bigamous marriage with her employer and the death by fire of his mad first wife derive from the rather different tradition of the Gothic novel. In *Shirley* (1849) Charlotte Brontë strove to be, in her own words, "as unromantic as Monday morning." In *Villette* (1853) the distinctive Gothic elements return to lend this study of the limits of stoicism an unexpected psychological intensity and drama.

Emily Brontë united these diverse traditions still more successfully in her only novel, *Wuthering Heights* (1847). Closely observed regional detail, precisely handled plot, and a sophisticated use of multiple internal narrators are combined with vivid imagery and an extravagantly Gothic theme. The result is a perfectly achieved study of elemental passions and the strongest possible refutation of the assumption that the age of the novel must also be an age of realism.

EARLY VICTORIAN VERSE

Despite the growing prestige and proliferation of fiction, this age of the novel was in fact also an age of great poetry. Alfred, Lord Tennyson made his mark very early with *Poems, Chiefly Lyrical* (1830) and *Poems* (1832; dated 1833), publications that led some critics to hail him as the natural successor to John Keats and Percy Bysshe Shelley. A decade later, in *Poems* (1842), Tennyson combined in two volumes the best of his early work with a second volume of more-recent writing. The collection established him as the outstanding poet of the era. In his early work Tennyson brought an exquisite lyric gift to late Romantic subject matter. The result is a poetry that, for all its debt to Keats, anticipates the French Symbolists of the 1880s.

ALFRED, LORD TENNYSON

Alfred Tennyson was the fourth of 12 children, born in 1809 into an old Lincolnshire family, his father a rector. Alfred, with two of his brothers, Frederick and Charles, was sent in 1815 to Louth grammar school—where he was unhappy. He left in 1820, but, though home conditions were difficult, his father managed to give him a wide literary education. Alfred was precocious, and before his teens he had composed in the styles of Alexander Pope, Sir Walter Scott, and John Milton. To his youth also belongs *The Devil and the Lady* (a collection of previously unpublished poems published posthumously in 1930), which shows an astonishing understanding of Elizabethan dramatic verse. Lord Byron was a dominant influence on the young Tennyson.

At the lonely rectory in Somersby the children were thrown upon their own resources. All writers on Tennyson emphasize the influence of the Lincolnshire countryside on his poetry: the plain, the sea about his home, "the sand-built ridge of heaped hills that mound the sea," and "the waste enormous marsh."

In 1824 the health of Tennyson's father began to break down, and he took refuge in drink. Alfred, though depressed by unhappiness at home, continued to write, collaborating with Frederick and Charles in *Poems by Two Brothers* (1826; dated 1827). His contributions (more than half the volume) are mostly in fashionable styles of the day.

In 1827 Alfred and Charles joined Frederick at Trinity College, Cambridge. There Alfred made friends with Arthur Hallam, the gifted son of the historian Henry Hallam. This was the deepest friendship of Tennyson's life. The friends became members of the Apostles, an exclusive undergraduate club of earnest intellectual interests. Tennyson's reputation as a poet increased at Cambridge. In 1829 he won the chancellor's gold medal with a poem called *Timbuctoo.* In 1830 *Poems, Chiefly Lyrical* was published; and in the same year Tennyson, Hallam, and other Apostles went to Spain to help in the unsuccessful revolution against Ferdinand VII. In the meantime, Hallam had become attached to Tennyson's sister Emily but was forbidden by her father to correspond with her for a year.

In 1831 Tennyson's father died. Alfred's misery was increased by his grandfather's discovery of his father's debts. He left Cambridge without taking a degree, and his grandfather made financial arrangements for the family. In the same year, Hallam published a eulogistic article on *Poems, Chiefly Lyrical* in *The Englishman's Magazine.* He went to Somersby in 1832 as the accepted suitor of Emily.

In 1832 Tennyson published another volume of his poems (dated 1833), including "The Lotos-Eaters," "The Palace of Art," and "The Lady of Shalott." Among them was a satirical epigram on the critic Christopher North (pseudonym of the Scottish writer John Wilson), who had attacked *Poems, Chiefly Lyrical* in *Blackwood's Magazine.* Tennyson's sally prompted a scathing attack on his new volume in the *Quarterly Review.* The attacks distressed Tennyson, but he continued to revise his old poems and compose new ones.

Alfred Tennyson began publishing verse in his teens, and he continued to publish even after reluctantly becoming a lord. Hulton Archive/Getty Images

In 1833 Hallam's engagement was recognized by his family, but while on a visit to Vienna in September he died suddenly. The shock to Tennyson was severe. It came at a depressing time; three of his brothers, Edward, Charles, and Septimus, were suffering from mental illness, and the bad reception of his own work added to the gloom. Yet it was in this period that he wrote some of his most characteristic work: "The Two Voices" (of which the original title, significantly, was "Thoughts of a Suicide"), "Ulysses," "St. Simeon Stylites," and, probably, the first draft of "Morte d'Arthur." To this period also belong some of the poems that became constituent parts of *In Memoriam,* celebrating Hallam's death, and lyrics later worked into *Maud.*

In May 1836 his brother Charles married Louisa Sellwood of Horncastle, and at the wedding Alfred fell in love with her sister Emily. For some years the lovers corresponded, but Emily's father disapproved of Tennyson because of his bohemianism, addiction to port and tobacco, and liberal religious views; and in 1840 he forbade the correspondence. Meanwhile the Tennysons had left Somersby and were living a rather wandering life nearer London. It was in this period that Tennyson made friends with many famous men, including the politician William Ewart Gladstone, the historian Thomas Carlyle, and the poet Walter Savage Landor.

In 1842 Tennyson published *Poems,* in two volumes, one containing a revised selection from the volumes of 1830 and 1832, the other, new poems. The new poems included "Morte d'Arthur," "The Two Voices," "Locksley Hall," and "The Vision of Sin" and other poems that reveal a strange naïveté, such as "The May Queen," "Lady Clara Vere de Vere," and "The Lord of Burleigh." The new volume was not on the whole well received. But the grant to him at this time, by the prime minister, Sir Robert Peel, of a pension of £200 helped to alleviate his financial worries. In 1847 he published his first long poem, *The Princess,* a singular anti-feminist fantasia.

The year 1850 marked a turning point. Tennyson resumed his correspondence with Emily Sellwood, and their engagement was renewed and followed by marriage. Meanwhile, Edward Moxon offered to publish the elegies on Hallam that Tennyson had been composing over the years. They appeared, at first anonymously, as *In Memoriam* (1850), which had a great success with both reviewers and the public, won him the friendship of Queen Victoria, and helped bring about, in the same year, his appointment as poet laureate.

In Memoriam is a vast poem of 131 sections of varying length, with a prologue and epilogue. Inspired by the grief Tennyson felt at the untimely death of his friend Hallam, the poem touches on many intellectual issues of the Victorian Age as the author searches for the meaning of life and death and tries to come to terms with his sense of loss. Most notably, *In Memoriam* reflects the struggle to reconcile traditional religious faith and belief in immortality with the emerging theories of evolution and modern geology. The verses show the development over three years of the poet's acceptance and understanding of his friend's death and conclude with an epilogue, a happy marriage song on the occasion of the wedding of Tennyson's sister Cecilia.

After his marriage, which was happy, Tennyson's life became more secure and outwardly uneventful. There were two sons, Hallam and Lionel. The times of wandering and unsettlement ended in 1853, when the Tennysons took a house, Farringford, in the Isle of Wight. Tennyson was to spend most of the rest of his life there and at Aldworth (near Haslemere, Surrey).

Tennyson's position as the national poet was confirmed by his *Ode on the Death of the Duke of Wellington* (1852) — though some critics at first thought it disappointing — and the famous poem on the charge of the Light Brigade at Balaklava, published in 1855 in *Maud and Other Poems*. *Maud* itself, a strange and turbulent "monodrama," provoked a storm of protest; many of the poet's admirers were shocked by the morbidity, hysteria, and bellicosity of the hero. Yet *Maud* was Tennyson's favourite among his poems.

A project that Tennyson had long considered at last issued in *Idylls of the King* (1859), a series of 12 connected poems broadly surveying the legend of King Arthur from his falling in love with Guinevere to the ultimate ruin of his kingdom. The poems concentrate on the introduction of evil to Camelot because of the adulterous love of Lancelot and Queen Guinevere, and on the consequent fading of the hope that had at first infused the Round Table fellowship. *Idylls of the King* had an immediate success, and Tennyson, who loathed publicity, had now acquired a sometimes embarrassing public fame. The *Enoch Arden* volume of 1864 perhaps represents the peak of his popularity. New Arthurian *Idylls* were published in *The Holy Grail, and Other Poems* in 1869 (dated 1870). These were again well received, though some readers were beginning to show discomfort at the "Victorian" moral atmosphere that Tennyson had introduced into his source material from Sir Thomas Malory.

In 1874 Tennyson decided to try his hand at poetic drama. *Queen Mary* appeared in 1875, and an abridged version was produced at the Lyceum in 1876 with only moderate success. It was followed by *Harold* (1876; dated 1877), *Becket* (not published in full until 1884), and the "village tragedy" *The Promise of May*, which proved a failure at the Globe in November 1882. This play—his only prose work—shows Tennyson's growing despondency and resentment at the religious, moral, and political tendencies of the age. He had already caused some sensation by publishing a poem called "Despair" in *The Nineteenth Century* (November 1881). A more positive indication of Tennyson's later beliefs appears in "The Ancient Sage," published in *Tiresias and Other Poems* (1885). Here the poet records his intimations of a life before and beyond this life.

Tennyson accepted a peerage (after some hesitation) in 1884. In 1886 he published a new volume containing "Locksley Hall Sixty Years After," consisting mainly of imprecations against modern decadence and liberalism and a retraction of the earlier poem's belief in inevitable human progress.

In 1889 Tennyson wrote the famous short poem "Crossing the Bar," during the crossing to the Isle of Wight. In the same year he published *Demeter and Other Poems,* which contains the charming retrospective "To Mary Boyle," "The Progress of Spring," a fine lyric written much earlier and rediscovered, and "Merlin and the Gleam," an allegorical summing-up of his poetic career. In 1892 his play *The Foresters* was successfully produced in New York City. Despite ill health, he was able to correct the proofs of his last volume, *The Death of Oenone, Akbar's Dream, and Other Poems* (1892).

G.K. Chesterton described Tennyson as "a suburban Virgil." The elegant Virgilian note was the last thing aimed at by Robert Browning. Browning's work was Germanic rather than Italianate, grotesque rather than idyllic, and colloquial rather than refined. The differences between Browning and Tennyson underline the creative diversity of the period.

Idyll

An idyll is a short poem of a pastoral or rural character in which something of the element of landscape is depicted or suggested. The word *idyll* is derived from the Greek word *eidyllion*, meaning "little picture." The term was used in Greco-Roman antiquity to designate a variety of brief poems on simple subjects in which the description of natural objects was introduced. The conventions of the pastoral were developed by the Alexandrian school of poetry, particularly by Theocritus, Bion, and Moschus, in the 3rd century BC, and the *Idylls* of Theocritus are the source of the popular idea of this type of poem.

The word was revived during the Renaissance, when some poets employed it to distinguish narrative pastorals from those in dialogue. The general use, or misuse, of the word arose in the 19th century from the popularity of two works, the *Idylles héroïques* (1858) of Victor-Richard de Laprade and the *Idylls of the King* (1859) of Alfred, Lord Tennyson, neither of which was related to the pastoral tradition. Thereafter the word was used indiscriminately to refer to works on a variety of subjects.

Although it is impossible to define the idyll as a definite literary form, the adjective idyllic has come to be synonymous with the rustic, pastoral, and tranquil, the mood first created by the Alexandrian poets.

ROBERT BROWNING AND ELIZABETH BARRETT BROWNING

Deeply influenced by Shelley, Robert Browning made two false starts. One was as a playwright in the 1830s and '40s. The other was as the late-Romantic poet of the confessional meditation *Pauline* (1833) and the difficult though innovatory narrative poem *Sordello* (1840).

Browning found his individual and distinctively modern voice in 1842, with the volume *Dramatic Lyrics*. As the

Robert Browning first tried his hand at writing plays, but later found his true calling as a poet. Hulton Archive/Getty Images

title suggests, it was a collection of dramatic monologues, among them "Porphyria's Lover," "Johannes Agricola in Meditation," and "My Last Duchess." The monologues make clear the radical originality of Browning's new manner: they involve the reader in sympathetic identification with the interior processes of criminal or unconventional minds, requiring active rather than merely passive engagement in the processes of moral judgment and self-discovery. More such monologues and some equally striking lyrics make up *Men and Women* (1855).

In 1846 Browning married Elizabeth Barrett. Though now remembered chiefly for her love poems *Sonnets from the Portuguese* (1850) and her experiment with the verse novel *Aurora Leigh* (1856; dated 1857), she was in her own lifetime far better known than her husband. Her *Poems* (1844) established her as a leading poet of the age. *Casa Guidi Windows* (1851) is a subtle reflection on her experience of Italian politics, and "A Musical Instrument" (1862) is one of the century's most memorable expressions of the difficulty of the poet's role.

Only with the publication of *Dramatis Personae* (1864) did Robert Browning achieve the sort of fame that Tennyson had enjoyed for more than 20 years. The volume contains, in "Rabbi Ben Ezra," the most extreme statement of Browning's celebrated optimism. Hand in hand with this reassuring creed, however, go the skeptical intelligence and the sense of the grotesque displayed in such poems as "Caliban upon Setebos" and "Mr. Sludge, 'The Medium.'"

His *The Ring and the Book* (1868–69) gives the dramatic monologue format unprecedented scope. Published in parts, like a Dickens novel, it tells a sordid murder story in a way that both explores moral issues and suggests the problematic nature of human knowledge. Browning's work after this date, though voluminous, is uneven.

In her lifetime, Elizabeth Barrett Browning found that the popularity of her collections of verse eclipsed those of her husband, Robert. Elliot & Fry/ Hulton Archive/Getty Images

Dramatic Monologue

A dramatic monologue is a poem written in the form of a speech of an individual character; it compresses into a single vivid scene a narrative sense of the speaker's history and psychological insight into his character. Though the form is chiefly associated with Robert Browning, who raised it to a highly sophisticated level in such poems as "My Last Duchess," "The Bishop Orders His Tomb at St. Praxed's Church," "Fra Lippo Lippi," and "Andrea del Sarto," it is actually much older. Many Old English poems are dramatic monologues—for instance, "The Wanderer" and "The Seafarer." The form is also common in folk ballads, a tradition that Robert Burns imitated with broad satiric effect in "Holy Willie's Prayer." Browning's contribution to the form is one of subtlety of characterization and complexity of the dramatic situation, which the reader gradually pieces together from the casual remarks or digressions of the speaker. The subject discussed is usually far less interesting than what is inadvertently revealed about the speaker himself. In "My Last Duchess," in showing off a painting of his late wife, an Italian aristocrat reveals his cruelty to her. The form parallels the novelistic experiments with point of view in which the reader is left to assess the intelligence and reliability of the narrator. Later poets who successfully used the form were Ezra Pound ("The River Merchant's Wife: A Letter"), T.S. Eliot ("Love Song of J. Alfred Prufrock"), and Robert Frost ("The Pauper Witch of Grafton").

CLOUGH AND ARNOLD

Arthur Hugh Clough died relatively young, at age 42, but managed nonetheless to produce three highly original poems. *The Bothie of Tober-na-Vuolich* (1848) is a narrative poem of modern life, written in hexameters. *Amours de Voyage* (1858) goes beyond this to the full-scale verse novel, using multiple internal narrators and vivid contemporary detail. *Dipsychus* (published posthumously in 1865 but not available in an unexpurgated version until 1951) is a remarkable closet drama that debates issues of belief and morality with a frankness, and a metrical liveliness, unequaled in Victorian verse.

Matthew Arnold's first volume of verse, *The Strayed Reveller, and Other Poems* (1849), combined lyric grace with an acute sense of the dark philosophical landscape of the period. The title poem of his next collection, *Empedocles on Etna* (1852), is a sustained statement of the modern dilemma and a remarkable poetic embodiment of the process that Arnold called "the dialogue of the mind with itself." Arnold, who was a friend of Clough, later suppressed this poem and attempted to write in a more impersonal manner. His greatest work ("Switzerland," "Dover Beach," "The Scholar-Gipsy") is, however, always elegiac in tone. In the 1860s he turned from verse to prose and became, with *Essays in Criticism* (1865), *Culture and Anarchy* (1869), and *Literature and Dogma* (1873), a lively and acute writer of literary, social, and religious criticism.

Born in 1822, Arnold was the eldest son of the renowned Thomas Arnold, who was appointed headmaster of Rugby School in 1828. Arnold entered Rugby (1837) and then attended Oxford as a scholar of Balliol College; there he won the Newdigate Prize with his poem *Cromwell* (1843) and was graduated with second-class honours in 1844. For Oxford Arnold retained an impassioned affection. His Oxford was the Oxford of John Henry Newman—of Newman just about to be received into the Roman Catholic Church; and although Arnold's own religious thought, like his father's, was strongly liberal, Oxford and Newman always remained for him joint symbols of spiritual beauty and culture.

In 1847 Arnold became private secretary to Lord
Lansdowne, who occupied a high Cabinet post during
Lord John Russell's Liberal ministries. And in 1851, in
order to secure the income needed for his marriage (June
1851) with Frances Lucy Wightman, he accepted from
Lansdowne an appointment as inspector of schools. This
was to be his routine occupation until within two years
of his death. He engaged in incessant travelling throughout the British provinces and also several times was sent
by the government to inquire into the state of education
in France, Germany, Holland, and Switzerland. Two of his
reports on schools abroad were reprinted as books, and
his annual reports on schools at home attracted wide
attention, written, as they were, in Arnold's own urbane
and civilized prose.

The work that gives Arnold his high place in the history of literature and the history of ideas was all
accomplished in the time he could spare from his official
duties. His first volume of verse was *The Strayed Reveller,
and Other Poems. By A.* (1849). This was followed (in 1852)
by another under the same initial, *Empedocles on Etna, and
Other Poems.* In 1853 appeared the first volume of poems
published under his own name. It consisted partly of
poems selected from the earlier volumes and also contained the well-known preface explaining (among other
things) why *Empedocles* was excluded from the selection.
It was, according to the preface, a dramatic poem "in
which the suffering finds no vent in action," in which
there is "everything to be endured, nothing to be done."
This preface foreshadows his later criticism in its insistence upon the classic virtues of unity, impersonality,
universality, and architectonic power and upon the value
of the classical masterpieces as models for "an age of spiritual discomfort"—an age "wanting in moral grandeur."

Other editions followed, and *Merope*, Arnold's classical tragedy, appeared in 1858, and *New Poems* in 1867. After that date, though there were further editions, Arnold wrote little additional verse.

Not much of Arnold's verse will stand the test of his own criteria; far from being classically poised, impersonal, serene, and grand, it is often intimate, personal, full of romantic regret, sentimental pessimism, and nostalgia. As a public and social character and as a prose writer, Arnold was sunny, debonair, and sanguine. But beneath ran the current of his buried life, and of this much of his poetry is the echo:

> *From the soul's subterranean depth upborne*
> *As from an infinitely distant land,*
> *Come airs, and floating echoes, and convey*
> *A melancholy into all our day.*

"I am past thirty," he wrote a friend in 1853, "and three parts iced over." The impulse to write poetry came typically when:

> *A bolt is shot back somewhere in the breast,*
> *And a lost pulse of feeling stirs again.*

Though he was "never quite benumb'd by the world's sway," these hours of insight became more and more rare, and the stirrings of buried feeling were associated with moods of regret for lost youth, regret for the freshness of the early world, moods of self-pity, moods of longing for:

> *The hills where his life rose*
> *And the sea where it goes.*

Yet, though much of Arnold's most characteristic verse is in this vein of soliloquy or intimate confession, he can sometimes rise, as in "Sohrab and Rustum," to epic severity and impersonality; to lofty meditation, as in "Dover Beach"; and to sustained magnificence and richness, as in "The Scholar Gipsy" and "Thyrsis"—where he wields an intricate stanza form without a stumble.

In 1857, assisted by the vote of his godfather (and predecessor) John Keble, Arnold was elected to the Oxford chair of poetry, which he held for 10 years. It was characteristic of him that he revolutionized this professorship. The keynote was struck in his inaugural lecture, "On the Modern Element in Literature." In this instance, "modern" was taken to mean not merely "contemporary" (for Greece was "modern"), but the spirit that, contemplating the vast and complex spectacle of life, craves for moral and intellectual "deliverance." Several of the lectures were afterward published as critical essays, but the most substantial fruits of his professorship were the three lectures *On Translating Homer* (1861)—in which he recommended Homer's plainness and nobility as medicine for the modern world, with its "sick hurry and divided aims" and condemned Francis Newman's recent translation as ignoble and eccentric—and the lectures *On the Study of Celtic Literature* (1867), in which, without much knowledge of his subject or of anthropology, he used the Celtic strain as a symbol of that which rejects the despotism of the commonplace and the utilitarian.

It is said that when the poet in Arnold died, the critic was born; and it is true that from this time onward he turned almost entirely to prose. Some of the leading ideas and phrases were early put into currency in *Essays in Criticism* (First Series, 1865; Second Series, 1888) and *Culture and Anarchy.* The first essay in the 1865 volume, "The Function of Criticism at the Present Time," is an overture announcing briefly most of the themes he developed more fully in later work. It is at once evident that he ascribes to "criticism" a scope and importance hitherto undreamed of. The function of criticism, in his sense, is "a disinterested endeavour to learn and propagate the best that is known and thought in the world, and thus to establish a current of fresh and true ideas." It is in fact a spirit that he is trying to foster, the spirit of an awakened and informed intelligence playing upon not "literature" merely but theology, history, art, science, sociology, and politics, and in every sphere seeking "to see the object as in itself it really is."

In this critical effort, thought Arnold, England lagged behind France and Germany, and the English accordingly remained in a backwater of provinciality and complacency. Even the great Romantic poets, with all their creative energy, suffered from the want of it. The English literary critic must know literatures other than his own and be in touch with European standards. This last line of thought Arnold develops in the second essay, "The Literary Influence of Academies," in which he dwells upon "the note of provinciality" in English literature, caused by remoteness from a "centre" of correct knowledge and correct taste. To realize how much Arnold widened the horizons of criticism requires only a glance at the titles of some of the other essays in *Essays in Criticism* (1865): "Maurice de Guérin," "Eugénie de Guérin," "Heinrich Heine," "Joubert," "Spinoza," "Marcus Aurelius"; in all these, as increasingly in his later books, he is "applying modern ideas to life" as well as to letters and "bringing all things under the point of view of the 19th century."

The first essay in the 1888 volume, "The Study of Poetry," was originally published as the general introduction to T.H. Ward's anthology, *The English Poets* (1880). It contains many of the ideas for which Arnold is best remembered. In an age of crumbling creeds, poetry will have to replace religion. More and more, we will "turn to poetry to interpret life for us, to console us, to sustain us." Therefore we must know how to distinguish the best poetry from the inferior, the genuine from the counterfeit; and to do this we must steep ourselves in the work of the acknowledged masters, using as "touchstones" passages exemplifying their "high seriousness," and their superiority of diction and movement.

The remaining essays, with the exception of the last two (on Tolstoy and Amiel), all deal with English poets: Milton, Gray, Keats, Wordsworth, Byron, and Shelley. All contain memorable things, and all attempt a serious and responsible assessment of each poet's "criticism of life" and his value as food for the modern spirit. Arnold has been taken to task for some of his judgments and omissions: for his judgment that Dryden and Pope were not "genuine" poets because they composed in their wits instead of "in the soul"; for calling Gray a "minor classic" in an age of prose and spiritual bleakness; for paying too much attention to the man behind the poetry (Gray, Keats, Shelley); for making no mention of Donne; and above all for saying that poetry is "at bottom a criticism of life." On this last point it should be remembered that he added "under the conditions fixed . . . by the laws of poetic truth and poetic beauty," and that if by "criticism" is understood (as Arnold meant) "evaluation," Arnold's dictum is seen to have wider significance than has been sometimes supposed.

Culture and Anarchy is in some ways Arnold's most central work. It is an expansion of his earlier attacks, in "The Function of Criticism" and "Heinrich Heine," upon the smugness, philistinism, and mammon worship of Victorian England. Culture, as "the study of perfection," is opposed to the prevalent "anarchy" of a new democracy without standards and without a sense of direction. By "turning a stream of fresh thought upon our stock notions and habits," culture seeks to make "reason and the will of God prevail."

Arnold's classification of English society into Barbarians (with their high spirit, serenity, and distinguished manners and their inaccessibility to ideas), Philistines (the stronghold of religious nonconformity, with plenty of energy and morality but insufficient "sweetness and light"), and Populace (still raw and blind) is well known. Arnold saw in the Philistines the key to the whole position; they were now the most influential section of society; their strength was the nation's strength, their crudeness its crudeness: Educate and humanize the Philistines, therefore. Arnold saw in the idea of "the State," and not in any one class of society, the true organ and repository of the nation's collective "best self." No summary can do justice to this extraordinary book; it can still be read with pure enjoyment, for it is written with an inward poise, a serene detachment, and an infusion of mental laughter, which make it a masterpiece of ridicule as well as a searching analysis of Victorian society. The same is true of its unduly neglected sequel, *Friendship's Garland* (1871).

Lastly Arnold turned to religion, the constant preoccupation and true centre of his whole life, and wrote *St. Paul and Protestantism* (1870), *Literature and Dogma* (1873), *God and the Bible* (1875), and *Last Essays on Church and Religion* (1877). He considered his religious writings to be constructive and conservative. Those who accused him of destructiveness did not realize how far historical and scientific criticism had already riddled the old foundations; and those who accused him of timidity failed to see that he regarded religion as the highest form of culture, the one indispensable without which all secular education is in vain. His attitude is best summed up in his own words (from the preface to *God and the Bible*): "At the present moment two things about the Christian religion must surely be clear to anybody with eyes in his head. One is, that men cannot do without it; the other, that they cannot do with it as it is." Convinced that much in popular religion was "touched with the finger of death" and convinced no less of the hopelessness of man without religion, he sought to find for religion a basis of "scientific fact" that even the positive modern spirit must accept.

Arnold died suddenly, of heart failure, in the spring of 1888. He died at Liverpool and was buried at Laleham with the three sons whose early loss had shadowed his life.

EARLY VICTORIAN NONFICTION PROSE

In an era increasingly flooded with fiction prose, the steady flow of nonfiction prose during the first half of the 19th century showed the vivid, probing directions in form and content in which writers could push their art. Most significant among these writers is the British historian and essayist Thomas Carlyle, who may be said to have initiated Victorian literature with *Sartor Resartus* (1833–34). He continued thereafter to have a powerful effect on its development. *The French Revolution* (1837), the book that made him famous, spoke very directly to this consciously postrevolutionary age. Carlyle's political writing, in *Chartism* (1839; dated 1840), *Past and Present* (1843), and the splenetic *Latter-Day Pamphlets* (1850), inspired other writers to similar "prophetic" denunciations of laissez-faire economics and utilitarian ethics.

The first importance of John Ruskin is as an art critic who, in *Modern Painters* (5 vol., 1843–60), brought Romantic theory to the study of painting and forged an appropriate prose for its expression. But in *The Stones of Venice* (3 vol., 1851–53), Ruskin took the political medievalism of Carlyle's *Past and Present* and gave it a poetic fullness and force. Carlyle and Ruskin together shaped both the nature of literature of the 19th century and its direction into the 20th century.

Among other prose writers of the early Victorian period, John Henry Newman was an influential poet, novelist, and theologian who wrote many of the tracts, published as *Tracts for the Times* (1833–41), that promoted the Oxford movement, which sought to reassert the Roman Catholic identity of the Church of England. His subsequent religious development is memorably described in his *Apologia pro Vita Sua* (1864), one of the many great autobiographies of this introspective century.

THOMAS CARLYLE

Carlyle, born in 1795, was the second son of James Carlyle, the eldest child of his second marriage. James Carlyle was a mason by trade and, later, a small farmer, a man of profound Calvinist convictions whose character and way of life had a profound and lasting influence on his son. Carlyle was equally devoted to his mother as well as to his eight brothers and sisters, and his strong affection for his family never diminished.

After attending the village school at Ecclefechan, Thomas was sent in 1805 to Annan Academy, where he apparently suffered from bullying, and later to the University of Edinburgh (1809), where he read widely but followed no precise line of study. His father had intended him to enter the ministry, but Thomas became increasingly doubtful of his vocation. He had an aptitude for mathematics, and in 1814 he obtained a mathematical teaching post at Annan. In 1816 he went to another school, at Kirkcaldy, where the Scottish preacher and mystic Edward Irving was teaching. He became one of the few men to whom Carlyle gave complete admiration and affection. "But for Irving," Carlyle commented sometime later, "I had never known what communion of man with man means." Their friendship continued even after Irving moved in 1822 to London, where he became famous as a preacher.

The next years were hard for Carlyle. Teaching did not suit him and he abandoned it. In December 1819 he returned to Edinburgh University to study law, and there he spent three miserable years, lonely, unable to feel certain of any meaning in life, and eventually abandoning the idea of entering the ministry. He did a little coaching (tutoring) and journalism, was poor and isolated, and was conscious of intense spiritual struggles. About 1821 he experienced a kind of conversion, which he described some years later in fictionalized account in *Sartor Resartus,* whose salient feature was that it was negative—hatred of the devil, not love of God, being the dominating idea. Though it may be doubted whether everything was really experienced as he described it, this violence is certainly characteristic of Carlyle's tortured and defiant spirit. In those lean years he began his serious study of German, which always remained the literature he most admired and enjoyed. For Goethe, especially, he had the greatest reverence, and he published a translation, *Wilhelm Meister's Apprenticeship*, in 1824. Meanwhile, he led a nomadic life, holding several brief tutorships at Edinburgh, Dunkeld, and elsewhere.

MARRIAGE AND LONDON

On Oct. 17, 1826, Carlyle married Jane Welsh, an intelligent, attractive, and somewhat temperamental daughter of a well-to-do doctor in Haddington. Welsh had been one of Irving's pupils, and she and Carlyle had known one another for five years. The hesitations and financial worries that beset them are recorded in their letters. It is interesting that Carlyle, usually so imperious, often adopted a weak, pleading tone to his future wife during the time of courtship, though this did not prevent him from being a masterful, difficult, and irritable husband; and, in spite of their strong mutual affection, their marriage was full of quarrels and misunderstandings. Those who knew him best believed Carlyle to be impotent.

In the early years of their marriage the Carlyles lived mostly at Craigenputtock, Dumfriesshire, and Carlyle contributed to the *Edinburgh Review* and worked on *Sartor Resartus*. Though this book eventually achieved great popular success, he had at first much difficulty in finding a publisher for it. Written with mingled bitterness and humour, it is a fantastic hodgepodge of autobiography and German philosophy. Its main theme is that the intellectual forms in which men's deepest convictions have been cast are dead and that new ones must be found to fit the time but that the intellectual content of this new religious system is elusive. Its author speaks of "embodying the Divine Spirit of religion in a new Mythus, in a new vehicle and vesture," but he never says very clearly what the new vesture is to be.

In 1834, after failing to obtain several posts he had desired, Carlyle moved to London with his wife and settled in Cheyne Row. Though he had not earned anything by his writings for more than a year and was fearful of the day when his savings would be exhausted, he refused to compromise but began an ambitious historical work, *The French Revolution*. The story of how the partially completed manuscript was lent to J.S. Mill and accidentally burned is well known. After the accident Carlyle wrote to Mill in a generous, almost gay, tone, which is truly remarkable when Carlyle's ambition, his complete dependence upon a successful literary career, his poverty, the months of wasted work, and his habitual melancholy and irritability are considered. The truth seems to be that he could bear grand and terrible trials more easily than petty annoyances. His habitual, frustrated melancholy arose, in part, from the fact that his misfortunes were not serious enough to match his tragic view of life; and he sought relief in intensive historical research, choosing subjects in which divine drama, lacking in his own life, seemed most evident. His book on the French Revolution is perhaps his greatest achievement. After the loss of the manuscript he worked furiously at rewriting it. It was finished early in 1837 and soon won both serious acclaim and popular success, besides bringing him many invitations to lecture, thus solving his financial difficulties.

True to his idea of history as a "Divine Scripture," Carlyle saw the French Revolution as an inevitable judgment upon the folly and selfishness of the monarchy and nobility. This simple idea was backed with an immense mass of well-documented detail and, at times, a memorable skill in sketching character. The following extract is characteristic of the contorted, fiery, and doom-laden prose, which is alternately colloquial, humorous, and grim:

> . . . *an august Assembly spread its pavilion; curtained by the dark infinite of discords; founded on the wavering bottomless of the Abyss; and keeps continual hubbub. Time is around it, and Eternity, and the Inane; and it does what it can, what is given it to do* (part 2, book 3, ch. 3).

Though many readers were thrilled by the drama of the narrative, it is not surprising that they were puzzled by Carlyle's prophetic harangues and their relevance to the contemporary situation.

In *Chartism* (1840) he appeared as a bitter opponent of conventional economic theory, but the radical-progressive and the reactionary elements were curiously blurred and mingled. With the publication of *On Heroes, Hero-Worship, and the Heroic in History* (1841) his reverence for strength, particularly when combined with the conviction of a God-given mission, began to emerge. He discussed the hero as divinity (pagan myths), as prophet (Muḥammad), as poet (Dante and Shakespeare), as priest (Luther and Knox), as man of letters (Johnson and Burns), and as king (Cromwell and Napoleon). It is perhaps in his treatment of poets that Carlyle shows to the best advantage. Perverse though he could be, he was never at the mercy of fashion; and he saw much more, particularly in Dante, than others did. Two years later this idea of the hero was elaborated in *Past and Present,* which strove "to penetrate...into a somewhat remote century...in hope of perhaps illustrating our own poor century thereby." He contrasts the wise and strong rule of a medieval abbot with the muddled softness and chaos of the 19th century, pronouncing in favour of the former, in spite of the fact that he had rejected dogmatic Christianity and had a special aversion to the Roman Catholic Church.

It was natural that Carlyle should turn to Cromwell as the greatest English example of his ideal man and should produce the bulky *Oliver Cromwell's Letters and Speeches. With Elucidations* in 1845. His next important work was *Latter-Day Pamphlets* (1850), in which the savage side of his nature was particularly prominent. In the essay on model prisons, for instance, he tried to persuade the public that the most brutal and useless sections of the population were being coddled in the new prisons of the 19th century. Though incapable of lying, Carlyle was completely unreliable as an observer, since he invariably saw what he had decided in advance that he ought to see.

In 1857 he embarked on a massive study of another of his heroes, Frederick the Great, and *The History of Friedrich II of Prussia, Called Frederick the Great* appeared between 1858 and 1865. Something of his political attitude at this time can be gathered from a letter written in April 1855 to the exiled Russian revolutionary A.I. Herzen, in which he says "I never had, and have now (if it were possible) less than ever, the least hope in 'Universal Suffrage' under any of its modifications" and refers to "the sheer Anarchy (as I reckon it sadly to be) which is got by 'Parliamentary eloquence,' Free Press, and counting of heads" (quoted from E.H. Carr, *The Romantic Exiles*).

Unfortunately, Carlyle was never able to respect ordinary men. Here, perhaps, rather than in any historical doubts about the veracity of the gospels, was the core of his quarrel with Christianity—it set too much value on the weak and sinful. His fierceness of spirit was composed of two elements, a serious Calvinistic desire to denounce evil and a habitual nervous ill temper, for which he often reproached himself but which he never managed to defeat.

FINAL YEARS

In 1865 he was offered the rectorship of Edinburgh University. The speech that he delivered at his installation in April 1866 was not very remarkable in itself but its tone of high moral exhortation made it an immediate success. It was published in 1866 under the title *On the Choice of Books*. Soon after his triumph in Edinburgh, Jane Carlyle died suddenly in London. She was buried in Haddington, and an epitaph by her husband was placed in the church.

Carlyle never completely recovered from her death. He lived another 15 years, weary, bored, and a partial recluse. A few public causes gained his support: he was active in the defense of Gov. E.J. Eyre of Jamaica, who was dismissed for his severity in putting down a black uprising in 1865. Carlyle commended him for "saving the West Indies and hanging one incendiary mulatto, well worth gallows, if I can judge." He was excited by the Franco-German War (1870–71), saying "Germany ought to be President of Europe," but such enthusiastic moments soon faded. In these last years he wrote little. His history *The Early Kings of Norway: Also an Essay on the Portraits of John Knox* came out in 1875, and *Reminiscences* was published in 1881. Later he edited his wife's letters, which appeared in 1883 under the title *Letters and Memorials of Jane Welsh Carlyle, Prepared for Publication by Thomas Carlyle*. Although Westminster Abbey was offered for his burial, he was buried, according to his wish, beside his parents at Ecclefechan.

John Ruskin

John Ruskin was born in 1819 into the commercial classes of the prosperous and powerful Britain of the years immediately following the Napoleonic Wars. His father, John James Ruskin, was a Scots wine merchant who had moved to London and made a fortune in the sherry trade. John Ruskin, an only child, was largely educated at home, where he was given a taste for art by his father's collecting of contemporary watercolours and a minute and comprehensive knowledge of the Bible by his piously Protestant mother.

This combination of the religious intensity of the Evangelical Revival and the artistic excitement of English Romantic painting laid the foundations of Ruskin's later views. In his formative years, painters such as J.M.W. Turner, John Constable, and John Sell Cotman were at the peak of their careers. At the same time religious writers and preachers such as Charles Simeon, John Keble, Thomas Arnold, and John Henry Newman were

establishing the spiritual and ethical preoccupations that
would characterize the reign of Queen Victoria. Ruskin's
family background in the world of business was significant, too: it not only provided the means for his extensive
travels to see paintings, buildings, and landscapes in
Britain and continental Europe but also gave him an
understanding of the newly rich, middle-class audience
for which his books would be written.

Ruskin discovered the work of Turner through the
illustrations to an edition of Samuel Rogers's poem *Italy*
given him by a business partner of his father in 1833. By the
mid-1830s he was publishing short pieces in both prose
and verse in magazines, and in 1836 he was provoked into
drafting a reply (unpublished) to an attack on Turner's
painting by the art critic of *Blackwood's Magazine*. After
five years at the University of Oxford, during which he
won the Newdigate Prize for poetry but was prevented by
ill health from sitting for an honours degree, Ruskin
returned, in 1842, to his abandoned project of defending
and explaining the late work of Turner.

ART AND ARCHITECTURAL CRITICISM

In 1843 Ruskin published the first volume of *Modern
Painters*, a book that would eventually consist of five volumes and occupy him for the next 17 years. His first
purpose was to insist on the "truth" of the depiction of
Nature in Turner's landscape paintings. Neoclassical critics had attacked the later work of Turner, with its
proto-Impressionist concern for effects of light and
atmosphere, for mimetic inaccuracy, and for a failure to
represent the "general truth" that had been an essential
criterion of painting in the age of Sir Joshua Reynolds.
Drawing on his serious amateur interests in geology, bot-
any, and meteorology, Ruskin made it his business to

demonstrate in detail that Turner's work was everywhere based on a profound knowledge of the local and particular truths of natural form. One after another, Turner's "truth of tone," "truth of colour," "truth of space," "truth of skies," "truth of earth," "truth of water," and "truth of vegetation" were minutely considered, in a laborious project that would not be completed until the appearance of the fifth and final volume of *Modern Painters* in 1860.

This shift of concern from general to particular conceptions of truth was a key feature of Romantic thought, and Ruskin's first major achievement was thus to bring the assumptions of Romanticism to the practice of art criticism. By 1843 avant-garde painters had been working in this new spirit for several decades, but criticism and public understanding had lagged behind. More decisively than any previous writer, Ruskin brought 19th-century English painting and 19th-century English art criticism into sympathetic alignment. As he did so, he alerted readers to the fact that they had, in Turner, one of the greatest painters in the history of Western art alive and working among them in contemporary London, and, in the broader school of English landscape painting, a major modern art movement.

Ruskin did this in a prose style peculiarly well adapted to the discussion of the visual arts in an era when there was limited reproductive illustration and no easy access to well-stocked public art galleries. In these circumstances the critic was obliged to create in words an effective sensory and emotional substitute for visual experience. Working in the tradition of the Romantic poetic prose of Charles Lamb and Thomas De Quincey, though more immediately influenced by the descriptive writing of Sir Walter Scott, the rhetoric of the Bible, and the blank verse of William Wordsworth, Ruskin vividly evoked the effect on the human eye and sensibility both of Turner's paintings and of the actual landscapes that Turner and other artists had sought to represent.

In the process Ruskin introduced the newly wealthy commercial and professional classes of the English-speaking world to the possibility of enjoying and collecting art. Since most of them had been shaped by an austerely puritanical religious tradition, Ruskin knew that they would be suspicious of claims for painting that stressed its sensual or hedonic qualities. Instead, he defined painting as "a noble and expressive language, invaluable as the vehicle of thought, but by itself nothing." What that language expressed, in Romantic landscape painting, was a Wordsworthian sense of a divine presence in Nature, a morally instructive natural theology in which God spoke through physical "types." Conscious of the spiritual significance of the natural world, young painters should "go to Nature in all singleness of heart . . . having no other thoughts but how best to penetrate her meaning, and remember her instruction; rejecting nothing, selecting nothing, and scorning nothing."

Three years later, in the second volume of *Modern Painters* (1846), Ruskin would specifically distinguish this strenuously ethical or Theoretic conception of art from the Aesthetic, undidactic, or art-for-art's-sake definition that would be its great rival in the second half of the 19th century. Despite his friendships with individual Aesthetes, Ruskin would remain the dominant spokesman for a morally and socially committed conception of art throughout his lifetime.

After the publication of the first volume of *Modern Painters* in 1843, Ruskin became aware of another avant-garde artistic movement: the critical rediscovery of the painting of the Gothic Middle Ages. He wrote about these

Idealist painters (especially Giotto, Fra Angelico, and Benozzo Gozzoli) at the end of the second volume of *Modern Painters*, and he belatedly added an account of them to the third edition of the first volume in 1846. These medieval religious artists could provide, he believed, in a way in which the Dutch, French, and Italian painters of the 17th and 18th centuries could not, an inspiring model for the art of the "modern" age.

This medievalist enthusiasm was one reason that Ruskin was so ready to lend his support to the Pre-Raphaelite Brotherhood (PRB), a group of young English artists formed in 1848 to reject the Neoclassical assumptions of contemporary art schools. Ruskin published an enthusiastic pamphlet about the PRB (in which he misleadingly identified them as the natural heirs of Turner) in 1851, wrote letters to the *Times* in 1851 and 1854 to defend them from their critics, and recommended their work in his Edinburgh Lectures of 1853 (published 1854).

But medievalism was even more important in the field of architecture, where the Gothic Revival was as direct an expression of the new Romantic spirit as the landscape painting of Turner or Constable. Ruskin had been involved in a major Gothic Revival building project in 1844, when George Gilbert Scott redesigned Ruskin's parents' parish church, St. Giles's Camberwell. In 1848, newly married to Euphemia (Effie) Gray, Ruskin went on a honeymoon tour of the Gothic churches of northern France and began to write his first major book on buildings, *The Seven Lamps of Architecture* (1849). Conceived in the disturbing context of the European revolutions of 1848, the book lays down seven moral principles (or "Lamps") to guide architectural practice, one of which, "The Lamp of Memory," articulates the scrupulous respect for the original fabric of old buildings that would inspire William Morris and, through him, the conservation movement of the 20th century. In November Ruskin went abroad again, this time to Venice to research a more substantial book on architecture.

The Stones of Venice was published in three volumes, one in 1851 and two more in 1853. In part it is a laboriously researched history of Venetian architecture, based on long months of direct study of the original buildings, then in a condition of serious neglect and decay. But it is also a book of moral and social polemic with the imaginative structure of a Miltonic or Wordsworthian sublime epic. Ruskin's narrative charts the fall of Venice from its medieval Eden, through the impiety and arrogance (as Ruskin saw it) of the Renaissance, to its modern condition of political impotence and social frivolity. As such, the book is a distinguished late example of the political medievalism found in the work of William Cobbett, Robert Southey, Thomas Carlyle, and the Young England movement of the 1840s. Ruskin differs from these predecessors both in the poetic power of his prose and in his distinctive—and widely influential—insistence that art and architecture are, necessarily, the direct expression of the social conditions in which they were produced. Here, as elsewhere, the Aesthetic movement, with its view of art as a rebellious alternative to the social norm and its enthusiasm for Renaissance texts and artifacts, stands in direct contrast to Ruskin's Theoretic views.

The Stones of Venice was influential in other ways as well. Its celebration of Italian Gothic encouraged the use of foreign models in English Gothic Revival architecture. By 1874 Ruskin would regret the extent to which architects had "dignified our banks and drapers' shops with Venetian tracery." But, for good or ill, his writing played a key part in establishing the view that the architectural style of Venice, the great maritime trading nation of the medieval world, was particularly appropriate for buildings in modern Britain. The other enduring influence derived, more subtly, from a single chapter in the second volume, "The Nature of Gothic." There Ruskin identified "imperfection" as an essential feature of Gothic art, contrasting it with the mechanical regularity of Neoclassical buildings and modern mass production. Gothic architecture, he believed, allowed a significant degree of creative freedom and artistic fulfillment to the individual workman. We could not, and should not, take pleasure in an object that had not itself been made with pleasure. In this proposition lay the roots both of Ruskin's own quarrel with industrial capitalism and of the Arts and Crafts movement of the later 19th century.

THE OUTSIDER

Turner died in 1851. Ruskin's marriage was dissolved, on grounds of nonconsummation, in 1854, leaving the former Effie Gray free to marry the Pre-Raphaelite painter John Everett Millais. Ruskin withdrew somewhat from society. He traveled extensively in Europe and, from 1856 to 1858, took on a considerable body of administrative work as the chief artistic executor of Turner's estate. He contributed both financially and physically to the construction of a major Gothic Revival building: Benjamin Woodward's Oxford University Museum.

In 1856 Rushkin published the third and fourth volumes of *Modern Painters*, with their penetrating inquiry into the reasons for the predominance of landscape painting in 19th-century art and their invention of the important critical term "pathetic fallacy." His annual *Academy Notes* (a series of pamphlets issued by an English publisher from 1855 to 1859) sustained his reputation as a persuasive commentator on contemporary painting. But by 1858 Ruskin was beginning to move on from the specialist criticism of art and architecture to a wider concern with the cultural condition of his age. His growing friendship with the historian and essayist Thomas Carlyle contributed to this process. Like Carlyle, Ruskin began to adopt the "prophetic" stance, familiar from the Bible, of a voice crying from the wilderness and seeking to call a lapsed people back into the paths of righteousness.

This marginal role as a disenchanted outsider both legitimized and, to an extent, required a ferocity and oddness that would be conspicuous features of Ruskin's later career. In 1858 Ruskin lectured on "The Work of Iron in Nature, Art and Policy" (published in *The Two Paths*, 1859), a text in which both the radical-conservative temper and the symbolic method of his later cultural criticism are clearly established. Beginning as an art critic, Ruskin contrasts the exquisite sculptured iron grilles of medieval Verona with the mass-produced metal security railings with which modern citizens protect their houses. The artistic contrast is, of course, also a social contrast, and Ruskin goes rapidly beyond this to a symbolic assertion of the "iron" values involved in his definition of the just society. By wearing the fetters of a benignly neofeudalist social order, men and women, Ruskin believed, might lead lives of greater aesthetic fulfillment, in an environment less degraded by industrial pollution.

These values are persistently restated in Ruskin's writings of the 1860s, sometimes in surprising ways. *Unto This Last* and *Munera Pulveris* (1862 and 1872 as books, though published in magazines in 1860 and 1862–63) are attacks on the classical economics of Adam Smith and John Stuart Mill. Neither book makes any significant technical contribution to the study of economics (though Ruskin thought otherwise). Both memorably express Ruskin's moral outrage at the extent to which the materialist and utilitarian ethical assumptions implicit in this new technique for understanding human behaviour had come to be accepted as normative. *Sesame and Lilies* (1865) would become notorious in the late 20th century as a stock example of Victorian male chauvinism. In fact, Ruskin was using the conventional construction of the feminine, as pacific, altruistic, and uncompetitive, to articulate yet another symbolic assertion of his anticapitalist social model. *The Crown of Wild Olive* (1866, enlarged in 1873) collects some of the best specimens of Ruskin's Carlylean manner, notably the lecture "Traffic" of 1864, which memorably draws its audience's attention to the hypocrisy manifested by their choice of Gothic architecture for their churches but Neoclassical designs for their homes.

The dogmatic Protestantism of Ruskin's childhood had been partially abandoned in 1858, after an "unconversion" experience in Turin. Ten years later, in a moving lecture on "The Mystery of Life and Its Arts," Ruskin reflected on his returning sense of the spiritual and transcendent. In *The Queen of the Air* (1869) he attempted to express his old concept of a divine power in Nature in new terms calculated for an age in which assent to the Christian faith was no longer automatic or universal. Through an account of the Greek myth of Athena, Ruskin sought to suggest an enduring human need for—and implicit recognition of—the supernatural authority on which the moral stresses of his artistic, political, and cultural views depend.

His father's death in 1864 had left Ruskin a wealthy man. He used his wealth, in part, to promote idealistic social causes, notably the Guild of St. George, a pastoral community first planned in 1871 and formally constituted seven years later. From 1866 to 1875 he was unhappily in love with a woman 30 years his junior, Rose La Touche, whose physical and mental deterioration caused him acute distress. During these years he began, himself, to show signs of serious psychological illness. In 1871 he bought Brantwood, a house in the English Lake District (now a museum of his work) and lived there for the rest of his life.

Ruskin's appointment as Slade Professor of Fine Art at Oxford in 1870 was a welcome encouragement at a troubled stage of his career, and in the following year he launched *Fors Clavigera*, a one-man monthly magazine in which, from 1871 to 1878 and 1880 to 1884 he developed his idiosyncratic cultural theories. Like his successive series of Oxford lectures (1870–79 and 1883–84), *Fors* is an unpredictable mixture of striking insights, powerful rhetoric, self-indulgence, bigotry, and occasional incoherence. As a by-product of the *Fors* project, however, Ruskin wrote his last major work: his autobiography, *Praeterita* (1885–89). Unfinished, shamelessly partial (it omits, for example, all mention of his marriage), and chronologically untrustworthy, it provides a subtle and memorable history of the growth of Ruskin's distinctive sensibility.

In November 1878 the painter James McNeill Whistler's action for libel against Ruskin—brought after Ruskin's attack on the impressionist manner of a Whistler *Nocturne*—came to trial. The trial made the conflict between Ruskin's moral view of art and Whistler's Aestheticism a matter of wide public interest. Whistler, awarded only a farthing's damages and no costs, was driven into bankruptcy. Ruskin suffered no financial ill effects, but his reputation as an art critic was seriously harmed. After this date there was a growing tendency to see him as an enemy of modern art: blinkered, eccentric, and out-of-date.

Modernist artists and critics rejected Ruskin. His stress on the moral, social, and spiritual purposes of art and his Naturalist theory of visual representation were unpopular in the era of Impressionism, Cubism, and Dada.

Amboise, *watercolour over pencil on paper by John Ruskin, 19th century. 44 × 28.5 cm.* In a private collection

Gothic Revival buildings became deeply unfashionable; the architecture critic Geoffrey Scott, in 1914, would dismiss Ruskin's architectural theory as "The Ethical Fallacy."

Subsequently, however, Ruskin was gradually rediscovered. His formative importance as a thinker about ecology, about the conservation of buildings and environments, about Romantic painting, about art education, and about the human cost of the mechanization of work became steadily more obvious. The outstanding quality of his own drawings and watercolours (modestly treated in his lifetime as working notes or amateur sketches) was increasingly acknowledged, as was his role as a stimulus to the flowering of British painting, architecture, and decorative art in the second half of the 19th century.

Above all, Ruskin was rediscovered as a great writer of English prose. Frequently self-contradictory, hectoringly moralistic, and insufficiently informed, Ruskin—much like Carlyle—was nonetheless gifted with exceptional powers of perception and expression. These are the gifts that the poet Matthew Arnold acknowledged when he spoke of "the genius, the feeling, the temperament" of the descriptive writing in the fourth volume of *Modern Painters*.

LATE VICTORIAN LITERATURE

"The modern spirit," Matthew Arnold observed in 1865, "is now awake." In 1859 Charles Darwin had published *On the Origin of Species by Means of Natural Selection*. Historians, philosophers, and scientists were all beginning to apply the idea of evolution to new areas of study of the human experience. Traditional conceptions of man's nature and place in the world were, as a consequence, under threat. Walter Pater summed up the process, in 1866, by stating that "Modern thought is distinguished from ancient by its cultivation of the 'relative' spirit in place of the 'absolute.'"

The economic crisis of the 1840s was long past. But the fierce political debates that led first to the Second Reform Act of 1867 and then to the battles for the enfranchisement of women were accompanied by a deepening crisis of belief.

THE NOVEL

Late Victorian fiction may express doubts and uncertainties, but in aesthetic terms it displays a new sophistication and self-confidence. The expatriate American novelist Henry James wrote in 1884 that until recently the English novel had "had no air of having a theory, a conviction, a consciousness of itself behind it." Its acquisition of these things was due in no small part to Mary Ann Evans, better known as George Eliot. Initially a critic and translator, she was influenced, after the loss of her Christian faith, by the ideas of Ludwig Feuerbach and Auguste Comte. Her advanced intellectual interests combined with her sophisticated sense of the novel form to shape her remarkable fiction, which culminated in her masterpiece, *Middlemarch*, an unprecedentedly full study of the life of a provincial town, focused on the thwarted idealism of her two principal characters. Eliot is the supreme realist of the Victorian era, but her realism involves a scientific analysis of the interior processes of social and personal existence.

GEORGE ELIOT

Mary Ann Evans was born in 1819 on an estate of her father's employer. She went as a boarder to Mrs. Wallington's School at Nuneaton (1828–32), where she came under the influence of Maria Lewis, the principal governess, who inculcated a strong evangelical piety in the young girl. At her last school (1832–35), conducted by the daughters of the Baptist minister at Coventry, her religious ardour increased. She dressed severely and engaged earnestly in good works. The school gave her a reading knowledge of French and Italian, and, after her mother's death had compelled her to return home to keep house for her father, he let her have lessons in Latin and German. In 1841 she moved with her father to Coventry.

There she became acquainted with a prosperous ribbon manufacturer, Charles Bray, a self-taught freethinker who campaigned for radical causes. His brother-in-law, Charles Hennell, was the author of *An Inquiry Concerning the Origin of Christianity* (1838), a book that precipitated Evans's break with orthodoxy that had been long in preparation. Various books on the relation between the Bible and science had instilled in her keen mind the very doubts they were written to dispel. In 1842 she told her father that she could no longer go to church. The ensuing storm raged for several months before they reached a compromise, leaving her free to think what she pleased so long as she appeared respectably at church, and she lived with him until his death in 1849.

The Brays and the Hennells quickly drew her from extreme provincialism, introducing her to many ideas in violent disagreement with her Tory father's religious and political views. When Charles Hennell married in 1843, she took over from his wife the translating of D.F. Strauss's *Das Leben Jesu kritisch bearbeitet*, which was published anonymously as *The Life of Jesus Critically Examined*, 3 vol. (1846), and had a profound influence on English rationalism. After the wedding Mrs. Hennell's father, R.H. Brabant, invited Evans to visit at Devizes. A rather silly man, he had worked for years on a book (never completed), which was to dispose of the supernatural elements in religion. They read German and Greek together and discussed theology on long walks; soon Mrs. Brabant became jealous of their intimacy, and, before the term of her visit, Evans was forced to leave. Mrs. Hennell felt that her father had acted ungenerously. Out of the humiliation of this episode George Eliot drew the horrible vividness of Mr. Casaubon in *Middlemarch*.

She spent the winter of 1849–50 at Geneva, reading extensively while living with the family of François d'Albert Durade, who painted a portrait of her. Like those by Mrs. Bray (1842) and Sir Frederic Burton (1865), all in the National Portrait Gallery, it shows her with light brown hair, gray-blue eyes, and a very fair complexion. Returning to Coventry, she spent the rest of 1850 with the Brays, pondering how to live on the £100 a year left by her father. After John Chapman, the publisher of *The Life of Jesus Critically Examined*, got her a chance to review R.W. Mackay's *The Progress of the Intellect* in *The Westminster Review* (January 1851), she decided to settle in London as a freelance writer, and in January 1851 she went to board with the Chapmans at 142, Strand.

Life with Lewes

Soon after her arrival in London, Mrs. Chapman and the children's governess, who was also John Chapman's mistress, became jealous of Marian, as she now signed her name, and after 10 weeks she returned to Coventry in tears. Doubtless her feelings were strongly attracted to the magnetic Chapman, whose diary supplies this information, but there is no evidence that she was ever his mistress. A few months later he bought *The Westminster Review*, and Evans, contrite at the domestic complications she had unwittingly caused, returned to London. For three years, until 1854, she served as subeditor of *The Westminster*, which under her influence enjoyed its most brilliant run since the days of John Stuart Mill. At the Chapmans' evening parties she met many notable literary figures in an atmosphere of political and religious radicalism. Across the Strand lived the subeditor of *The Economist*, Herbert Spencer, whose *Social Statics* (1851) Chapman had just published. Evans shared many of Spencer's interests and saw so much of him that it was soon rumoured that they were engaged. Though he did not become her husband, he introduced her to the two men who did.

George Henry Lewes was the most versatile of Victorian journalists. In 1841 he had married Agnes Jervis, by whom he had four sons. In 1850 Lewes and a friend, the journalist Thornton Leigh Hunt, founded a radical weekly called *The Leader*, for which he wrote the literary and theatrical sections. In April 1850, two weeks after the first number appeared, Agnes Lewes gave birth to a son whose father was Thornton Hunt. Lewes, being a man of liberal views, had the child registered as Edmund Lewes and remained on friendly terms with his wife and Hunt. But after she bore Hunt a second child in October 1851, Lewes ceased to regard her as his wife, though, having condoned the adultery, he was precluded from suing for divorce. At this moment of dejection, his home hopelessly broken, he met Marian Evans. They consulted about articles and went to plays and operas that Lewes reviewed for *The Leader*. Convinced that his break with Agnes was irrevocable, Evans determined to live openly with Lewes as his wife. In July 1854, after the publication of her translation of Feuerbach's *Essence of Christianity*, they went to Germany together. In all but the legal form it was a marriage, and it continued happily until Lewes's death in 1878. "Women who are content with light and easily broken ties," she told

Mrs. Bray, "do *not* act as I have done. They obtain what they desire and are still invited to dinner."

At Weimar and Berlin she wrote some of her best essays for *The Westminster* and translated Spinoza's *Ethics* (still unpublished), while Lewes worked on his groundbreaking life of Goethe. By his pen alone he had to support his three surviving sons at school in Switzerland as well as Agnes, whom he gave £100 a year, which was continued until her death in 1902. She had four children by Hunt, the last born in 1857, all registered under Lewes's name. The few friends who knew the facts agreed that toward Agnes his conduct was more than generous, but there was a good deal of malicious gossip about the "strong-minded woman" who had "run off with" her husband. Evans's deepest regret was that her act isolated her from her family in Warwickshire. She turned to early memories and, encouraged by Lewes, wrote a story about a childhood episode in Chilvers Coton parish. Published in *Blackwood's Magazine* (1857) as *The Sad Fortunes of the Reverend Amos Barton,* it was an instant success. Two more tales, *Mr. Gilfil's Love-Story* and *Janet's Repentance,* also based on local events, appeared serially in the same year, and Blackwood republished all three as *Scenes of Clerical Life,* 2 vol. (1858), under the pseudonym George Eliot.

Adam Bede, 3 vol. (1859), her first long novel, she described as "a country story—full of the breath of cows and the scent of hay." Its masterly realism—"the faithful representing of commonplace things"—brought to English fiction the same truthful observation of minute detail that Ruskin was commending in the Pre-Raphaelites. The book is rich in humour. The germ of the plot was an anecdote her Methodist aunt told of visiting a girl condemned for child murder. The dialect of the Bedes she had heard in the conversations of her Derbyshire uncles with her father, some of whose early experiences she assigned to Adam. But what was new in English fiction was the combination of deep human sympathy and rigorous moral judgment. *Adam Bede* went through eight printings within a year, and Blackwood doubled the £800 paid for it and returned the copyright.

In *The Mill on the Floss*, 3 vol. (1860), she returned again to the scenes of her early life. The first half of the book, with its remarkable portrayal of childhood, is irresistibly appealing, and throughout there are scenes that reach a new level of psychological subtlety.

At this time historical novels were in vogue, and during their visit to Florence in 1860 Lewes suggested Savonarola as a good subject, George Eliot grasped it enthusiastically and began to plan *Romola* (1862–63). First, however, she wrote *Silas Marner* (1861), which had thrust itself between her and the Italian material. Its brevity and perfection of form made this story of the weaver whose lost gold is replaced by a strayed child the best known of her books, though it has suffered unfairly from being forced on generations of schoolchildren. *Romola* was planned as a serial for *Blackwood's*, until an offer of £10,000 from *The Cornhill Magazine* induced George Eliot to desert her old publisher; but rather than divide the book into the 16 installments the editor wanted, she accepted £3,000 less, an evidence of artistic integrity few writers would have shown. Details of Florentine history, setting, costume, and dialogue were scrupulously studied at the British Museum and during a second trip to Italy in 1861. It was published in 14 parts between July 1862 and August 1863. Though the book lacks the spontaneity of the English stories, it has been unduly disparaged.

George Eliot's next two novels are laid in England at the time of agitation for passage of the Reform Bill. In *Felix Holt, the Radical*, 3 vol. (1866), she drew the election riot from recollection of one she saw at Nuneaton in December 1832. The initial impulse of the book was not the political theme but the tragic character of Mrs. Transome, who was one of her greatest triumphs. The intricate plot popular taste then demanded now tells against the novel. *Middlemarch* (8 parts, 1871–72) is by general consent George Eliot's masterpiece. Under her hand the novel had developed from a mere entertainment into a highly intellectual form of art. Every class of Middlemarch society is depicted from the landed gentry and clergy to the manufacturers and professional men, the shopkeepers, publicans, farmers, and labourers. Several strands of plot are interwoven to reinforce each other by contrast and parallel. Yet the story depends not on close-knit intrigue but on showing the incalculably diffusive effect of the unhistoric acts of those who "lived faithfully a hidden life and rest in unvisited tombs."

Daniel Deronda (8 parts, 1876), in which George Eliot comes nearest the contemporary scene, is built on the contrast between Mirah Cohen, a poor Jewish girl, and the upper class Gwendolen Harleth, who marries for money and regrets it. The less convincingly realized hero, Daniel, after discovering that he is Jewish, marries Mirah and departs for Palestine to establish a home for his nation. The picture of the Cohen family evoked grateful praise from Jewish readers. But the best part of *Daniel Deronda* is the keen analysis of Gwendolen's character, which seems to many critics the peak of George Eliot's achievement.

Final Years

In 1863 the Leweses bought the Priory, 21, North Bank, Regent's Park, where their Sunday afternoons became a brilliant feature of Victorian life. There on Nov. 30, 1878, Lewes died. For nearly 25 years he had fostered her genius and managed all the practical details of life, which now fell upon her. Most of all she missed the encouragement that alone made it possible for her to write. For months she saw no one but his son Charles Lee Lewes. She devoted herself to completing the last volume of his *Problems of Life and Mind* (1873–79) and founded the George Henry Lewes Studentship in Physiology at Cambridge. For some years her investments had been in the hands of John Walter Cross (1840–1924), a banker introduced to the Leweses by Herbert Spencer. Cross's mother had died a week after Lewes. Drawn by sympathy and the need for advice, George Eliot soon began to lean on him for affection too. On May 6, 1880, they were married in St. George's, Hanover Square. Cross was 40; she was in her 61st year. After a wedding trip in Italy they returned to her country house at Witley before moving to 4, Cheyne Walk, Chelsea, where she died in December.

THOMAS HARDY

Rivaling Eliot for title of greatest novelist of the late Victorian era was Thomas Hardy. His first published novel, *Desperate Remedies*, appeared in 1871 and was followed by 13 more before he abandoned prose to publish (in the 20th century) only poetry. His major fiction consists of the tragic novels of rural life, *The Mayor of Casterbridge*, *Tess of the D'Urbervilles*, and *Jude the Obscure*. In these novels his brilliant evocation of the landscape and people of his fictional Wessex is combined with a sophisticated sense of the "ache of modernism."

Hardy was born in 1840, the eldest of the four children of Thomas Hardy, a stonemason and jobbing builder, and his wife, Jemima (née Hand). He grew up in an isolated cottage on the edge of open heathland. Though he was often ill as a child, his early experience of rural life, with its

Thomas Hardy forsook a career as an architect to write poetry and fiction. Today, Hardy is considered one of the preeminent novelists of his generation. Hulton Archive/Getty Images

seasonal rhythms and oral culture, was fundamental to much of his later writing. He spent a year at the village school at age eight and then moved on to schools in Dorchester, the nearby county town, where he received a good grounding in mathematics and Latin. In 1856 he was apprenticed to John Hicks, a local architect, and in 1862, shortly before his 22nd birthday, he moved to London and became a draftsman in the busy office of Arthur Blomfield, a leading ecclesiastical architect. Driven back to Dorset by ill health in 1867, he worked for Hicks again and then for the Weymouth architect G.R. Crickmay.

Though architecture brought Hardy both social and economic advancement, it was only in the mid-1860s that lack of funds and declining religious faith forced him to abandon his early ambitions of a university education and eventual ordination as an Anglican priest. His habits of intensive private study were then redirected toward the reading of poetry and the systematic development of his own poetic skills. The verses he wrote in the 1860s would emerge in revised form in later volumes (e.g., "Neutral Tones," "Retty's Phases"), but when none of them achieved immediate publication, Hardy reluctantly turned to prose.

In 1867–68 he wrote the class-conscious novel *The Poor Man and the Lady*, which was sympathetically considered by three London publishers but never published. George Meredith, as a publisher's reader, advised Hardy to write a more shapely and less opinionated novel. The result was the densely plotted *Desperate Remedies* (1871), which was influenced by the contemporary "sensation" fiction of Wilkie Collins. In his next novel, however, the brief and affectionately humorous idyll *Under the Greenwood Tree* (1872), Hardy found a voice much more distinctively his own. In this book he evoked, within the simplest of marriage plots, an episode of social change (the displacement of a group of church musicians) that was a direct reflection of events involving his own father shortly before Hardy's own birth.

In March 1870 Hardy had been sent to make an architectural assessment of the lonely and dilapidated Church of St. Juliot in Cornwall. There—in romantic circumstances later poignantly recalled in prose and verse—he first met the rector's vivacious sister-in-law, Emma Lavinia Gifford, who became his wife four years later. She actively encouraged and assisted him in his literary endeavours, and his next novel, *A Pair of Blue Eyes* (1873), drew heavily upon the circumstances of their courtship for its wild Cornish setting and its melodramatic story of a young woman (somewhat resembling Emma Gifford) and the two men, friends become rivals, who successively pursue, misunderstand, and fail her.

Hardy's break with architecture occurred in the summer of 1872, when he undertook to supply *Tinsley's Magazine* with the 11 monthly installments of *A Pair of Blue Eyes*—an initially risky commitment to a literary career that was soon validated by an invitation to contribute a serial to the far more prestigious *Cornhill Magazine*. The resulting novel, *Far from the Madding Crowd* (1874), introduced Wessex for the first time and made Hardy famous by its agricultural settings and its distinctive blend of humorous, melodramatic, pastoral, and tragic elements. The book is a vigorous portrayal of the beautiful and impulsive Bathsheba Everdene and her marital choices among Sergeant Troy, the dashing but irresponsible soldier; William Boldwood, the deeply obsessive farmer; and Gabriel Oak, her loyal and resourceful shepherd.

Middle Period

Hardy and Emma Gifford were married, against the wishes of both their families, in September 1874. At first they moved rather restlessly about, living sometimes in

London, sometimes in Dorset. His record as a novelist during this period was somewhat mixed. *The Hand of Ethelberta* (1876), an artificial social comedy turning on versions and inversions of the British class system, was poorly received and has never been widely popular. *The Return of the Native* (1878), on the other hand, was increasingly admired for its powerfully evoked setting of Egdon Heath, which was based on the sombre countryside Hardy had known as a child. The novel depicts the disastrous marriage between Eustacia Vye, who yearns romantically for passionate experiences beyond the hated heath, and Clym Yeobright, the returning native, who is blinded to his wife's needs by a naively idealistic zeal for the moral improvement of Egdon's impervious inhabitants. Hardy's next works were *The Trumpet-Major* (1880), set in the Napoleonic period, and two more novels generally considered "minor"—*A Laodicean* (1881) and *Two on a Tower* (1882). The serious illness which hampered completion of *A Laodicean* decided the Hardys to move to Wimborne in 1881 and to Dorchester in 1883.

It was not easy for Hardy to establish himself as a member of the professional middle class in a town where his humbler background was well known. He signaled his determination to stay by accepting an appointment as a local magistrate and by designing and building Max Gate, the house just outside Dorchester in which he lived until his death. Hardy's novel *The Mayor of Casterbridge* (1886) incorporates recognizable details of Dorchester's history and topography. The busy market-town of Casterbridge becomes the setting for a tragic struggle, at once economic and deeply personal, between the powerful but unstable Michael Henchard, who has risen from workman to mayor by sheer natural energy, and the more shrewdly calculating Donald Farfrae, who starts out in Casterbridge as Henchard's protégé but ultimately dispossesses him of everything that he had once owned and loved. In Hardy's next novel, *The Woodlanders* (1887), socioeconomic issues again become central as the permutations of sexual advance and retreat are played out among the very trees from which the characters make their living, and Giles Winterborne's loss of livelihood is integrally bound up with his loss of Grace Melbury and, finally, of life itself.

Wessex Tales (1888) was the first collection of the short stories that Hardy had long been publishing in magazines. His subsequent short-story collections are *A Group of Noble Dames* (1891), *Life's Little Ironies* (1894), and *A Changed Man* (1913). Hardy's short novel *The Well-Beloved* (serialized 1892, revised for volume publication 1897) displays a hostility to marriage that was related to increasing frictions within his own marriage.

The closing phase of Hardy's career in fiction was marked by the publication of *Tess of the d'Urbervilles* (1891) and *Jude the Obscure* (1895), which are generally considered his finest novels. Though *Tess* is the most richly "poetic" of Hardy's novels, and *Jude* the most bleakly written, both books offer deeply sympathetic representations of working-class figures: Tess Durbeyfield, the erring milkmaid, and Jude Fawley, the studious stonemason. In powerful, implicitly moralized narratives, Hardy traces these characters' initially hopeful, momentarily ecstatic, but persistently troubled journeys toward eventual deprivation and death.

Though technically belonging to the 19th century, these novels anticipate the 20th century in regard to the nature and treatment of their subject matter. *Tess* profoundly questions society's sexual mores by its compassionate portrayal and even advocacy of a heroine who is seduced, and perhaps raped, by the son of her employer.

She has an illegitimate child, suffers rejection by the man she loves and marries, and is finally hanged for murdering her original seducer. In *Jude the Obscure* the class-ridden educational system of the day is challenged by the defeat of Jude's earnest aspirations to knowledge, while conventional morality is affronted by the way in which the sympathetically presented Jude and Sue change partners, live together, and have children with little regard for the institution of marriage. Both books encountered some brutally hostile reviews, and Hardy's sensitivity to such attacks partly precipitated his long-contemplated transition from fiction to poetry.

Poetry

Hardy seems always to have rated poetry above fiction, and *Wessex Poems* (1898), his first significant public appearance as a poet, included verse written during his years as a novelist as well as revised versions of poems dating from the 1860s. As a collection it was often perceived as miscellaneous and uneven—an impression reinforced by the author's own idiosyncratic illustrations—and acceptance of Hardy's verse was slowed, then and later, by the persistence of his reputation as a novelist. *Poems of the Past and the Present* (1901) contained nearly twice as many poems as its predecessor, most of them newly written. Some of the poems are explicitly or implicitly grouped by subject or theme. There are, for example, 11 "War Poems" prompted by the South African War (e.g., "Drummer Hodge," "The Souls of the Slain") and a sequence of disenchantedly "philosophical" poems (e.g., "The Mother Mourns," "The Subalterns," "To an Unborn Pauper Child"). In *Time's Laughingstocks* (1909), the poems are again arranged under headings, but on principles that often remain elusive. Indeed, there is no clear line of development in Hardy's poetry from immaturity to maturity; his style undergoes no significant change over time. His best poems can be found mixed together with inferior verse in any particular volume, and new poems are often juxtaposed to reworkings of poems written or drafted years before. The range of poems within any particular volume is also extremely broad—from lyric to meditation to ballad to satirical vignette to dramatic monologue or dialogue—and Hardy persistently experiments with different, often invented, stanza forms and metres.

In 1903, 1905, and 1908 Hardy successively published the three volumes of *The Dynasts,* a huge poetic drama that is written mostly in blank verse and subtitled "an epic-drama of the War with Napoleon"—though it was not intended for actual performance. The sequence of major historical events—Trafalgar, Austerlitz, Waterloo, and so on—is diversified by prose episodes involving ordinary soldiers and civilians and by an ongoing cosmic commentary from such personified "Intelligences" as the "Spirit of the Years" and the "Spirit of the Pities." Hardy, who once described his poems as a "series of seemings" rather than expressions of a single consistent viewpoint, found in the contrasted moral and philosophical positions of the various Intelligences a means of articulating his own intellectual ambiguities. *The Dynasts* as a whole served to project his central vision of a universe governed by the purposeless movements of a blind, unconscious force that he called the Immanent Will. Though subsequent criticism has tended to find its structures cumbersome and its verse inert, *The Dynasts* remains an impressive—and highly readable—achievement, and its publication certainly reinforced both Hardy's "national" image (he was appointed to the Order of Merit in 1910) and his enormous fame worldwide.

The sudden death of Emma Hardy in 1912 brought to an end some 20 years of domestic estrangement. It also stirred Hardy to profundities of regret and remorse and to the composition of "After a Journey," "The Voice," and the other "Poems of 1912–13," which are by general consent regarded as the peak of his poetic achievement. In 1914 Hardy married Florence Emily Dugdale, who was 38 years his junior. While his second wife sometimes found her situation difficult—as when the inclusion of "Poems of 1912–13" in the collection *Satires of Circumstance* (1914) publicly proclaimed her husband's continuing devotion to her predecessor—her attention to Hardy's health, comfort, and privacy made a crucial contribution to his remarkable productivity in old age. Late in his eighth decade he published a fifth volume of verse, *Moments of Vision* (1917), and wrote in secret an official "life" of himself for posthumous publication under the name of his widow. In his ninth decade Hardy published two more poetry collections, *Late Lyrics and Earlier* (1922) and *Human Shows* (1925), and put together the posthumously published *Winter Words* (1928). Following his death, on Jan. 11, 1928, his cremated remains were interred with national pomp in Westminster Abbey, while his separated heart was buried in the churchyard of his native parish.

GEORGE MEREDITH

Another major novelist of the 1870s was George Meredith, who also worked as a poet, a journalist, and a publisher's reader. His prose style is distinct from that of his contemporaries, and his achievement is uneven; his reputation in the 20th and 21st centuries has suffered as a result. His novels, however, are distinguished by their wit, brilliant dialogue, and aphoristic quality of language as well as by their psychological studies of character. Meredith also presented a highly subjective view of life that, far ahead of his time, regarded women as truly the equals of men. His

Anthony Trollope

(b. April 24, 1815, London, Eng.—d. Dec. 6, 1882, London)

The English novelist Anthony Trollope worked for the postal service in England and Ireland from 1834 to 1867. Beginning in 1844 he produced nearly 50 novels, writing mainly before breakfast at a fixed rate of 1,000 words an hour. His best-loved and most famous works are the six interconnected Barsetshire novels, including *Barchester Towers* (1857) and *The Last Chronicle of Barset* (1867). Depicting the social scene in an imaginary English county, they abound in memorable characters and atmosphere. The Palliser novels, dealing with political issues and featuring the character Plantagenet Palliser, include the sharply satirical *The Eustace Diamonds* (1873). Other works, such as *He Knew He Was Right* (1869), show great psychological penetration. *The Way We Live Now* (1875), with its ironic view of the Victorian upper classes, is especially highly regarded. Trollope's *Autobiography* (1883) is a uniquely candid account of the working life of a Victorian writer.

greatest work of fiction, *The Egoist*, is an incisive comic novel that embodies the distinctive theory of the corrective and therapeutic powers of laughter expressed in his lecture "The Idea of Comedy" (1877).

Meredith, the son and grandson of tailors, was born in 1828 above the family tailor shop in Portsmouth. The name Meredith is Welsh in origin, and family tradition held that its bearers were descendants of Welsh kings and chieftains. A small inheritance from his mother, who died when he was five, enabled Meredith to attend a superior local seminary and thus early to assume the role of a young "gentleman." Yet the sensitive boy must gradually have become conscious of the contrast between this role and his actual social status. And the reality was to become even harsher with the bankruptcy of the tailoring shop when he was about 11 and his father's subsequent marriage to the young woman who had been their housekeeper.

In 1840 a second legacy, this time from an aunt, enabled him to go first to a boarding school and then, in 1842, to the Moravian School at Neuwied on the Rhine River, which was to leave its stamp upon the remainder of his life. Tolerant religious instruction was combined with humanism. The monotony of study was broken by daily sports, storytelling, and playacting and on vacations by week-long expeditions or boating trips down the Rhine. All of these influences except the religious remained with Meredith throughout life. After "a spasm of religion which lasted about six weeks," he later said, he never "swallowed the Christian fable" and thereafter called himself a freethinker.

Meredith's return to England in 1844, at the age of 16, ended his formal education. Like all of the other great Victorian novelists, he was to be largely self-educated. After several false starts, he was apprenticed at 18 to a London solicitor named Richard Charnock and was ostensibly launched upon a career in law. There is no evidence, however, that he ever pursued it.

He was steeped in *The Arabian Nights* and German legends and literature; he had already written verse, and he soon found that Charnock's interests were more literary than legal and that he had gathered around him a coterie of young friends whose interests were also literary. Perhaps all of these were influences. At any rate, among the Charnock circle was Edward "Ned" Peacock, son of Thomas Love Peacock, the eccentric author, and through Edward he met Edward's sister, Mary Ellen Nicolls, a widow with a small daughter. She was brilliant, witty, handsome, and about eight years older than he. In the course of editing and writing for a manuscript literary magazine conducted by the Charnock circle, he fell in love with her. Shortly after he reached his majority and came into the remainder of his little inheritance, they were married.

On their return, the Merediths took lodgings at Weybridge, Surrey, near Peacock's house at Lower Halliford, Middlesex, and George busied himself writing poems and articles and making translations. Unfortunately, they brought in little money. Somehow, nevertheless, he managed to pay the publication costs of a little collection of verse, entitled *Poems,* in 1851. Though the writer and critic William Michael Rossetti praised it, Charles Kingsley, the novelist, found "very high promise" in it, and the poet Alfred Tennyson said kindly that he wished he might have written the beautiful "Love in the Valley," praise added nothing to the family coffers.

Beset by creditors, the Merediths had to take refuge in Peacock's house, where their only child, Arthur, was born in 1853. Understandably, Peacock soon preferred to rent a cottage for them across the village green from him. As poetry did not pay, Meredith now in desperation turned his hand to prose, writing a fantasy entitled *The Shaving of Shagpat: An Arabian Entertainment,* published in 1855. Original in conception but imitative of *The Arabian Nights* in manner, it baffled most readers, who did not know whether to regard it as allegory or fairy tale. But the most perceptive of the critics, the novelist George Eliot, praised it as "a work of genius, and of poetical genius."

Poverty, disappointment, and the growing antagonism between two highly strung, critical natures placed an unbearable strain upon the marriage of the Merediths. Little more is known of this period in their lives, except that Meredith's wife was in Wales, in the company of an artist friend of the couple, Henry Wallis, during the summer of 1857. In April 1858 she gave birth to a son, whose father was registered as "George Meredith, author," but whose paternity Meredith always denied. Subsequently, Meredith's wife and Wallis went off to Capri together. She died in 1861, leaving Meredith with his eight-year-old son, Arthur.

Work was Meredith's only solace, and he was feverishly working upon a novel, *The Ordeal of Richard Feverel* (published in 1859), with which he hoped to win fame and fortune. It was characteristic of his best work in many respects: in form it is a romantic comedy (but with a tragic ending, as is frequent in Meredith); it deals with the relationship between a baronet and his son; the son falls in love with a lower class girl and is subjected to an ordeal—a recurring motif in Meredith—by his father; the novel is rich in allusion, image, and metaphor; the dialogue is sparkling, witty, and elliptical as in life; there are frequent intrusions by the author; three of the chapters are written in highly lyric prose; and the psychology of motive and rationalization is explored in depth. Though not without faults, the novel nevertheless remains Meredith's most moving and most widely read novel. But delicate readers found it prurient and had it banned by the influential lending libraries, scattering Meredith's hopes of affluence. He was forced to accept employment as a reader of manuscripts for a publisher and as a writer of editorials and news items for a provincial newspaper. His own writing had to be done in what spare time remained.

Feverel was followed by *Evan Harrington* (1860), an amusing comedy in which Meredith used the family tailoring establishment and his own relatives for subject matter. Taking up poetry again, Meredith next published a volume of poems, *Modern Love, and Poems of the English Roadside, with Poems and Ballads,* in 1862. If *Evan Harrington* had exorcised the tailor demon that haunted him, "Modern

Love" doubtless served a similar purpose for his own disastrous marriage. Semi-autobiographical, it is concerned with the tragedy of marital infidelity and its nemesis, though his own wound was now sufficiently healed for him to write compassionately.

After a walking tour on the Continent, he once more turned to prose. The theme of his next novel, *Emilia in England* (later renamed *Sandra Belloni*), was the contrast between a simple but passionate girl and some sentimental English social climbers. Its publication in 1864 was made the occasion of the first general consideration of all his works up to this point in an article in the *Westminster Review* by the Irish journalist and writer Justin M'Carthy. A second event of importance in 1864 was his remarriage. Arthur had been placed in boarding school, and Meredith's own loneliness was intensified. Luckily, he met an attractive, well-bred young woman of Anglo-French descent, Marie Vulliamy, fell in love with her, and, after undergoing his own ordeal in persuading her father of his respectability, married her in September 1864. Thus ended a period in his life: he was no longer unknown and no longer lonely.

A son was born to the couple in 1865 and a daughter in 1871. With a family to support and popularity still elusive, Meredith had to keep hard at work for the next 15 years, with only occasional walking expeditions on the Continent. In 1866, however, he was sent out by *The Morning Post* to report the Italian campaign in the Austro-Prussian War, which lasted only seven weeks but enabled him to spend three months in his beloved Italy. After his return he was able to purchase a comfortable cottage near the bottom of Box Hill, Surrey, where he was to live quietly until his death.

During the next 20 years, from 1865 to 1885, Meredith continued the drudgery of reading manuscripts but substituted weekly readings to an elderly rich widow for the newspaper work. It was, however, a period marked by the birth of the children, the publication of seven novels and a volume of poems, and, in the 1880s, by growing public recognition. After two mediocre novels in the 1860s, Meredith returned to what was his forte—romantic comedy—with *The Adventures of Harry Richmond* (1871). Once more he wrote a close study of a father–son relationship, only this time the father is an impostor who out-Micawbers Dickens' Mr. Micawber in his belief that something will "turn up" to make his fortune. The son's ordeal is that he must perceive and reject the world of fantasy in which his father lives and achieve maturity through painful experience. After an interval of about four years came *Beauchamp's Career.* Its hero is a self-deluded idealist who is converted to radicalism and whose ordeal is both political and personal. It is one of Meredith's better novels and confirmed what was clear by now, that one of his greatest strengths was the creation of spirited, flesh-and-blood women who think for themselves.

The next two novels of consequence, *The Egoist* (1879) and *Diana of the Crossways* (1885), marked the beginning of Meredith's acceptance by a wider reading public and a more favourable reception by critics. Both are comedies, full of Meredithian wit and brilliant dialogue and notable for women characters who prove their right to be accepted as individuals, equal with men, rather than puppets. In *The Egoist* the enemy is egoism, and the egoist is tested by a succession of ordeals before joining the ranks of humanity. While that novel is concerned with the dangers of wrong choice before marriage, *Diana* is the first of a series of studies of mismating in marriage. Diana herself is a memorable character of spirit and brains, although Meredith is less successful in persuading readers that she could naively be guilty of a grave breach of confidence. In both novels, however, the men that Meredith approves of and hands the heroines over to are rather flat and uninteresting.

A new period now began in Meredith's life. Fame, if not popularity, and financial independence had come at last. Yet his enjoyment of them was to be tempered by the death of his wife in 1885 and of Arthur in 1890, by the beginning of deafness, and by the onset of ataxia that was first to limit his ability to walk and finally to render him immobile. Honours and testimonials came in plenty: an honorary LL.D. degree from the University of St. Andrews, Fife, Scot.; election to the prestigious office of President of the Society of Authors; and in 1905 the Order of Merit, strictly limited to 24 members, was conferred upon him by order of the King. Meredith had become a public institution, his home at Box Hill almost a literary shrine. After 1885 his work was done except for three novels and five volumes of poems that were increasingly more philosophic than poetic. On his 80th birthday he was presented with another testimonial, with 250 signatures of the great ones of the world, and both King Edward VII and Pres. Theodore Roosevelt sent congratulations.

ROBERT LOUIS STEVENSON

In the 1880s the three-volume novel, with its panoramic vistas and proliferating subplots, began to give way to more narrowly focused one-volume novels. At the same time, a gap started to open between popular fiction and the "literary" or "art" novel. The flowering of realist fiction was also accompanied, perhaps inevitably, by a revival of its opposite, the romance. The 1860s had produced a new subgenre, the sensation novel, seen at its best in the work of Wilkie Collins. Gothic novels and romances by Sheridan Le Fanu, Robert Louis Stevenson, William Morris, and Oscar Wilde; utopian fiction by Morris and

Samuel Butler; and the early science fiction of H.G. Wells make it possible to speak of a full-scale romance revival. Stevenson's best-known novels represent the clearest and most consistent expression of the concerns of the late Victorian romance novel.

Stevenson was born in Edinburgh in 1850, the only son of Thomas Stevenson, a prosperous civil engineer, and his wife, Margaret Isabella Balfour. His poor health made regular schooling difficult, but he attended Edinburgh Academy and other schools before, at 17, entering Edinburgh University, where he was expected to prepare himself for the family profession of lighthouse engineering. But Stevenson had no desire to be an engineer, and he eventually agreed with his father, as a compromise, to prepare instead for the Scottish bar.

He had shown a desire to write early in life, and once in his teens he had deliberately set out to learn the writer's craft by imitating a great variety of models in prose and verse. His youthful enthusiasm for the Covenanters (i.e., those Scotsmen who banded together to defend their version of Presbyterianism in the 17th century) led to his writing *The Pentland Rising,* his first printed work. During his years at the university he rebelled against his parents' religion and set himself up as a liberal bohemian who abhorred the alleged cruelties and hypocrisies of bourgeois respectability.

In 1873, in the midst of painful differences with his father, he visited a married cousin in Suffolk, England, where he met Sidney Colvin, the English scholar, who became a lifelong friend, and Fanny Sitwell (who later married Colvin). Sitwell, an older woman of charm and talent, drew the young man out and won his confidence. Soon Stevenson was deeply in love, and on his return to Edinburgh he wrote her a series of letters in which he played the part first of lover, then of worshipper, then of

Finely crafted essays and literary critiques marked Robert Louis Stevenson's earliest forays into professional writing. Hulton Archive/Getty Images

son. One of the several names by which Stevenson
addressed her in these letters was "Claire," a fact that
many years after his death was to give rise to the erroneous
notion that Stevenson had had an affair with a humbly
born Edinburgh girl of that name. Eventually the passion
turned into a lasting friendship.

Later in 1873 Stevenson suffered severe respiratory illness and was sent to the French Riviera, where Colvin
later joined him. He returned home the following spring.
In July 1875 he was called to the Scottish bar, but he never
practiced. Stevenson was frequently abroad, most often in
France. Two of his journeys produced *An Inland Voyage*
(1878) and *Travels with a Donkey in the Cévennes* (1879). His
career as a writer developed slowly. His essay "Roads"
appeared in the *Portfolio* in 1873, and in 1874 "Ordered
South" appeared in *Macmillan's Magazine*, a review of Lord
Lytton's *Fables in Song* appeared in the *Fortnightly*, and his
first contribution (on Victor Hugo) appeared in *The
Cornhill Magazine*, then edited by Leslie Stephen, a critic
and biographer. It was these early essays, carefully wrought,
quizzically meditative in tone, and unusual in sensibility,
that first drew attention to Stevenson as a writer.

Stephen brought Stevenson into contact with Edmund
Gosse, the poet and critic, who became a good friend.
Later, when in Edinburgh, Stephen introduced Stevenson
to the writer W.E. Henley. The two became warm friends
and were to remain so until 1888, when a letter from
Henley to Stevenson containing a deliberately implied
accusation of dishonesty against the latter's wife precipitated a quarrel that Henley, jealous and embittered,
perpetuated after his friend's death in a venomous review
of a biography of Stevenson.

In 1876 Stevenson met Fanny Vandegrift Osbourne, an
American lady separated from her husband, and the two
fell in love. Stevenson's parents' horror at their son's

involvement with a married woman subsided somewhat when she returned to California in 1878, but it revived with greater force when Stevenson decided to join her in August 1879. Stevenson reached California ill and penniless (the record of his arduous journey appeared later in *The Amateur Emigrant,* 1895, and *Across the Plains,* 1892). His adventures, which included coming very near death and eking out a precarious living in Monterey and San Francisco, culminated in marriage to Fanny Osbourne (who was by then divorced from her first husband) early in 1880. About the same time a telegram from his relenting father offered much-needed financial support, and after a honeymoon by an abandoned silver mine (recorded in *The Silverado Squatters,* 1883) the couple sailed for Scotland to achieve reconciliation with the Thomas Stevensons.

Soon after his return, Stevenson, accompanied by his wife and his stepson, Lloyd Osbourne, went, on medical advice (he had tuberculosis), to Davos, Switz. The family left there in April 1881 and spent the summer in Pitlochry and then in Braemar, Scot. There, in spite of bouts of illness, Stevenson embarked on *Treasure Island* (begun as a game with Lloyd), which started as a serial in *Young Folks,* under the title *The Sea-Cook,* in October 1881. Stevenson finished the story in Davos, to which he had returned in the autumn, and then started on *Prince Otto* (1885), a more complex but less successful work. *Treasure Island* is an adventure presented with consummate skill, with atmosphere, character, and action superbly geared to one another. The book is at once a gripping adventure tale and a wry comment on the ambiguity of human motives.

In 1881 Stevenson published *Virginibus Puerisque,* his first collection of essays, most of which had appeared in *The Cornhill.* The winter of 1881 he spent at a chalet in Davos. In April 1882 he left Davos; but a stay in the Scottish Highlands, while it resulted in two of his finest short stories, "Thrawn Janet" and "The Merry Men," produced lung hemorrhages, and in September he went to the south of France. There the Stevensons finally settled at a house in Hyères, where, in spite of intermittent illness, Stevenson was happy and worked well. He revised *Prince Otto,* worked on *A Child's Garden of Verses* (first called *Penny Whistles*), and began *The Black Arrow: A Tale of the Two Roses* (1888), a historical adventure tale deliberately written in anachronistic language.

The threat of a cholera epidemic drove the Stevensons from Hyères back to England. They lived at Bournemouth from September 1884 until July 1887, but his frequent bouts of dangerous illness proved conclusively that the British climate, even in the south of England, was not for him. The Bournemouth years were fruitful, however. There he got to know and love the American novelist Henry James. There he revised *A Child's Garden* (first published in 1885) and wrote "Markheim," *Kidnapped,* and *Strange Case of Dr. Jekyll and Mr. Hyde.* The poems in *A Child's Garden* represent with extraordinary fidelity an adult's recapturing of the emotions and sensations of childhood; there is nothing quite like them in English literature. In *Kidnapped* the fruit of his researches into 18th-century Scottish history and of his feeling for Scottish landscape, history, character, and local atmosphere mutually illuminate one another. But it was *Dr. Jekyll*—both moral allegory and thriller—that established his reputation with the ordinary reader.

In August 1887, still in search of health, Stevenson set out for America with his wife, mother, and stepson. On arriving in New York, he found himself famous, with editors and publishers offering lucrative contracts. He stayed for a while in the Adirondack Mountains, where he wrote essays for *Scribner's* and began *The Master of Ballantrae.* This novel, another exploration of moral ambiguities, contains some of his most impressive writing, although marred by its contrived conclusion.

In June 1888 Stevenson, accompanied by his family, sailed from San Francisco in the schooner yacht *Casco,* which he had chartered, on what was intended to be an excursion for health and pleasure. In fact, he was to spend the rest of his life in the South Seas. They went first to the Marquesas Islands, then to Fakarava Atoll, then to Tahiti, then to Honolulu, where they stayed nearly six months, leaving in June 1889 for the Gilbert Islands, and then to Samoa, where he spent six weeks.

During his months of wandering around the South Sea islands, Stevenson made intensive efforts to understand the local scene and the inhabitants. As a result, his writings on the South Seas (*In the South Seas,* 1896; *A Footnote to History,* 1892) are admirably pungent and perceptive. He was writing first-rate journalism, deepened by the awareness of landscape and atmosphere, such as that so notably rendered in his description of the first landfall at Nuku Hiva in the Marquesas.

In October 1890 he returned to Samoa from a voyage to Sydney and established himself and his family in patriarchal status at Vailima, his house in Samoa. The climate suited him; he led an industrious and active life; and, when he died suddenly, it was of a cerebral hemorrhage, not of the long-feared tuberculosis.

His work during those years was moving toward a new maturity. While *Catriona* (U.S. title, *David Balfour,* 1893) marked no advance in technique or imaginative scope on *Kidnapped,* to which it is a sequel, *The Ebb-Tide* (1894), a grim and powerful tale written in a dispassionate style (it was a complete reworking of a first draft by Lloyd Osbourne), showed that Stevenson had reached an important transition in his literary career. The next phase was demonstrated triumphantly in *Weir of Hermiston* (1896), the

Stevenson drew on his travels, including an extended journey to Samoa (pictured), to create several of his adventure tales. Kean Collection/Hulton Archive/Getty Images

unfinished masterpiece on which he was working on the day of his death. "The Beach of Falesá" (first published 1892; included in *Island Night's Entertainments,* 1893), a story with a finely wrought tragic texture, as well as the first part of *The Master of Ballantrae,* pointed in this direction, but neither approaches *Weir.* Stevenson achieved in this work a remarkable richness of tragic texture in a style stripped of all superfluities. The dialogue contains some of the best Scots prose in modern literature. Fragment though it is, *Weir of Hermiston* stands as a great work.

NEW WOMAN FICTION

Amidst the revival of romance epitomized by Stevenson, however, realism continued to flourish, sometimes encouraged by the example of European realist and naturalist novelists. Both George Moore and George Gissing were influenced by the French novelist Émile Zola, though both also reacted against him.

The 1890s saw intense concern with the social role of women, reflected in the New Woman fiction of Grant Allen (*The Woman Who Did,* 1895), Sarah Grand (*The Heavenly Twins,* 1893), and George Egerton (*Keynotes,* 1893). The heroines of such texts breach conventional assumptions by supporting woman suffrage, smoking, adopting "rational" dress, and rejecting traditional double standards in sexual behaviour.

VERSE

The Pre-Raphaelite Brotherhood, formed in 1848 and unofficially reinforced a decade later, was founded as a group of painters but also functioned as a school of writers who linked the incipient Aestheticism of Keats and De Quincey to the Decadent movement of the fin de siècle. Dante Gabriel Rossetti collected his early writing in *Poems* (1870), a volume that led the critic Robert Buchanan to attack him as the leader of "The Fleshly School of Poetry." Rossetti combined some subtle treatments of contemporary life with a new kind of medievalism, seen also in *The Defence of Guenevere* (1858) by William Morris. The earnest political use of the Middle Ages found in Carlyle and Ruskin did not die out—Morris himself continued it and linked it, in the 1880s, with Marxism. But these writers also used medieval settings as a context that made possible an uninhibited treatment of sex and violence. The shocking subject matter and vivid imagery of Morris's first volume were further developed by Algernon Charles Swinburne, who, in *Atalanta in Calydon* (1865) and *Poems and Ballads* (1866), combined them with an intoxicating metrical power. His second series of *Poems and Ballads* (1878), with its moving elegies for Charles Baudelaire and Théophile Gautier, displays a sophisticated command of recent developments in avant-garde French verse.

The carefully wrought religious poetry of Christina Rossetti is perhaps truer to the original, pious purposes of the Pre-Raphaelite Brotherhood. Her first collection, *Goblin Market, and Other Poems* (1862), with its vivid but richly ambiguous title poem, established her status as one of the outstanding lyric poets of the century. The other outstanding religious poet of this period is Gerard Manley Hopkins, a Jesuit priest whose work was first collected as *Poems* in 1918, nearly 30 years after his death.

Robert Browning's experiments with the dramatic monologue were further developed in the 1860s by Augusta Webster, who used the form in *Dramatic Studies* (1866), *A Woman Sold and Other Poems* (1867), and *Portraits* (1870) to produce penetrating accounts of female experience. Her posthumously published sonnet sequence

Mother & Daughter (1895) is a lucid and unsentimental account of that relationship.

The 1890s witnessed a flowering of lyric verse, influenced intellectually by the critic and novelist Walter Pater and formally by contemporary French practice. Such writing was widely attacked as "decadent" for its improper subject matter and its consciously amoral doctrine of "art for art's sake." This stress upon artifice and the freedom of art from conventional moral constraints went hand in hand, however, with an exquisite craftsmanship and a devotion to intense emotional and sensory effects. Outstanding among the numerous poets publishing in the final decade of the century were John Davidson, Arthur Symons, Francis Thompson, Ernest Dowson, Lionel Johnson, and A.E. Housman. In *The Symbolist Movement in Literature* (1899), Symons suggested the links between this writing and European Symbolism and Impressionism. Thompson provides a vivid example of the way in which a decadent manner could, paradoxically, be combined with fierce religious enthusiasm. A rather different note was struck by Rudyard Kipling, who combined polemical force and sharp observation (particularly of colonial experience) with a remarkable metrical vigour.

RUDYARD KIPLING

Kipling was born in 1865 in India. His father, John Lockwood Kipling, was an artist and scholar who had considerable influence on his son's work, became curator of the Lahore museum, and is described presiding over this "wonder house" in the first chapter of *Kim*, Rudyard's most famous novel. His mother was Alice Macdonald, two of whose sisters married the highly successful 19th-century painters Sir Edward Burne-Jones and Sir Edward Poynter, while a third married Alfred Baldwin and became the mother of Stanley Baldwin, later prime minister. These connections were of lifelong importance to Kipling.

Much of his childhood was unhappy. Kipling was taken to England by his parents at the age of six and was left for five years at a foster home at Southsea, the horrors of which he described in the story *Baa Baa, Black Sheep* (1888). He then went on to the United Services College at Westward Ho, north Devon, a new, inexpensive, and inferior boarding school. It haunted Kipling for the rest of his life—but always as the glorious place celebrated in *Stalky & Co.* (1899) and related stories: an unruly paradise in which the highest goals of English education are met amid a tumult of teasing, bullying, and beating. The Stalky saga is one of Kipling's great imaginative achievements. Readers repelled by a strain of brutality—even of cruelty—in his writings should remember the sensitive and shortsighted boy who was brought to terms with the ethos of this deplorable establishment through the demands of self-preservation.

Kipling returned to India in 1882 and worked for seven years as a journalist. His parents, although not officially important, belonged to the highest Anglo-Indian society, and Rudyard thus had opportunities for exploring the whole range of that life. All the while he had remained keenly observant of the thronging spectacle of native India, which had engaged his interest and affection from earliest childhood. He was quickly filling the journals he worked for with prose sketches and light verse. He published the verse collection *Departmental Ditties* in 1886, the short-story collection *Plain Tales from the Hills* in 1888, and between 1887 and 1889 he brought out six paper-covered volumes of short stories. Among the latter were *Soldiers Three*, *The Phantom Rickshaw* (containing the story *The Man Who Would Be King*), and *Wee Willie Winkie* (containing *Baa, Baa, Black Sheep*). When Kipling returned to

Rudyard Kipling is noted for writing poetry and prose. He is arguably best remembered—and best-loved—for his children's books, which include The Jungle Books. Hulton Archive/Getty Images

England in 1889, his reputation had preceded him, and within a year he was acclaimed as one of the most brilliant prose writers of his time. His fame was redoubled upon the publication in 1892 of the verse collection *Barrack-Room Ballads*, which contained such popular poems as "Mandalay," "Gunga Din," and "Danny Deever." Not since the English poet Lord Byron had such a reputation been achieved so rapidly. When the poet laureate Alfred, Lord Tennyson died in 1892, it may be said that Kipling took his place in popular estimation.

In 1892 Kipling married Caroline Balestier, the sister of Wolcott Balestier, an American publisher and writer with whom he had collaborated in *The Naulahka* (1892), a facile and unsuccessful romance. That year the young couple moved to the United States and settled on Mrs. Kipling's property in Vermont, but their manners and attitudes were considered objectionable by their neighbours. Unable or unwilling to adjust to life in America, the Kiplings returned to England in 1896. Ever after Kipling remained very aware that Americans were "foreigners," and he extended to them, as to the French, no more than a semiexemption from his proposition that only "lesser breeds" are born beyond the English Channel.

Besides numerous short-story collections and poetry collections such as *The Seven Seas* (1896), Kipling published his best-known novels in the 1890s and immediately thereafter. His novel *The Light That Failed* (1890) is the story of a painter going blind and spurned by the woman he loves. *Captains Courageous* (1897), in spite of its sense of adventure, is often considered a poor novel because of the excessive descriptive writing. *Kim* (1901), although essentially a children's book, must be considered a classic. *The Jungle Books* (1894 and 1895) is a stylistically superb collection of stories linked by poems for children. These books give further proof that Kipling excelled at telling a story but was inconsistent in producing balanced, cohesive novels.

In 1902 Kipling bought a house at Burwash, Sussex, which remained his home until his death. Sussex was the background of much of his later writing—especially in *Puck of Pook's Hill* (1906) and *Rewards and Fairies* (1910), two volumes that, although devoted to simple dramatic presentations of English history, embodied some of his deepest intuitions. In 1907 he received the Nobel Prize for Literature, the first Englishman to be so honoured. In South Africa, where he spent much time, he was given a house by Cecil Rhodes, the diamond magnate and South African statesman. This association fostered Kipling's imperialist persuasions, which were to grow stronger with the years. These convictions are not to be dismissed in a word; they were bound up with a genuine sense of a civilizing mission that required every Englishman, or, more broadly, every white man, to bring European culture to the heathen natives of the uncivilized world. Kipling's ideas were not in accord with much that was liberal in the thought of the age, and as he became older he was an increasingly isolated figure. When he died, two days before King George V, he must have seemed to many a far less representative Englishman than his sovereign.

Kipling's poems and stories were extraordinarily popular in the late 19th and early 20th century, but after World War I his reputation as a serious writer suffered through his being widely viewed as a jingoistic imperialist, a reputation that survives to today. As a poet he scarcely ranks high, although his rehabilitation was attempted by so distinguished a critic as T.S. Eliot. His verse is indeed vigorous, and in dealing with the lives and colloquial speech of common soldiers and sailors it broke new ground. But balladry, music-hall song, and popular hymnology provide its unassuming basis; and even at its most serious—as in "Recessional" (1897) and similar pieces in which Kipling addressed himself to his fellow countrymen in times of crisis—the effect is rhetorical rather than imaginative.

But it is otherwise with Kipling's prose. In the whole sweep of his adult storytelling, he displays a steadily developing art, from the early volumes of short stories set in India through the collections *Life's Handicap* (1891), *Many Inventions* (1893), *The Day's Work* (1898), *Traffics and Discoveries* (1904), *Actions and Reactions* (1909), *Debits and Credits* (1926), and *Limits and Renewals* (1932). While his later stories cannot exactly be called better than the earlier ones, they are as good—and they bring a subtler if less dazzling technical proficiency to the exploration of deeper though sometimes more perplexing themes. Kipling's critical reputation declined steadily during his lifetime—a decline that, some critics argue, can be accounted for solely in terms of political prejudice. Paradoxically, postcolonial critics later rekindled an intense interest in his work, viewing it as both symptomatic and critical of imperialist attitudes.

Kipling, it should be noted, wrote much and successfully for children; for the very young in *Just So Stories* (1902), and for others in *The Jungle Books* and in *Puck of Pook's Hill* and *Rewards and Fairies*. Of his miscellaneous works, the more notable are a number of early travel sketches collected in two volumes in *From Sea to Sea* (1899) and the unfinished *Something of Myself*, posthumously published in 1941, a reticent essay in autobiography.

Christina Rossetti

Christina Rossetti is one of the most important of English women poets both in range and quality. She excelled in works of fantasy, in poems for children, and in religious poetry.

Despite financial hardship, caring for her mother, and battling physical ailments, poet Christina Rossetti persevered in her work. Critics place her among the most significant English women poets. Hulton Archive/Getty Images

Born in 1830, Christina was the youngest child of Gabriele Rossetti and was the sister of the painter-poet Dante Gabriel Rossetti. In 1847 her grandfather, Gaetano Polidori, printed on his private press a volume of her *Verses*, in which signs of poetic talent are already visible. In 1850, under the pseudonym Ellen Alleyne, she contributed seven poems to the Pre-Raphaelite journal *The Germ*. In 1853, when the Rossetti family was in financial difficulties, Christina helped her mother keep a school at Frome, Somerset, but it was not a success, and in 1854 the pair returned to London, where Christina's father died. In straitened circumstances, Christina entered on her life work of companionship to her mother, devotion to her religion, and the writing of her poetry. She was a firm High Church Anglican, and in 1850 she broke her engagement to the artist James Collinson, an original member of the Pre-Raphaelite Brotherhood, because he had become a Roman Catholic. For similar reasons she rejected Charles Bagot Cayley in 1864, though a warm friendship remained between them.

In 1862 Christina published *Goblin Market, and Other Poems* and in 1866 *The Prince's Progress, and Other Poems*, both with frontispiece and decorations by her brother Dante Gabriel. These two collections, which contain most of her finest work, established her among the poets of her day. The stories in her first prose work, *Commonplace, and Other Short Stories* (1870), are of no great merit, but *Sing-Song: A Nursery Rhyme Book* (1872; enlarged 1893), with illustrations by Arthur Hughes, takes a high place among children's books of the 19th century.

In 1871 Christina was stricken by Graves' disease, a thyroid disorder that marred her appearance and left her life in danger. She accepted her affliction with courage and resignation, sustained by religious faith, and she continued to publish, issuing one collection of poems in 1875 and

A Pageant, and Other Poems in 1881. But after the onset of her illness she mostly concentrated on devotional prose writings. *Time Flies* (1885), a reading diary of mixed verse and prose, is the most personal of these works. Christina was considered a possible successor to Alfred, Lord Tennyson, as poet laureate, but she developed a fatal cancer in 1891. *New Poems* (1896), published by her brother, contained unprinted and previously uncollected poems.

Though she was haunted by an ideal of spiritual purity that demanded self-denial, Christina resembled her brother Dante Gabriel in certain ways, for beneath her humility, her devotion, and her quiet, saintlike life lay a passionate and sensuous temperament, a keen critical perception, and a lively sense of humour. Part of her success as a poet arises from the fact that, while never straining the limits of her sympathy and experience, she succeeded in uniting these two seemingly contradictory sides of her nature. There is a vein of the sentimental and didactic in her weaker verse, but at its best her poetry is strong, personal, and unforced, with a metrical cadence that is unmistakably her own. The transience of material things is a theme that recurs throughout her poetry, and the resigned but passionate sadness of unhappy love is often a dominant note.

DANTE GABRIEL ROSSETTI

Dante Gabriel Rossetti, one of Christina Rossetti's brothers, was a painter and poet who remains best known for helping found the Pre-Raphaelite Brotherhood, a group of painters treating religious, moral, and medieval subjects in a nonacademic manner. Through his exploration of new themes and his break with academic convention, Rossetti remains an important figure in the history of 19th-century English art. But his enduring worth probably lies as much in his poetry as in his painting.

Gerard Manley Hopkins

(b. July 28, 1844, Stratford, Essex, Eng.—d. June 8, 1889,
Dublin, Ire.)

The poet and Jesuit priest Gerard Manley Hopkins was one of
the most individual of Victorian writers.

Hopkins was the eldest of the nine children of Manley
Hopkins, an Anglican, who had been British consul general in
Hawaii. Hopkins won the poetry prize at the Highgate grammar
school and in 1863 was awarded a grant to study at Balliol College,
Oxford, where he continued writing poetry while studying
classics. In 1866, he was received into the Roman Catholic
Church by John Henry (later Cardinal) Newman. The following
year, he left Oxford with a distinguished academic record and
decided to become a priest. He entered the Jesuit novitiate in
1868 and burned his youthful verses, determining "to write no
more, as not belonging to my profession."

In 1874 Hopkins went to St. Beuno's College in North Wales
to study theology. There he learned Welsh, and, under the impact
of the language itself as well as that of the poetry and encouraged by his superior, he began to write poetry again. Moved by
the death of five Franciscan nuns in a shipwreck in 1875, he broke
his seven-year silence to write the long poem "The Wreck of the
Deutschland," in which he succeeded in realizing "the echo of a
new rhythm" that had long been haunting his ear. He also wrote
a series of sonnets strikingly original in their richness of language and use of rhythm, including "The Windhover." He
continued to write poetry, but it was read only in manuscript by
his friends and fellow poets.

Ordained to the priesthood in 1877, Hopkins served as mis-
sioner, occasional preacher, and parish priest in various Jesuit
churches and institutions in London, Oxford, Liverpool, and
Glasgow and taught classics at Stonyhurst College, Lancashire.
From 1885 he wrote another series of sonnets, beginning with
"Carrion Comfort." These poems, known as the "terrible sonnets," reveal strong tensions between his delight in the sensuous

world and his urge to express it and his equally powerful sense of religious vocation.

Overworked and in poor health, Hopkins died of typhoid fever at the age of 44 and was buried in the Glasnevin Cemetery, Dublin. After his death, Robert Bridges began to publish a few of Hopkins's most mature poems in anthologies. By 1918, Bridges, then poet laureate, judged the time opportune for the first collected edition. It appeared but sold slowly. Not until 1930 was a second edition issued, and thereafter Hopkins's work was deemed to be among the most original, powerful, and influential literary accomplishments of the 20th century by those on whom it had a marked influence, including T.S. Eliot, Dylan Thomas, W.H. Auden, Stephen Spender, and C. Day-Lewis.

Born in 1828, he received a general education in the junior department of King's College (1836–41), but he then hesitated between poetry and painting as a vocation. When about 14 he went to "Sass's," an old-fashioned drawing school in Bloomsbury (central London), and thence, in 1845, to the Royal Academy schools, where he became a full student.

Meanwhile, he read omnivorously—romantic and poetic literature, William Shakespeare, J.W. von Goethe, Lord Byron, Sir Walter Scott, and Gothic tales of horror. He was fascinated by the work of the American writer Edgar Allan Poe. In 1847 he discovered the 18th-century English painter-poet William Blake through the purchase of a volume of Blake's designs and writings in prose and verse; the volume has since been known as the Rossetti manuscript. Blake's diatribes against the painter Sir Joshua Reynolds encouraged Rossetti to attempt lampoons of his own against the triviality of early Victorian paintings of anecdotal subjects, those of Sir Edwin Landseer being a special target of his derision.

As a successful painter, Dante Gabriel Rossetti (left) collaborated with his sister, Christina (second from left), to create frontispieces for her early verse collections. His own poems received a lukewarm response from critics. Lewis Carroll/Hulton Archive/Getty Images

By the time Rossetti was 20, he had already done a number of translations of Italian poets and had composed some original verse, but he was also much in and out of artists' studios and for a short time was, in an informal way, a pupil of the painter Ford Madox Brown. He acquired some of Brown's admiration for the German "Pre-Raphaelites," the nickname of the austere Nazarenes, who had sought to bring back into German art a pre-Renaissance purity of style and aim. It remained to initiate a similar reform in England.

Largely through Rossetti's efforts, the English Pre-Raphaelite Brotherhood was formed in 1848 with seven members, all Royal Academy students except for William

Michael Rossetti. They aimed at "truth to nature," which was to be achieved by minuteness of detail and painting from nature outdoors. This was, more especially, the purpose of the two other principal members, William Holman Hunt and John Everett Millais. Rossetti expanded the Brotherhood's aims by linking poetry, painting, and social idealism and by interpreting the term Pre-Raphaelite as synonymous with a romanticized medieval past.

While Rossetti's first two oil paintings—"The Girlhood of Mary" (1849; Tate Gallery, London) and "Ecce Ancilla Domini" ("The Annunciation"; 1850, Tate Gallery)—were simple in style, they were elaborate in symbolism. Some of the same atmosphere is felt in the rich word-painting and emotional force of his poem "The Blessed Damozel," published in 1850 in the first issue of *The Germ,* the Pre-Raphaelite magazine. When it was exhibited in 1850, "Ecce Ancilla Domini" received severe criticism, which Rossetti could never bear with equanimity. In consequence, he ceased to show in public and gave up oils in favour of watercolours, which he could more easily dispose of to personal acquaintances. He also turned from traditional religious themes to painting scenes from Shakespeare, Robert Browning, and Dante, which allowed more freedom of imaginative treatment. A typical example of his work from this period is "How They Met Themselves" (1851–60; Fitzwilliam Museum, Cambridge). After 1856 Rossetti was led by Sir Thomas Malory's *Morte Darthur* and Tennyson's *Idylls of the King* to evoke in his paintings an imaginary Arthurian epoch, with heraldic glow and pattern of colour and medieval accessories of armour and dress.

The 1850s were eventful years for Rossetti. They began with the introduction into the Pre-Raphaelite circle of the beautiful Elizabeth Siddal, who served at first as model for the whole group but was soon attached to Rossetti alone and, in 1860, married him. Many portrait drawings testify to his affection for her.

In 1854 he gained a powerful but exacting patron in the art critic John Ruskin. By then the Pre-Raphaelite Brotherhood was at an end, splintered by the different interests and temperaments of its members. But Rossetti's magnetic personality aroused a fresh wave of enthusiasm. In 1856 he came into contact with the then-Oxford undergraduates Edward Burne-Jones and William Morris. With these two young disciples he initiated a second phase of the Pre-Raphaelite movement. The two main aspects of this fresh departure were a romantic enthusiasm for a legendary past instead of the realism of "truth to nature" and the ambition of reforming the applied arts of design. Rossetti's influence not only led to easel pictures illustrating Arthurian legend but also into other fields of art. A new era of book decoration was foreshadowed by Rossetti's illustration for the Moxon edition of the *Poems* (1857) of Alfred, Lord Tennyson. His commission in 1856 to paint a triptych ("The Seed of David") for Llandaff Cathedral was a prelude to the ambitious scheme of 1857 to decorate the Oxford Union debating chamber with mural paintings of Arthurian themes. Though Rossetti and his helpers (Burne-Jones, Morris, and others) failed through want of technical knowledge and experience, the enterprise was fruitful in suggesting that the scope of art could be expanded to include the crafts.

From 1860 onward, trials were part of Rossetti's much-disturbed life. His marriage to Elizabeth Siddal, clouded by her constant ill health, ended tragically in 1862 with her death from an overdose of laudanum. Grief led him to bury with her the only complete manuscript of his poems. That he considered his love for his wife similar to Dante's mystical and idealized love for Beatrice is evident from the symbolic "Beata Beatrix," painted in 1863 and now in the Tate Gallery.

Rossetti's life and art were now greatly changed. He moved from riverside premises in London's Blackfriars to Chelsea. The influence of new friends—Algernon Charles Swinburne and the American painter James McNeill Whistler—led to a more aesthetic and sensuous approach to art. Literary themes gave way to pictures of mundane beauties, such as his mistress, Fanny Cornforth, gorgeously appareled and painted with a command of oils he had not previously shown. Among these works are "The Blessed Damozel" (1871–79), "The Bower Meadow" (1872), "Proserpine" (1874; Tate Gallery), and "La Pia de' Tolomei" (1881). The luxuriant colours and rhythmic design of these paintings enhance the effect of their languid, sensuous female subjects, all of whom bear a distinctive "Pre-Raphaelite" facial type. The paintings proved popular with collectors, and Rossetti grew affluent enough to employ studio assistants to make copies and replicas. He also collected antiques and filled his large Chelsea garden with a menagerie of animals and birds.

Rossetti had enjoyed a modest success in 1861 with his published translations, *The Early Italian Poets;* and toward the end of the 1860s his thoughts turned to poetry again. He began composing new poems and planned the recovery of the manuscript poems buried with his wife in Highgate Cemetery. Carried out in 1869 through the agency of his unconventional man of business, Charles Augustus Howell, the exhumation visibly distressed the superstitious Rossetti. The publication of these poems followed in 1870. The *Poems* were well enough received until a misdirected, savage onslaught by "Thomas Maitland" (pseudonym of the journalist-critic Robert Buchanan) on "The Fleshly School of Poetry" singled out Rossetti for attack. Rossetti responded temperately in "The Stealthy School of Criticism," published in the *Athenaeum;* but the attack, combined with remorse and the amount of chloral and alcohol he now took for insomnia, brought about his collapse in 1872. He recovered sufficiently to paint and write, but his life in Chelsea was subsequently that of a semi-invalid and recluse. Until 1874 he spent much time at Kelmscott Manor (near Oxford), of which he took joint tenancy with William Morris in 1871. His lovingly idealized portraits of Jane Morris at this time were a return to his more poetic and mystical style.

In the early 1880s Rossetti occupied himself with a replica of an early watercolour, "Dante's Dream" (1880), a revised edition of *Poems* (1881), and *Ballads and Sonnets* (1881), containing the completed sonnet sequence of "The House of Life," in which he described the love between man and woman with tragic intensity. The lawyer and man of letters Theodore Watts-Dunton meanwhile did his best to put Rossetti's financial affairs in order. From a visit to Keswick (in northwestern England) in 1881, Rossetti returned in worse health than before, and he died the following spring.

Rossetti was a natural master of the sonnet, and his finest achievement, "The House of Life," is a sonnet sequence unique in the intensity of its evocation of the mysteries of physical and spiritual love. Here, as he claimed against his detractors, "the passionate and just delights of the body are declared to be as naught if not ennobled by the concurrence of the soul at all times." The poem's memorable lines are created with simplicity of diction:

> *Oh! clasp we to our hearts, for deathless dower,*
> *This close-companioned inarticulate hour*
> *When twofold silence was the song of love.*
> ("Silent Noon," *The House of Life*, sonnet XIX)

Pre-Raphaelite Brotherhood

The Pre-Raphaelite Brotherhood was a group of young British painters who banded together in 1848 in reaction against what they conceived to be the unimaginative and artificial historical painting of the Royal Academy and who purportedly sought to express a new moral seriousness and sincerity in their works. They were inspired by Italian art of the 14th and 15th centuries, and their adoption of the name Pre-Raphaelite expressed their admiration for what they saw as the direct and uncomplicated depiction of nature typical of Italian painting before the High Renaissance and, particularly, before the time of Raphael. Although the Brotherhood's active life lasted not quite five years, its influence on painting in Britain, and ultimately on the decorative arts and interior design, was profound.

The Pre-Raphaelite Brotherhood was formed by three Royal Academy students: Dante Gabriel Rossetti, William Holman Hunt, and John Everett Millais, all under 25 years of age. The painter James Collinson, the painter and critic F.G. Stephens, the sculptor Thomas Woolner, and the critic William Michael Rossetti (Dante Gabriel's brother) joined them by invitation. The painters William Dyce and Ford Madox Brown, who acted in part as mentors to the younger men, came to adapt their own work to the Pre-Raphaelite style.

The Brotherhood immediately began to produce highly convincing and significant works. Their pictures of religious and medieval subjects strove to revive the deep religious feeling and naive, unadorned directness of 15th-century Florentine and Sienese painting. The style that Hunt and Millais evolved featured sharp and brilliant lighting, a clear atmosphere, and a near-photographic reproduction of minute details. They also frequently introduced a private poetic symbolism into their representations of biblical subjects and medieval literary themes. Rossetti's work differed from that of the others in its more arcane aesthetic and in the artist's general lack of interest in copying the precise appearance of objects in nature. Vitality and freshness of vision are the most admirable qualities of these early Pre-Raphaelite paintings.

Some of the founding members exhibited their first works anonymously, signing their paintings with the monogram PRB. When their identity and youth were discovered in 1850, their work was harshly criticized by the novelist Charles Dickens, among others, not only for its disregard of academic ideals of beauty but also for its apparent irreverence in treating religious themes with an uncompromising realism. Nevertheless, the leading art critic of the day, John Ruskin, stoutly defended Pre-Raphaelite art, and the members of the group were never without patrons.

By 1854 the members of the Pre-Raphaelite Brotherhood had gone their individual ways, but their style had a wide influence and gained many followers during the 1850s and early '60s. In the late 1850s Dante Gabriel Rossetti became associated with the younger painters Edward Burne-Jones and William Morris and moved closer to a sensual and almost mystical romanticism. Millais, the most technically gifted painter of the group, went on to become an academic success. Hunt alone pursued the same style throughout most of his career and remained true to Pre-Raphaelite principles. Pre-Raphaelitism in its later stage is epitomized by the paintings of Burne-Jones, characterized by a jewel-toned palette, elegantly attenuated figures, and highly imaginative subjects and settings.

ALGERNON CHARLES SWINBURNE

The characteristic qualities of Algernon Charles Swinburne's verse are insistent alliteration, unflagging rhythmic energy, sheer melodiousness, great variation of pace and stress, effortless expansion of a given theme, and evocative (if rather imprecise) use of imagery. His poetic style is highly individual and his command of word-colour and word-music striking. Swinburne's technical gifts and capacity for prosodic invention were extraordinary, but too often his poems' remorseless rhythms have a narcotic effect, and he has been accused of paying more attention to the melody of words than to their meaning.

Swinburne's father was an admiral, and his mother was a daughter of the 3rd Earl of Ashburnham. Born in 1837, he attended Eton and Balliol College, Oxford, which he left in 1860 without taking a degree. There he met William Morris, Edward Burne-Jones, and Dante Gabriel Rossetti and was attracted to their Pre-Raphaelite Brotherhood. An allowance from his father enabled him to follow a literary career.

In 1861 he met Richard Monckton Milnes (later Lord Houghton), who encouraged his writing and fostered his reputation. In the early 1860s Swinburne apparently suffered from an unhappy love affair about which little is known. Literary success came with the verse drama *Atalanta in Calydon* (1865), in which he attempted to re-create in English the spirit and form of Greek tragedy; his lyric powers are at their finest in this work. *Atalanta* was followed by the first series of *Poems and Ballads* in 1866, which clearly display Swinburne's preoccupation with masochism, flagellation, and paganism. This volume contains some of his finest poems, among them "Dolores" and "The Garden of Proserpine." The book was vigorously attacked for its "feverish carnality"—the magazine *Punch* referred to the poet as "Mr. Swineborn"—though it was enthusiastically welcomed by the younger generation. In 1867 Swinburne met his idol, Giuseppe Mazzini, and the poetry collection *Songs Before Sunrise* (1871), which is principally concerned with the theme of political liberty, shows the influence of that Italian patriot. The second series of *Poems and Ballads,* less hectic and sensual than the first, appeared in 1878.

During this time Swinburne's health was being undermined by alcoholism and by the excesses resulting from his temperament and masochistic tendencies; he experienced periodic fits of intense nervous excitement, from which, however, his remarkable powers of recuperation long enabled him to recover quickly. In 1879 he collapsed completely and was rescued and restored to health by his friend Theodore Watts-Dunton. The last 30 years of his life were spent at The Pines, Putney, under the guardianship of Watts-Dunton, who maintained a strict regimen and encouraged Swinburne to devote himself to writing. Swinburne eventually became a figure of respectability and adopted reactionary views. He published 23 volumes of poetry, prose, and drama during these years, but, apart from the long poem *Tristram of Lyonesse* (1882) and the verse tragedy *Marino Faliero* (1885), his most important poetry belongs to the first half of his life.

Swinburne was also an important and prolific English literary critic of the later 19th century. Among his best critical writings are *Essays and Studies* (1875) and his monographs on William Shakespeare (1880), Victor Hugo (1886), and Ben Jonson (1889). His devotion to Shakespeare and his unrivaled knowledge of Elizabethan and Jacobean drama are reflected in his early play *Chastelard* (1865). The latter work was the first of a trilogy on Mary, queen of Scots, who held a peculiar fascination for him; *Bothwell* (1874) and *Mary Stuart* (1881) followed. He also wrote on William Blake, Percy Bysshe Shelley, and Charles Baudelaire, and his elegy on the latter, *Ave Atque Vale* (1867–68), is among his finest works.

THE VICTORIAN THEATRE

Early Victorian drama was a popular art form, appealing to an uneducated audience that demanded emotional excitement rather than intellectual subtlety. Vivacious melodramas did not, however, hold exclusive possession of the stage. The mid-century saw lively comedies by Dion Boucicault and Tom Taylor. In the 1860s T.W. Robertson pioneered a new realist drama, an achievement later celebrated by Arthur Wing Pinero in his charming sentimental comedy *Trelawny of the "Wells"* (1898). The 1890s were, however, the outstanding decade of dramatic innovation. Oscar Wilde crowned his brief career as a playwright with one of the few great high comedies in English, *The Importance of Being Earnest* (1895). At the same time, the influence of Norwegian playwright Henrik Ibsen was helping to produce a new genre of serious "problem plays," such as Pinero's *The Second Mrs. Tanqueray* (1893). J.T. Grein founded the Independent Theatre in 1891 to foster such work and staged there the first plays of George Bernard Shaw and translations of Ibsen.

Oscar Wilde

Oscar Wilde's reputation rests on his only novel, *The Picture of Dorian Gray* (1891), and on the comic masterpieces he created for the theatre: *Lady Windermere's Fan* (1892) and *The Importance of Being Earnest* (1895). He was a spokesman for the late 19th-century Aesthetic movement in England, which advocated art for art's sake, and he was the object of celebrated civil and criminal suits involving homosexuality and ending in his imprisonment (1895–97).

Wilde was born in 1854 in Dublin to professional and literary parents. His father, Sir William Wilde, was Ireland's leading ear and eye surgeon, who also published books on archaeology, folklore, and the satirist Jonathan Swift; his mother, who wrote under the name Speranza, was a revolutionary poet and an authority on Celtic myth and folklore.

After attending Portora Royal School, Enniskillen (1864–71), Wilde went, on successive scholarships, to

An ardent aesthete, Oscar Wilde was a witty novelist and playwright who was not adverse to trading on his flamboyant reputation to promote himself and his works. Hulton Archive/Getty Images

Trinity College, Dublin (1871–74), and Magdalen College, Oxford (1874–78), which awarded him a degree with honours. During these four years, he distinguished himself not only as a classical scholar, a poseur, and a wit but also as a poet by winning the coveted Newdigate Prize in 1878 with a long poem, *Ravenna*. He was deeply impressed by the teachings of the English writers John Ruskin and Walter Pater on the central importance of art in life and particularly by the latter's stress on the aesthetic intensity by which life should be lived. Like many in his generation, Wilde was determined to follow Pater's urging "to burn always with [a] hard, gemlike flame." But Wilde also delighted in affecting an aesthetic pose; this, combined with rooms at Oxford decorated with objets d'art, resulted in his famous remark: "Oh, would that I could live up to my blue china!"

In the early 1880s, when Aestheticism was the rage and despair of literary London, Wilde established himself in social and artistic circles by his wit and flamboyance. Soon the periodical *Punch* made him the satiric object of its antagonism to the Aesthetes for what was considered their unmasculine devotion to art; and in their comic opera *Patience,* Gilbert and Sullivan based the character Bunthorne, a "fleshly poet," partly on Wilde. Wishing to reinforce the association, Wilde published, at his own expense, *Poems* (1881), which echoed, too faithfully, his discipleship to the poets Algernon Swinburne, Dante Gabriel Rossetti, and John Keats. Eager for further acclaim, Wilde agreed to lecture in the United States and Canada in 1882, announcing on his arrival at customs in New York City that he had "nothing to declare but his genius." Despite widespread hostility in the press to his languid poses and aesthetic costume of velvet jacket, knee breeches, and black silk stockings, Wilde for 12 months exhorted the

Americans to love beauty and art; then he returned to Great Britain to lecture on his impressions of America.

In 1884 Wilde married Constance Lloyd, daughter of a prominent Irish barrister; two children, Cyril and Vyvyan, were born, in 1885 and 1886. Meanwhile, Wilde was a reviewer for the *Pall Mall Gazette* and then became editor of *Woman's World* (1887–89). During this period of apprenticeship as a writer, he published *The Happy Prince and Other Tales* (1888), which reveals his gift for romantic allegory in the form of the fairy tale.

In the final decade of his life, Wilde wrote and published nearly all of his major work. In his only novel, *The Picture of Dorian Gray* (published in *Lippincott's Magazine*, 1890, and in book form, revised and expanded by six chapters, 1891), Wilde combined the supernatural elements of the Gothic novel with the unspeakable sins of French decadent fiction. Critics charged immorality despite Dorian's self-destruction; Wilde, however, insisted on the amoral nature of art regardless of an apparently moral ending. *Intentions* (1891), consisting of previously published essays, restated his aesthetic attitude toward art by borrowing ideas from the French poets Théophile Gautier and Charles Baudelaire and the American painter James McNeill Whistler. In the same year, two volumes of stories and fairy tales also appeared, testifying to his extraordinary creative inventiveness: *Lord Arthur Savile's Crime, and Other Stories* and *A House of Pomegranates*.

But Wilde's greatest successes were his society comedies. Within the conventions of the French "well-made play" (with its social intrigues and artificial devices to resolve conflict), he employed his paradoxical, epigrammatic wit to create a form of comedy new to the 19th-century English theatre. His first success, *Lady Windermere's Fan*, demonstrated that this wit could revitalize the rusty machinery of French drama. In the same year, rehearsals of his macabre play *Salomé,* written in French and designed, as he said, to make his audience shudder by its depiction of unnatural passion, were halted by the censor because it contained biblical characters. It was published in 1893, and an English translation appeared in 1894 with Aubrey Beardsley's celebrated illustrations.

A second society comedy, *A Woman of No Importance* (produced 1893), convinced the critic William Archer that Wilde's plays "must be taken on the very highest plane of modern English drama." In rapid succession, Wilde's final plays, *An Ideal Husband* and *The Importance of Being Earnest,* were produced early in 1895. In the latter, his greatest achievement, the conventional elements of farce are transformed into satiric epigrams—seemingly trivial but mercilessly exposing Victorian hypocrisies.

> *I suppose society is wonderfully delightful. To be in it is merely a bore. But to be out of it simply a tragedy.*

> *I never travel without my diary. One should always have something sensational to read in the train.*

> *All women become like their mothers. That is their tragedy. No man does. That's his.*

In many of his works, exposure of a secret sin or indiscretion and consequent disgrace is a central design. If life imitated art, as Wilde insisted in his essay "The Decay of Lying" (1889), he was himself approximating the pattern in his reckless pursuit of pleasure. In addition, his close friendship with Lord Alfred Douglas, whom he had met in 1891, infuriated the Marquess of Queensberry, Douglas' father. Accused, finally, by the marquess of being a sodomite, Wilde, urged by Douglas, sued for criminal libel. Wilde's case collapsed, however, when the evidence went against him, and he dropped the suit. Urged to flee to France by his friends, Wilde refused, unable to believe that his world was at an end. He was arrested and ordered to stand trial.

Wilde testified brilliantly, but the jury failed to reach a verdict. In the retrial he was found guilty and sentenced, in May 1895, to two years at hard labour. Most of his sentence was served at Reading Gaol, where he wrote a long letter to Douglas (published in 1905 in a drastically cut version as *De Profundis*) filled with recriminations against the younger man for encouraging him in dissipation and distracting him from his work.

In May 1897 Wilde was released, a bankrupt, and immediately went to France, hoping to regenerate himself as a writer. His only remaining work, however, was *The Ballad of Reading Gaol* (1898), revealing his concern for inhumane prison conditions. Despite constant money problems he maintained, as George Bernard Shaw said, "an unconquerable gaiety of soul" that sustained him, and he was visited by such loyal friends as Max Beerbohm and Robert Ross, later his literary executor; he was also reunited with Douglas. He died suddenly in Paris of acute meningitis brought on by an ear infection. In his semiconscious final moments, he was received into the Roman Catholic church, which he had long admired.

ARTHUR WING PINERO

Arthur Wing Pinero made an important contribution toward creating a self-respecting English theatre by helping to found a "social" drama that drew a fashionable audience. It is his farces—literate, superbly constructed, with a precise, clockwork inevitability of plot and a brilliant use of coincidence—that have proved to be of more lasting value than his other plays.

Born in 1855 into an English family descended from Portuguese Jews, Pinero abandoned legal studies at age 19 to become an actor; and, though still a young man, he played older character parts for the leading theatre company headed by Henry Irving. His first play, *£200 a Year*, was produced in 1877.

His best farces, such as *The Magistrate* (1885), *The Schoolmistress* (1886), and *Dandy Dick* (1887), were written for the Royal Court Theatre in London. They combine wildly improbable events with likable characters and a consistently amusing style. Pinero was at the same time studying serious drama by adapting plays from the French (including *The Iron Master*, 1884, and *Mayfair*, 1885) and also mining a profitable vein of sentiment of his own, as in *The Squire* (1881) and *Sweet Lavender* (1888). Seriousness and sentiment fused in *The Profligate* (1889) and—most sensationally—in *The Second Mrs. Tanqueray* (1893), which established Pinero as an important playwright. This was the first of several plays depicting women battling with their situation in society. These plays not only created good parts for actresses but also demanded sympathy for women, who were judged by stricter standards than men in Victorian society.

In a less serious vein, *Trelawny of the "Wells"* (written for the Royal Court Theatre and produced in 1898) portrayed theatrical company life in the old style of the 1860s—already then a vanishing tradition—and *The Gay Lord Quex* (1899) was about a theatrical rake of no placeable period but having great panache. Pinero was knighted in 1909, an honour that reflected a level of public respectability that

Wilde never achieved during his lifetime. Yet it is Wilde whose plays have survived most vibrantly into the 21st century and which remain the clearest expression of late Victorian theatre.

VICTORIAN LITERARY COMEDY

Victorian literature began with such humorous books as *Sartor Resartus* and *The Pickwick Papers*. Despite the crisis of faith, the "Condition of England" question, and the "ache of modernism," this note was sustained throughout the century. The comic novels of Dickens and Thackeray, the squibs, sketches, and light verse of Thomas Hood and Douglas Jerrold, the nonsense of Edward Lear and Lewis Carroll, and the humorous light fiction of Jerome K. Jerome and George Grossmith and his brother Weedon Grossmith are proof that this age, so often remembered for its gloomy rectitude, may in fact have been the greatest era of comic writing in English literature.

CHAPTER 2

THE 20TH CENTURY: FROM 1900 TO 1945

The 20th century opened with great hope but also with some apprehension, for the new century marked the final approach to a new millennium. For many, humankind was entering upon an unprecedented era. H.G. Wells's utopian studies, the aptly titled *Anticipations of the Reaction of Mechanical and Scientific Progress upon Human Life and Thought* (1901) and *A Modern Utopia* (1905), both captured and qualified this optimistic mood and gave expression to a common conviction that science and technology would transform the world in the century ahead. To achieve such transformation, outmoded institutions and ideals had to be replaced by ones more suited to the growth and liberation of the human spirit. The death of Queen Victoria in 1901 and the accession of Edward VII seemed to confirm that a franker, less inhibited era had begun.

EDWARDIAN NOVELISTS

Many writers of the Edwardian period drew widely upon the realistic and naturalistic conventions of the 19th century, and many novelists in particular were eager to use such conventions to explore the shortcomings of English social life. Wells—in *Love and Mr. Lewisham* (1900); *Kipps* (1905); *Ann Veronica* (1909), his pro-suffragist novel; and *The History of Mr. Polly* (1910)—captured the frustrations of lower- and middle-class existence, even though he relieved his accounts with many comic touches. In *Anna of the Five Towns* (1902), Arnold Bennett detailed the constrictions of provincial life among the self-made business classes in the area of England known as the Potteries; in *The Man of Property* (1906), the first volume of *The Forsyte Saga*, Galsworthy described the destructive possessiveness of the professional bourgeoisie; and, in *Where Angels Fear to Tread* (1905) and *The Longest Journey* (1907), E.M. Forster portrayed with irony the insensitivity, self-repression, and philistinism of the English middle classes.

These novelists, however, wrote more memorably when they allowed themselves a larger perspective. In *The Old Wives' Tale* (1908), Bennett showed the destructive effects of time on the lives of individuals and communities and evoked a quality of pathos that he never matched in his other fiction; in *Tono-Bungay* (1909), Wells showed the ominous consequences of the uncontrolled developments taking place within a British society still dependent upon the institutions of a long-defunct landed aristocracy; and in *Howards End* (1910), Forster showed how little the rootless and self-important world of contemporary commerce cared for the more rooted world of culture, although he acknowledged that commerce was a necessary evil. Nevertheless, even as they perceived the difficulties of the present, most Edwardian novelists, like their counterparts in the theatre, held firmly to the belief not only that constructive change was possible but also that this change could in some measure be advanced by their writing.

Other writers, including Thomas Hardy and Rudyard Kipling, who had established their reputations during the previous century, and Hilaire Belloc, G.K. Chesterton, and Edward Thomas, who established their reputations in the first decade of the new century, were less confident about the future and sought to revive the traditional forms—the ballad, the narrative poem, the satire, the fantasy, the topographical poem, and the essay—that in their view preserved traditional sentiments and perceptions. The revival of traditional forms in the late 19th and early 20th century was not a unique event. There were many such revivals during the 20th century, and the traditional poetry of A.E. Housman (whose book *A Shropshire Lad*, originally published in 1896, enjoyed huge popular success during World War I), Walter de la Mare, John Masefield, Robert Graves, and Edmund Blunden represents an important and often neglected strand of English literature in the first half of the century.

G.K. Chesterton

Chesterton was to become known as much for his exuberant personality and rotund figure as for his fiction, verse, and essays. Born in 1874, he was educated at St. Paul's School and later studied art at the Slade School and literature at University College, London. His writings to 1910 were of three kinds. First, his social criticism, largely in his voluminous journalism, was gathered in *The Defendant* (1901), *Twelve Types* (1902), and *Heretics* (1905). In it he expressed strongly pro-Boer views in the South African War. Politically, he began as a Liberal but after a brief radical period became, with his Christian and medievalist friend Hilaire Belloc, a Distributist, favouring the distribution of land. This phase of his thinking is exemplified by *What's Wrong with the World* (1910).

His second preoccupation was literary criticism. *Robert Browning* (1903) was followed by *Charles Dickens* (1906) and *Appreciations and Criticisms of the Works of Charles Dickens* (1911), prefaces to the individual novels, which are among his finest contributions to criticism. His *George Bernard Shaw* (1909) and *The Victorian Age in Literature*

G.K. Chesterton, *chalk drawing by James Gunn, 1932; in the National Portrait Gallery, London.* Courtesy of the National Portrait Gallery, London

(1913) together with *William Blake* (1910) and the later monographs *William Cobbett* (1925) and *Robert Louis Stevenson* (1927) have a spontaneity that places them above the works of many academic critics.

Chesterton's third major concern was theology and religious argument. He was converted from Anglicanism to Roman Catholicism in 1922. Although he had written on Christianity earlier, as in his book *Orthodoxy* (1909), his conversion added edge to his controversial writing, notably *The Catholic Church and Conversion* (1926), his writings in *G.K.'s Weekly*, and *Avowals and Denials* (1934). Other works arising from his conversion were *St. Francis of Assisi* (1923), the essay in historical theology *The Everlasting Man* (1925), and *St. Thomas Aquinas* (1933).

In his verse Chesterton was a master of ballad forms, as shown in the stirring "Lepanto" (1911). When it was not uproariously comic, his verse was frankly partisan and didactic. His essays developed his shrewd, paradoxical irreverence to its ultimate point of real seriousness. He is seen at his happiest in such essays as "On Running After One's Hat" (1908) and "A Defence of Nonsense" (1901), in which he says that nonsense and faith are "the two supreme symbolic assertions of truth" and "to draw out the soul of things with a syllogism is as impossible as to draw out Leviathan with a hook."

Many readers value Chesterton's fiction most highly. *The Napoleon of Notting Hill* (1904), a romance of civil war in suburban London, was followed by the loosely knit collection of short stories, *The Club of Queer Trades* (1905), and the popular allegorical novel *The Man Who Was Thursday* (1908). But the most successful association of fiction with social judgment is in Chesterton's series on the priest-sleuth Father Brown: *The Innocence of Father Brown* (1911), followed by *The Wisdom . . .* (1914), *The Incredulity . . .* (1926), *The Secret . . .* (1927), and *The Scandal of Father Brown* (1935).

Chesterton's friendships were with men as diverse as H.G. Wells, Shaw, Belloc, and Max Beerbohm. His *Autobiography* was published in 1936, the year of his death.

WRITING FOR THE NEW CENTURY

The most significant writing of the period, traditionalist or modern, was inspired by neither hope nor apprehension but by bleaker feelings that the new century would witness the collapse of a whole civilization. The new century had begun with Great Britain involved in the South African War (the Boer War; 1899–1902), and it seemed to some that the British Empire was as doomed to destruction, both from within and from without, as had been the Roman Empire. In his poems on the South African War, Hardy (whose achievement as a poet in the 20th century rivaled his achievement as a novelist in the 19th) questioned simply and sardonically the human cost of empire building and established a tone and style that many British poets were to use in the course of the century, while Kipling, who had done much to engender pride in empire, began to speak in his verse and short stories of the burden of empire and the tribulations it would bring.

JOSEPH CONRAD

The expatriate novelist Joseph Conrad (pseudonym of Józef Teodor Konrad Korzeniowski, born in the Ukraine of Polish parents) also expressed a sense of crisis in works written near the turn of the 20th century. He attributed the crisis not so much to the decline of a specific civilization as to human failings. Man was a solitary, romantic creature of will who at any cost imposed his meaning upon the world because he could not endure a world that did not reflect his central place within it. In *Lord Jim*, he had seemed to sympathize with this predicament; but in *Heart of Darkness*, *Nostromo*, *The Secret Agent*, and *Under Western Eyes*, he detailed such imposition, and the psychological pathologies he increasingly associated with it, without sympathy. He did so as a philosophical novelist whose concern with the mocking limits of human knowledge affected not only the content of his fiction but also its very structure. Conrad's writing itself is marked by gaps in the narrative, by narrators who do not fully grasp the significance of the events they are retelling, and by characters who are unable to make themselves understood.

Conrad's father, Apollo Nałęcz Korzeniowski, a poet and an ardent Polish patriot, was one of the organizers of the committee that went on in 1863 to direct the Polish insurrection against Russian rule. He was arrested in late 1861 and was sent into exile at Vologda in northern Russia. His wife and four-year-old son followed him there, and the harsh climate hastened his wife's death from tuberculosis in 1865. In *A Personal Record* Conrad relates that his first introduction to the English language was at the age of eight, when his father was translating the works of Shakespeare and Victor Hugo in order to support the household. In those solitary years with his father he read the works of Sir Walter Scott, James Fenimore Cooper, Charles Dickens, and William Makepeace Thackeray in Polish and French. Apollo was ill with tuberculosis and died in Cracow in 1869. Responsibility for the boy was assumed by his maternal uncle, Tadeusz Bobrowski, a lawyer, who provided his nephew with advice, admonition, financial help, and love. He sent Conrad to school at Cracow and then to Switzerland, but the boy was bored by school and yearned to go to sea. In 1874 Conrad left for Marseille with the intention of going to sea.

Joseph Conrad's seafarer stories have at their root the author's own voyages while in the French and the British merchant navies. George C. Beresford/Hulton Archive/Getty Images

Bobrowski made him an allowance of 2,000 francs a year and put him in touch with a merchant named Delestang, in whose ships Conrad sailed in the French merchant service. His first voyage, on the *Mont-Blanc* to Martinique, was as a passenger; on her next voyage he sailed as an apprentice. In July 1876 he again sailed to the West Indies, as a steward on the *Saint-Antoine*. On this voyage Conrad seems to have taken part in some unlawful enterprise, probably gunrunning, and to have sailed along the coast of Venezuela.

Conrad became heavily enmeshed in debt upon returning to Marseille and apparently unsuccessfully attempted to commit suicide. As a sailor in the French merchant navy he was liable to conscription when he came of age, so after his recovery he signed on in April 1878 as a deckhand on a British freighter bound for Constantinople with a cargo of coal. After the return journey his ship landed him at Lowestoft, Eng., in June 1878. It was Conrad's first English landfall, and he spoke only a few words of the language of which he was to become a recognized master. Conrad remained in England, and in the following October he shipped as an ordinary seaman aboard a wool clipper on the London–Sydney run.

Conrad was to serve 16 years in the British merchant navy, and his experiences would serve as the basis for much of his fiction. While in London in the summer of 1889, between voyages and waiting for a command, Conrad took rooms near the Thames and began to write what would be his first novel, *Almayer's Folly.* The task was interrupted by the strangest and probably the most important of his adventures. As a child in Poland, he had stuck his finger on the centre of the map of Africa and said, "When I grow up I shall go there." In 1889 the Congo Free State was four years old as a political entity and already notorious as a sphere of imperialistic exploitation. Conrad's childhood dream took positive shape in the ambition to command a Congo River steamboat. Using what influence he could, he went to Brussels and secured an appointment. What he saw, did, and felt in the Congo are largely recorded in "Heart of Darkness," his most famous, finest, and most enigmatic story, the title of which signifies not only the heart of Africa, the dark continent, but also the heart of evil—everything that is corrupt, nihilistic, malign—and perhaps the heart of man. The story is central to Conrad's work and vision, and it is difficult not to think of his Congo experiences as traumatic. He may have exaggerated when he said, "Before the Congo I was a mere animal," but in a real sense the dying Kurtz's cry, "The horror! The horror!" was Conrad's. He suffered psychological, spiritual, even metaphysical shock in the Congo, and his physical health was also damaged; for the rest of his life, he was racked by recurrent fever and gout.

Conrad was in the Congo for four months, returning to England in January 1891. He made several more voyages as a first mate, but by 1894, when his guardian Tadeusz Bobrowski died, his sea life was over. In the spring of 1894 Conrad sent *Almayer's Folly* to the London publisher Fisher Unwin, and the book was published in April 1895. It was as the author of this novel that Conrad adopted the name by which he is known.

Almayer's Folly was followed in 1896 by *An Outcast of the Islands*. These two novels provoked a misunderstanding of Conrad's talents and purpose which dogged him the rest of his life. Set in the Malayan archipelago, they caused him to be labeled a writer of exotic tales, a reputation which a series of novels and short stories about the sea—*The Nigger of the "Narcissus"* (1897), *Lord Jim* (1900), *Youth* (1902), *Typhoon* (1902), and others—seemed only to confirm. But words of his own about the *"Narcissus"* give the real reason for his choice of settings: "the problem . . . is not a problem of the sea, it is merely a problem that has risen on board a ship where the conditions of complete isolation from all land entanglements make it stand out with a particular force and colouring." This is equally true of his other works; the latter part of *Lord Jim* takes place in a jungle village not because the emotional and moral problems that interest Conrad are those peculiar to jungle villages, but because there Jim's feelings of guilt, responsibility, and insecurity—feelings common to humankind—work themselves out with a logic and inevitability that are enforced by his isolation. It is this purpose, rather than a taste for the outlandish, that distinguishes Conrad's work from that of many novelists of the 19th and early 20th centuries.

In 1895 Conrad married the 22-year-old Jessie George, by whom he had two sons. He thereafter resided mainly in the southeast corner of England, where his life as an author was plagued by poor health, near poverty, and difficulties of temperament. It was not until 1910, after he had written what are now considered his finest novels—*Lord Jim* (1900), *Nostromo* (1904), *The Secret Agent* (1907), and *Under Western Eyes* (1911), the last being three novels of political intrigue and romance—that his financial situation became relatively secure. Though hampered by rheumatism, Conrad continued to write for the remaining years of his life. In April 1924 he refused an offer of knighthood from Prime Minister Ramsay MacDonald, and he died shortly thereafter.

In his own time Conrad was praised for his power to depict life at sea and in the tropics and for his works' qualities of "romance"—a word used basically to denote his power of using an elaborate prose style to cast a film of illusory splendour over somewhat sordid events. Conrad's view of life is indeed deeply pessimistic. In every idealism are the seeds of corruption, and the most honourable individuals find their unquestioned standards totally inadequate to defend themselves against the assaults of evil. It is significant that Conrad repeats again and again situations in which such men are obliged to admit emotional kinship with those whom they have expected only to despise. This despairing vision gains much of its force from the feeling that Conrad accepted it reluctantly, rather than with morbid enjoyment. This vision also helped to confirm his centrality to Modernism and to the general understanding of it.

EDWARDIAN PLAYWRIGHTS

In tune with the anti-Aestheticism unleashed by the trial of the archetypal Aesthete, Oscar Wilde, both novelists and playwrights saw their task in the new century to be an unashamedly didactic one. In a series of wittily iconoclastic plays, of which *Man and Superman* and *Major Barbara* are the most substantial, George Bernard Shaw turned the Edwardian theatre into an arena for debate upon the principal concerns of the day: the question of political organization, the morality of armaments and war, the function of class and of the professions, the validity of the family and of marriage, and the issue of female emancipation.

GEORGE BERNARD SHAW

Born in 1856 in Dublin, Shaw was the third and youngest child (and only son) of George Carr Shaw and Lucinda Elizabeth Gurly Shaw. Technically, he belonged to the Protestant "ascendancy"—the landed Irish gentry—but his impractical father was first a sinecured civil servant and then an unsuccessful grain merchant, and George Bernard grew up in an atmosphere of genteel poverty, which to him was more humiliating than being merely poor. At first tutored by a clerical uncle, Shaw basically rejected the schools he then attended, and by age 16 he was working in a land agent's office.

Shaw developed a wide knowledge of music, art, and literature as a result of his mother's influence and his visits to the National Gallery of Ireland. In 1872 his mother left her husband and took her two daughters to London, following her music teacher, George John Vandeleur Lee, who from 1866 had shared households in Dublin with the Shaws. In 1876 Shaw resolved to become a writer, and he joined his mother and elder sister (the younger one having died) in London. Shaw in his 20s suffered continuous frustration and poverty. He depended upon his mother's pound a week from her husband and her earnings as a music teacher. He spent his afternoons in the British Museum reading room, writing novels and reading what he had missed at school, and his evenings in search of additional self-education in the lectures and debates that characterized contemporary middle-class London intellectual activities.

His fiction failed utterly. The semiautobiographical and aptly titled *Immaturity* (1879; published 1930) repelled every publisher in London. His next four novels were similarly refused, as were most of the articles he submitted to the press for a decade. Shaw's initial literary work earned him less than 10 shillings a year. A fragment posthumously published as *An Unfinished Novel* in 1958 (but written 1887–88) was his final false start in fiction.

Despite his failure as a novelist in the 1880s, Shaw found himself during this decade. He became a vegetarian, a socialist, a spellbinding orator, a polemicist, and tentatively a playwright. He became the force behind the newly

Among Edwardian playwrights, George Bernard Shaw was the most success-ful, and his works are the most enduring. Ernest H. Mills/Hulton Archive/ Getty Images

founded (1884) Fabian Society, a middle-class socialist group that aimed at the transformation of English society not through revolution but through "permeation" (in Sidney Webb's term) of the country's intellectual and political life. Shaw involved himself in every aspect of its activities, most visibly as editor of one of the classics of British socialism, *Fabian Essays in Socialism* (1889), to which he also contributed two sections.

Eventually, in 1885 the drama critic William Archer found Shaw steady journalistic work. His early journalism ranged from book reviews in the *Pall Mall Gazette* (1885–88) and art criticism in the *World* (1886–89) to brilliant musical columns in the *Star* (as "Corno di Bassetto"—basset horn) from 1888 to 1890 and in the *World* (as "G.B.S.") from 1890 to 1894. Shaw had a good understanding of music, particularly opera, and he supplemented his knowledge with a brilliance of digression that gives many of his notices a permanent appeal. But Shaw truly began to make his mark when he was recruited by Frank Harris to the *Saturday Review* as theatre critic (1895–98); in that position he used all his wit and polemical powers in a campaign to displace the artificialities and hypocrisies of the Victorian stage with a theatre of vital ideas. He also began writing his own plays.

FIRST PLAYS

When Shaw began writing for the English stage, its most prominent dramatists were Sir A.W. Pinero and H.A. Jones. Both men were trying to develop a modern realistic drama, but neither had the power to break away from the type of artificial plots and conventional character types expected by theatregoers. The poverty of this sort of drama had become apparent with the introduction of several of Henrik Ibsen's plays onto the London stage around 1890, when *A Doll's House* was played in London; his *Ghosts* followed in 1891, and the possibility of a new freedom and seriousness on the English stage was introduced. Shaw, who was about to publish *The Quintessence of Ibsenism* (1891), rapidly refurbished an abortive comedy, *Widowers' Houses*, as a play recognizably "Ibsenite" in tone, making it turn on the notorious scandal of slum landlordism in London. The result (performed 1892) flouted the threadbare romantic conventions that were still being exploited even by the most daring new playwrights. In the play a well-intentioned young Englishman falls in love and then discovers that his prospective father-in-law's fortune and his own private income derive from exploitation of the poor. Potentially this is a tragic situation, but Shaw seems to have been always determined to avoid tragedy. The unamiable lovers do not attract sympathy; it is the social evil and not the romantic predicament on which attention is concentrated, and the action is kept well within the key of ironic comedy.

The same dramatic predispositions control *Mrs. Warren's Profession*, written in 1893 but not performed until 1902 because the lord chamberlain, the censor of plays, refused it a license. Its subject is organized prostitution, and its action turns on the discovery by a well-educated young woman that her mother has graduated through the "profession" to become a part-proprietor of brothels throughout Europe. Again, the economic determinants of the situation are emphasized, and the subject is treated remorselessly and without the titillation of fashionable comedies about "fallen women." As with many of Shaw's works, the play is, within limits, a drama of ideas, but the vehicle by which these are presented is essentially one of high comedy.

Shaw called these first plays "unpleasant," because "their dramatic power is used to force the spectator to face unpleasant facts." He followed them with four "pleasant" plays in an effort to find the producers and audiences that his mordant comedies had offended. Both groups of plays were revised and published in *Plays Pleasant and Unpleasant* (1898). The first of the second group, *Arms and the Man* (performed 1894), has a Balkan setting and makes light-hearted, though sometimes mordant, fun of romantic falsifications of both love and warfare. The second, *Candida* (performed 1897), was important for English theatrical history, for its successful production at the Royal Court Theatre in 1904 encouraged Harley Granville-Barker and J.E. Vedrenne to form a partnership that resulted in a series of brilliant productions there. The play represents its heroine as forced to choose between her clerical husband—a worthy but obtuse Christian socialist—and a young poet who has fallen wildly in love with her. She chooses her confident-seeming husband because she discerns that he is actually the weaker. The poet is immature and hysterical but, as an artist, has a capacity to renounce personal happiness in the interest of some large creative purpose. This is a significant theme for Shaw; it leads on to that of the conflict between man as spiritual creator and woman as guardian of the biological continuity of the human race that is basic to *Man and Superman*. In *Candida* such speculative issues are only lightly touched on, and this is true also of *You Never Can Tell* (performed 1899), in which the hero and heroine, who believe themselves to be respectively an accomplished amorist and an utterly rational and emancipated woman, find themselves in the grip of a vital force that takes little account of these notions.

The strain of writing these plays, while his critical and political work went on unabated, so sapped Shaw's strength that a minor illness became a major one. In 1898, during the process of recuperation, he married his unofficial nurse, Charlotte Payne-Townshend, an Irish heiress and friend of Beatrice and Sidney Webb. The apparently celibate marriage lasted all their lives, Shaw satisfying his emotional needs in paper-passion correspondences with Ellen Terry, Mrs. Patrick Campbell, and others.

Shaw's next collection of plays, *Three Plays for Puritans* (1901), continued what became the traditional Shavian preface—an introductory essay in an electric prose style dealing as much with the themes suggested by the plays as the plays themselves. *The Devil's Disciple* (performed 1897) is a play set in New Hampshire during the American Revolution and is an inversion of traditional melodrama. *Caesar and Cleopatra* (performed 1901) is Shaw's first great play. In the play Cleopatra is a spoiled and vicious 16-year-old child rather than the 38-year-old temptress of Shakespeare's *Antony and Cleopatra*. The play depicts Caesar as a lonely and austere man who is as much a philosopher as he is a soldier. The play's outstanding success rests upon its treatment of Caesar as a credible study in magnanimity and "original morality" rather than as a superhuman hero on a stage pedestal. The third play, *Captain Brassbound's Conversion* (performed 1900), is a sermon against various kinds of folly masquerading as duty and justice.

International Importance

In *Man and Superman* (performed 1905) Shaw expounded his philosophy that humanity is the latest stage in a purposeful and eternal evolutionary movement of the "life force" toward ever-higher life forms. The play's hero, Jack Tanner, is bent on pursuing his own spiritual development in accordance with this philosophy as he flees the determined marital pursuit of the heroine, Ann Whitefield. In the end Jack ruefully allows himself to be captured in marriage by Ann upon recognizing that she herself is a powerful instrument of the "life force," since the continuation and thus the destiny of the human race lies ultimately in her and other women's reproductive capacity. The play's nonrealistic third act, the "Don Juan in Hell" dream scene, is spoken theatre at its most operatic and is often performed independently as a separate piece.

Shaw had already become established as a major playwright on the Continent by the performance of his plays there, but, curiously, his reputation lagged in England. It was only with the production of *John Bull's Other Island* (performed 1904) in London, with a special performance for Edward VII, that Shaw's stage reputation was belatedly made in England.

Shaw continued, through high comedy, to explore religious consciousness and to point out society's complicity in its own evils. In *Major Barbara* (performed 1905), Shaw has his heroine, a major in the Salvation Army, discover that her estranged father, a munitions manufacturer, may be a dealer in death but that his principles and practice, however unorthodox, are religious in the highest sense, while those of the Salvation Army require the hypocrisies of often-false public confession and the donations of the distillers and the armourers against which it inveighs. In *The Doctor's Dilemma* (performed 1906), Shaw produced a satire upon the medical profession (representing the self-protection of professions in general) and upon both the artistic temperament and the public's inability to separate it from the artist's achievement. In *Androcles and the Lion* (performed 1912), Shaw dealt with true and false religious exaltation in a philosophical play about early Christianity. Its central theme, examined through a group of early Christians condemned to the arena, is that one must have something worth dying for—an end outside oneself—in order to make life worth living.

A scene from the 1938 film version of Pygmalion. *Shaw wrote the screenplay for this incarnation of the story based on his popular stage play of the same name.* Hulton Archive/Getty Images

Possibly Shaw's comedic masterpiece, and certainly his funniest and most popular play, is *Pygmalion* (performed 1913). It was claimed by Shaw to be a didactic drama about phonetics, and its antiheroic hero, Henry Higgins, is a phonetician, but the play is a humane comedy about love and the English class system. The play is about the training Higgins gives to a Cockney flower girl to enable her to pass as a lady and is also about the repercussions of the experiment's success. The scene in which Eliza Doolittle appears in high society when she has acquired a correct accent but no notion of polite conversation is one of the funniest in English drama. *Pygmalion* has been both filmed (1938), winning an Academy Award for Shaw for his screenplay, and adapted into an immensely popular musical, *My Fair Lady* (1956; motion-picture version, 1964).

WORKS AFTER WORLD WAR I

World War I was a watershed for Shaw. At first he ceased writing plays, publishing instead a controversial pamphlet, "Common Sense About the War," which called Great Britain and its Allies equally culpable with the Germans and argued for negotiation and peace. His antiwar speeches made him notorious and the target of much criticism. In *Heartbreak House* (performed 1920), Shaw exposed, in a country-house setting on the eve of war, the spiritual bankruptcy of the generation responsible for the war's bloodshed. Attempting to keep from falling into "the bottomless pit of an utterly discouraging pessimism," Shaw wrote five linked plays under the collective title *Back to Methuselah* (1922). They expound his philosophy of creative evolution in an extended dramatic parable that progresses through time from the Garden of Eden to AD 31,920.

The canonization of Joan of Arc in 1920 reawakened within Shaw ideas for a chronicle play about her. In the resulting masterpiece, *Saint Joan* (performed 1923), the Maid is treated not only as a Catholic saint and martyr but as a combination of practical mystic, heretical saint, and inspired genius. Joan, as the superior being "crushed between those mighty forces, the Church and the Law," is the personification of the tragic heroine; her death embodies the paradox that humankind fears—and often kills—its saints and heroes and will go on doing so until the very higher moral qualities it fears become the general condition of man through a process of evolutionary change. Acclaim for *Saint Joan* led to the awarding of the 1925 Nobel Prize for Literature to Shaw (he refused the award).

In his later plays Shaw intensified his explorations into tragicomic and nonrealistic symbolism. For the next five years, he wrote nothing for the theatre but worked on his collected edition of 1930–38 and the encyclopaedic political tract "The Intelligent Woman's Guide to Socialism and Capitalism" (1928). Then he produced *The Apple Cart* (performed 1929), a futuristic high comedy that emphasized Shaw's inner conflicts between his lifetime of radical politics and his essentially conservative mistrust of the common man's ability to govern himself. Shaw's later, minor plays included *Too True to Be Good* (performed 1932), *On The Rocks* (performed 1933), *The Simpleton of the Unexpected Isles* (performed 1935), *Geneva* (performed 1938), and *In Good King Charles's Golden Days* (1939). After a wartime hiatus, Shaw, then in his 90s, produced several more plays, including *Farfetched Fables* (performed 1950), *Shakes Versus Shav* (performed 1949), and *Why She Would Not* (1956), which is a fantasy with only flashes of the earlier Shaw.

Impudent, irreverent, and always a showman, Shaw used his buoyant wit to keep himself in the public eye to the end of his 94 years; his wiry figure, bristling beard, and dandyish cane were as well-known throughout the world as his plays. When his wife, Charlotte, died of a lingering illness in 1943, in the midst of World War II, Shaw, frail and feeling the effects of wartime privations, made permanent his retreat from his London apartment to his country home at Ayot St. Lawrence, a Hertfordshire village in which he had lived since 1906. He died there in 1950, widely acclaimed as the best comic dramatist of his time.

HARLEY GRANVILLE-BARKER

Shaw was not alone in transforming the theatre into a venue in which to explore the primary concerns of his day, even if he was alone in the brilliance of his comedy. John Galsworthy, for instance, made use of the theatre in *Strife* (1909) to explore the conflict between capital and labour, and in *Justice* (1910) he lent his support to reform of the penal system. Similarly, Harley Granville-Barker dissected in *The Voysey Inheritance* and *Waste* the hypocrisies and deceit of upper-class and professional life. But Barker would also become known for his revolutionary approach to stage direction, which did much to change theatrical production in the 20th century.

Born in 1877, Barker was the eldest child and only son of Albert James Barker, a property developer, and Mary Elisabeth Bozzi Granville; his mother, a popular performer celebrated for her bird calls, largely supported the family with her work. Barker began his stage training at 13 years of age and first appeared on the London stage two years later. He preferred work with William Poel's Elizabethan Stage Society and Ben Greet's Shakespeare repertory company to a West End career, and in 1900 he joined the experimental Stage Society. His first major play, *The Marrying of Ann Leete* (1900), was produced by the society. In 1904 he became manager of the Court Theatre with J.E. Vedrenne and introduced the public to the plays of Galsworthy, Henrik Ibsen, Maurice Maeterlinck, and John Masefield, as well as Gilbert Murray's translations from Greek. His original productions of the early plays of Shaw were especially important. His wife, Lillah McCarthy, played leading roles in many of the plays he produced. Among new plays produced at the Court Theatre were several of his own: *The Voysey Inheritance* (1905), the most famous, showing Shaw's influence; *Prunella* (1906), a charming fantasy written with Laurence Housman; *Waste* (1907); and *The Madras House* (1910).

Also revolutionary was his treatment of Shakespeare. Instead of traditional scenic decor and declamatory elocution, Barker successfully introduced, in the Savoy productions (1912–14) of *The Winter's Tale* and *Twelfth Night*, continuous action on an open stage and rapid, lightly stressed speech. He and William Archer were active in promoting a national theatre, and by 1914 Barker had every prospect of a brilliant career.

After World War I, however, during which he served with the Red Cross, he found the mood of the postwar theatre alien and contented himself with work behind the scenes, including presidency of the British Drama League. He settled in Paris with his second wife, an American, collaborating with her in translating Spanish plays and writing his five series of *Prefaces to Shakespeare* (1927–48), a contribution to Shakespearean criticism that analyzed the plays from the point of view of a practical playwright with first-hand stage experience.

In 1937 Barker became director of the British Institute of the University of Paris. He fled to Spain in 1940 and then went to the United States, where he worked for British Information Services and lectured at Harvard University. He returned to Paris in 1946 and died there that year. A selection of his letters was published in 1986 as *Granville Barker and His Correspondents*.

ANGLO-AMERICAN MODERNISM: POUND, LEWIS, LAWRENCE, AND ELIOT

From 1908 to 1914 there was a remarkably productive period of innovation and experiment as novelists and poets undertook, in anthologies and magazines, to challenge the literary conventions not just of the recent past but of the entire post-Romantic era. For a brief moment, London, which up to that point had been culturally one of the dullest of the European capitals, boasted an avant-garde to rival those of Paris, Vienna, and Berlin, even if its leading personality, Ezra Pound, and many of its most notable figures were American.

The spirit of Modernism—a radical and utopian spirit stimulated by new ideas in anthropology, psychology, philosophy, political theory, and psychoanalysis—was in the air, expressed rather mutedly by the pastoral and often anti-Modern poets of the Georgian movement (1912–22) and more authentically by the English and American poets of the Imagist movement, to which Pound first drew attention in *Ripostes* (1912), a volume of his own poetry, and in *Des Imagistes* (1914), an anthology. Prominent among the Imagists were the English poets T.E. Hulme, F.S. Flint, and Richard Aldington and the Americans Hilda Doolittle (H.D.) and Amy Lowell.

Reacting against what they considered to be an exhausted poetic tradition, the Imagists wanted to refine the language of poetry in order to make it a vehicle not for pastoral sentiment or imperialistic rhetoric but for the exact description and evocation of mood. To this end they experimented with free or irregular verse and made the image their principal instrument. In contrast to the leisurely Georgians, they worked with brief and economical forms.

Meanwhile, painters and sculptors, grouped together by the painter and writer Wyndham Lewis under the banner of Vorticism, combined the abstract art of the Cubists with the example of the Italian Futurists who conveyed in their painting, sculpture, and literature the new sensations of movement and scale associated with modern developments such as automobiles and airplanes. With the typographically arresting *Blast: Review of the Great English Vortex* (two editions, 1914 and 1915) Vorticism found its polemical mouthpiece and in Lewis, its editor, its most active propagandist and accomplished literary exponent. His experimental play *Enemy of the Stars,* published in *Blast* in 1914, and his experimental novel *Tarr* (1918) can still surprise with their violent exuberance.

World War I brought this first period of the Modernist revolution to an end and, while not destroying its radical and utopian impulse, made the Anglo-American Modernists all too aware of the gulf between their ideals and the chaos of the present. Novelists and poets parodied received forms and styles, in their view made redundant by the immensity and horror of the war, but, as can be seen most clearly in Pound's angry and satirical *Hugh Selwyn Mauberley* (1920), with a note of anguish and with the wish that writers might again make form and style the bearers of authentic meanings.

In his two most innovative novels, *The Rainbow* (1915) and *Women in Love* (1920), D.H. Lawrence traced the sickness of modern civilization—a civilization in his view only too eager to participate in the mass slaughter of the war—to the effects of industrialization upon the human psyche. Yet as he rejected the conventions of the fictional tradition, which he had used to brilliant effect in his deeply felt autobiographical novel of working-class family life, *Sons and Lovers* (1913), he drew upon myth and symbol to hold out the hope that individual and collective rebirth could come through human intensity and passion.

On the other hand, the poet and playwright T.S. Eliot, another American resident in London, in his most innovative poetry, *Prufrock and Other Observations* (1917) and *The Waste Land* (1922), traced the sickness of modern civilization—a civilization that, on the evidence of the war, preferred death or death-in-life to life—to the spiritual emptiness and rootlessness of modern existence. As he rejected the conventions of the poetic tradition, Eliot, like Lawrence, drew upon myth and symbol to hold out the hope of individual and collective rebirth, but he differed sharply from Lawrence by supposing that rebirth could come through self-denial and self-abnegation. Even so, their satirical intensity, no less than the seriousness and scope of their analyses of the failings of a civilization that had voluntarily entered upon the First World War, ensured that Lawrence and Eliot became the leading and most authoritative figures of Anglo-American Modernism in England in the whole of the postwar period.

During the 1920s Lawrence (who had left England in 1919) and Eliot began to develop viewpoints at odds with the reputations they had established through their early work. In *Kangaroo* (1923) and *The Plumed Serpent* (1926), Lawrence revealed the attraction to him of charismatic, masculine leadership, while, in *For Lancelot Andrewes: Essays on Style and Order* (1928), Eliot (whose influence as a literary critic now rivaled his influence as a poet) announced that he was a "classicist in literature, royalist in politics and anglo-catholic in religion" and committed himself to hierarchy and order. Elitist and paternalistic, they did not, however, adopt the extreme positions of Pound (who left England in 1920 and settled permanently in Italy in 1925) or Lewis. Drawing upon the ideas of the left and of the right, Pound and Lewis dismissed democracy as a sham and argued that economic and ideological manipulation was the dominant factor. For some, the antidemocratic views of the Anglo-American Modernists simply made explicit the reactionary tendencies inherent in the movement from its beginning; for others, they came from a tragic loss of balance occasioned by World War I. This issue is a complex one, and judgments upon the literary merit and political status of Pound's ambitious but immensely difficult Imagist epic *The Cantos* (1917–70) and Lewis's powerful sequence of politico-theological novels *The Human Age* (*The Childermass*, 1928; *Monstre Gai* and *Malign Fiesta*, both 1955) are sharply divided.

CELTIC MODERNISM: YEATS, JOYCE, JONES, AND MACDIARMID

Pound, Lewis, Lawrence, and Eliot were the principal male figures of Anglo-American Modernism, but important contributions also were made by the Irish poet and playwright William Butler Yeats and the Irish novelist James Joyce. By virtue of nationality, residence, and, in Yeats's case, an unjust reputation as a poet still steeped in Celtic mythology, they had less immediate impact upon the British literary intelligentsia in the late 1910s and early 1920s than Pound, Lewis, Lawrence, and Eliot, although by the mid-1920s their influence had become direct and substantial. Many critics today argue that Yeats's work as a poet and Joyce's work as a novelist are the most important Modernist achievements of the period.

In his early verse and drama, Yeats, who had been influenced as a young man by the Romantic and Pre-Raphaelite movements, evoked a legendary and supernatural Ireland in language that was often vague and grandiloquent. As an adherent of the cause of Irish nationalism, he had hoped to instill pride in the Irish past. The poetry of *The Green Helmet* (1910) and *Responsibilities* (1914), however, was marked not only by a more concrete and colloquial style but also by a growing isolation from the nationalist movement, for Yeats celebrated an aristocratic Ireland epitomized for him by the family and country house of his friend and patron, Lady Gregory.

The grandeur of his mature reflective poetry in *The Wild Swans at Coole* (1917), *Michael Robartes and the Dancer* (1921), *The Tower* (1928), and *The Winding Stair* (1929) derived in large measure from the way in which (caught up by the violent discords of contemporary Irish history) he accepted the fact that his idealized Ireland was illusory. At its best his mature style combined passion and

168

precision with powerful symbol, strong rhythm, and lucid diction; and even though his poetry often touched upon public themes, he never ceased to reflect upon the Romantic themes of creativity, selfhood, and the individual's relationship to nature, time, and history.

Joyce, who spent his adult life on the continent of Europe, expressed in his fiction his sense of the limits and possibilities of the Ireland he had left behind. In his collection of short stories, *Dubliners* (1914), and his largely autobiographical novel *A Portrait of the Artist as a Young Man* (1916), he described in fiction at once realist and symbolist the individual cost of the sexual and imaginative oppressiveness of life in Ireland. As if by provocative contrast, his panoramic novel of urban life, *Ulysses* (1922), was sexually frank and imaginatively profuse. (Copies of the first edition were burned by the New York postal authorities, and British customs officials seized the second edition in 1923.) Employing extraordinary formal and linguistic inventiveness, including the stream-of-consciousness method, Joyce depicted the experiences and the fantasies of various men and women in Dublin on a summer's day in June 1904. Yet his purpose was not simply documentary, for he drew upon an encyclopaedic range of European literature to stress the rich universality of life buried beneath the provincialism of pre-independence Dublin, in 1904 a city still within the British Empire.

In his even more experimental *Finnegans Wake* (1939), extracts of which had already appeared as *Work in Progress* from 1928 to 1937, Joyce's commitment to cultural universality became absolute. By means of a strange, polyglot idiom of puns and portmanteau words, he not only explored the relationship between the conscious and the unconscious but also suggested that the languages and myths of Ireland were interwoven with the languages and myths of many other cultures.

Portrait of a writer as a young man: James Joyce in his early 20s. Joyce experimented with form and language, tweaking the social consciousness of his fellow Dubliners in the process. C.P. Curran/Hulton Archive/Getty Images

The example of Joyce's experimentalism was followed by the Anglo-Welsh poet David Jones and by the Scottish poet Hugh MacDiarmid (pseudonym of Christopher Murray Grieve). Whereas Jones concerned himself, in his complex and allusive poetry and prose, with the Celtic, Saxon, Roman, and Christian roots of Great Britain, MacDiarmid sought not only to recover what he considered to be an authentically Scottish culture but also to establish, as in his *In Memoriam James Joyce* (1955), the truly cosmopolitan nature of Celtic consciousness and achievement. MacDiarmid's masterpiece in the vernacular, *A Drunk Man Looks at the Thistle* (1926), helped to inspire the Scottish renaissance of the 1920s and '30s.

Stream of Consciousness

The term *stream of consciousness* refers to a narrative technique in nondramatic fiction intended to render the flow of myriad impressions—visual, auditory, physical, associative, and subliminal—that impinge on the consciousness of an individual and form part of his awareness along with the trend of his rational thoughts. The term was first used by the psychologist William James in *The Principles of Psychology* (1890). As the psychological novel developed in the 20th century, some writers attempted to capture the total flow of their characters' consciousness, rather than limit themselves to rational thoughts. To represent the full richness, speed, and subtlety of the mind at work, the writer incorporates snatches of incoherent thought, ungrammatical constructions, and free association of ideas, images, and words at the pre-speech level.

The stream-of-consciousness novel commonly uses the narrative techniques of interior monologue. Probably the most famous example is James Joyce's *Ulysses* (1922), a complex evocation of the inner states of the characters Leopold and Molly

Bloom and Stephen Dedalus. Other notable examples include *Leutnant Gustl* (1901) by Arthur Schnitzler, an early use of stream of consciousness to re-create the atmosphere of pre-World War I Vienna; William Faulkner's *The Sound and the Fury* (1929), which records the fragmentary and impressionistic responses in the minds of three members of the Compson family to events that are immediately being experienced or events that are being remembered; and Virginia Woolf's *The Waves* (1931), a complex novel in which six characters recount their lives from childhood to old age.

THE LITERATURE OF WORLD WAR I AND THE INTERWAR PERIOD

The impact of World War I upon the Anglo-American Modernists has been noted. In addition the war brought a variety of responses from the more-traditionalist writers, predominantly poets, who saw action. Rupert Brooke caught the idealism of the opening months of the war (and died in service); Siegfried Sassoon and Ivor Gurney caught the mounting anger and sense of waste as the war continued; and Isaac Rosenberg (perhaps the most original of the war poets), Wilfred Owen, and Edmund Blunden not only caught the comradely compassion of the trenches but also addressed themselves to the larger moral perplexities raised by the war (Rosenberg and Owen were killed in action). It was not until the 1930s, however, that much of this poetry became widely known, and it is the poetry of Brooke and Sassoon that has become amongst the most iconic of these poets. Yet the best-known poetry of these two men express opposite reactions to the war: Brooke's idealism is counterbalanced by Sassoon's pacifism.

BROOKE AND SASSOON

At school at Rugby, where his father was a master, Brooke distinguished himself as a cricket and football (soccer) player as well as a scholar. At King's College, Cambridge, where he matriculated in 1906, he was prominent in the Fabian (Socialist) Society and attracted innumerable friends. He studied in Germany and traveled in Italy, but his favourite pastime was rambling in the English country-side. In 1911 his *Poems* were published.

He spent a year (1913–14) wandering in the United States, Canada, and the South Seas. With the outbreak of World War I, he received a commission in the Royal Navy. After taking part in a disastrous expedition to Antwerp that ended in a harrowing retreat, he sailed for the Dardanelles, which he never reached. In 1915 he died of septicemia on a hospital ship off Skyros and was buried in an olive grove on that island.

Brooke's wartime sonnets, *1914* (1915), brought him immediate fame. They express an idealism in the face of death that is in strong contrast to the later poetry of trench warfare. One of his most popular sonnets, "The Soldier," begins with the lines:

> *If I should die, think only this of me:*
> *That there's some corner of a foreign field*
> *That is for ever England.*

Whereas Brooke died while serving in World War I, Sassoon survived the war and lived until the 1960s. Sassoon enlisted in World War I and was twice wounded seriously while serving as an officer in France. It was his antiwar poetry, such as *The Old Huntsman* (1917) and *Counterattack* (1918), and his public affirmation of pacifism, after he had won the Military Cross and was still in the army, that made him widely known.

His antiwar protests were at first attributed to shell shock, and he was confined for a time in a sanatorium, where he met and influenced another pacifist soldier-poet, Wilfred Owen, whose works he published after Owen was killed at the front.

Sassoon's autobiographical works include *The Memoirs of George Sherston*, 3 vol. (1928–36), and *Siegfried's Journey*, 3 vol. (1945), and more of his poems were published as *Collected Poems* (1947) and *The Path to Peace* (1960).

ALDOUS HUXLEY

In the wake of the war the dominant tone, at once cynical and bewildered, was set by Aldous Huxley's satirical novel *Crome Yellow*. Drawing upon Lawrence and Eliot, he concerned himself in his novels of ideas with the fate of the individual in rootless modernity. His pessimistic vision found its most complete expression in the 1930s, however, in his most famous and inventive novel, the anti-utopian fantasy *Brave New World*, and his account of the anxieties of middle-class intellectuals of the period, *Eyeless in Gaza*.

Huxley was a grandson of the prominent biologist T.H. Huxley and was the third child of the biographer and man of letters Leonard Huxley. He was educated at Eton, during which time he became partially blind owing to keratitis. He retained enough eyesight to read with difficulty, and he graduated from Balliol College, Oxford, in 1916. He published his first book in 1916 and worked on the periodical *Athenaeum* from 1919 to 1921. Thereafter he devoted himself largely to his own writing and spent much of his time in Italy until the late 1930s, when he settled in California.

Aldous Huxley, 1959. Robert M. Quittner/Black Star

Huxley established himself as a major author in his first two published novels, *Crome Yellow* (1921) and *Antic Hay* (1923); these are witty and malicious satires on the pretensions of the English literary and intellectual coteries of his day. *Those Barren Leaves* (1925) and *Point Counter Point* (1928) are works in a similar vein. Huxley's deep distrust of 20th-century trends in both politics and technology found expression in *Brave New World* (1932), a nightmarish vision of a future society in which psychological conditioning forms the basis for a scientifically determined and immutable caste system. The novel *Eyeless in Gaza* (1936) continues to shoot barbs at the emptiness and aimlessness experienced in contemporary society, but it also shows Huxley's growing interest in Hindu philosophy and mysticism as a viable alternative. Many of his subsequent works reflect this preoccupation, notably *The Perennial Philosophy* (1946).

Huxley's most important later works are *The Devils of Loudun* (1952), a brilliantly detailed psychological study of a historical incident in which a group of 17th-century French nuns were allegedly the victims of demonic possession; and *The Doors of Perception* (1954), a book about Huxley's experiences with the hallucinogenic drug mescaline. The author's lifelong preoccupation with the negative and positive impacts of science and technology on 20th-century life make him one of the representative writers and intellectuals of that century.

THE OLD AND NEW GUARD

Huxley's frank and disillusioned manner was echoed by the dramatist Noël Coward in *The Vortex* (1924), which established his reputation; by the poet Robert Graves in his autobiography, *Good-Bye to All That* (1929); and by the poet Richard Aldington in his *Death of a Hero* (1929), a semiautobiographical novel of prewar bohemian London and the trenches. Exceptions to this dominant mood were found among writers too old to consider themselves, as did Graves and Aldington, members of a betrayed generation. In *A Passage to India* (1924), E.M. Forster examined the quest for and failure of human understanding among various ethnic and social groups in India under British rule. In *Parade's End* (1950; comprising *Some Do Not*, 1924;

No More Parades, 1925; *A Man Could Stand Up,* 1926; and *Last Post*, 1928) Ford Madox Ford, with an obvious debt to James and Conrad, examined the demise of aristocratic England in the course of the war, exploring on a larger scale the themes he had treated with brilliant economy in his short novel *The Good Soldier* (1915). And in *Wolf Solent* (1929) and *A Glastonbury Romance* (1932), John Cowper Powys developed an eccentric and highly erotic mysticism.

These were, however, writers of an earlier, more confident era. A younger and more contemporary voice belonged to members of the Bloomsbury group. Setting themselves against the humbug and hypocrisy that, they believed, had marked their parents' generation in upper-class England, they aimed to be uncompromisingly honest in personal and artistic life. In Lytton Strachey's iconoclastic biographical study *Eminent Victorians* (1918), this amounted to little more than amusing irreverence, even though Strachey had a profound effect upon the writing of biography.

Noël Coward

(b. Dec. 16, 1899, Teddington, near London, Eng.—d. March 26, 1973, St. Mary, Jamaica)

The playwright, actor, and composer Noël Coward remains best known for highly polished comedies of manners.

Coward appeared professionally as an actor from the age of 12. Between acting engagements he wrote such light comedies as *I'll Leave It to You* (1920) and *The Young Idea* (1923), but his reputation as a playwright was not established until the serious play *The Vortex* (1924), which was highly successful in London. In 1925 the first of his durable comedies, *Hay Fever*, opened in London.

Coward ended the decade with his most popular musical play, *Bitter Sweet* (1929).

Another of his classic comedies, *Private Lives* (1930), is often revived. It shares with *Design for Living* (1933) a worldly milieu and characters unable to live with or without one another. His patriotic pageant of British history, *Cavalcade* (1931), traced an English family from the time of the South African (Boer) War through the end of World War I. Other successes included *Tonight at Eight-Thirty* (1936), a group of one-act plays performed by Coward and Gertrude Lawrence, with whom he often played. He rewrote one of the short plays, *Still Life,* as the film *Brief Encounter* (1946). *Present Laughter* (1939) and *Blithe Spirit* (1941;

Noël Coward, 1963. Horst Tappe/EB Inc.

film 1945; musical version, *High Spirits,* 1964) are usually listed among his better comedies.

In his plays Coward caught the clipped speech and brittle disillusion of the generation that emerged from World War I. His songs and revue sketches also struck the world-weary note of his times. Coward had another style, sentimental but theatrically effective, that he used for romantic, backward-glancing musicals and for plays constructed around patriotism or some other presumably serious theme. He performed almost every function in the theatre—including producing, directing, dancing, and singing in a quavering but superbly timed and articulate baritone—and acted in, wrote, and directed motion pictures as well.

E.M. FORSTER

Forster's father, an architect, died when the son, born in 1879, was a baby. Forster was brought up by his mother and paternal aunts. The difference between the two families, his father's being strongly evangelical with a high sense of moral responsibility, his mother's more feckless and generous-minded, gave him an enduring insight into the nature of domestic tensions, while his education as a dayboy (day student) at Tonbridge School, Kent, was responsible for many of his later criticisms of the English public school (private) system. At King's College, Cambridge, he enjoyed a sense of liberation. For the first time he was free to follow his own intellectual inclinations; and he gained a sense of the uniqueness of the individual, of the healthiness of moderate skepticism, and of the importance of Mediterranean civilization as a counterbalance to the more straitlaced attitudes of northern European countries.

On leaving Cambridge, Forster decided to devote his life to writing. His first novels and short stories were redolent of an age that was shaking off the shackles of Victorianism. While adopting certain themes (the importance of women in their own right, for example) from earlier English novelists such as George Meredith, he broke with the elaborations and intricacies favoured in the late 19th century and wrote in a freer, more colloquial style. From the first his novels included a strong strain of social comment, based on acute observation of middle-class life. There was also a deeper concern, however, a belief, associated with Forster's interest in Mediterranean "paganism," that, if men and women were to achieve a satisfactory life, they needed to keep contact with the earth and to cultivate their imaginations. In an early novel, *The Longest Journey* (1907), he suggested that cultivation of either in isolation is not enough, reliance on the earth alone leading to a genial brutishness and exaggerated development of imagination undermining the individual's sense of reality.

The same theme runs through *Howards End* (1910), a more ambitious novel that brought Forster his first major success. The novel is conceived in terms of an alliance between the Schlegel sisters, Margaret and Helen, who embody the liberal imagination at its best, and Ruth Wilcox, the owner of the house Howards End, which has remained close to the earth for generations; spiritually they recognize a kinship against the values of Henry Wilcox and his children, who conceive life mainly in terms of commerce. In a symbolic ending, Margaret Schlegel marries Henry Wilcox and brings him back, a broken man, to Howards End, reestablishing there a link (however heavily threatened by the forces of progress around it) between the imagination and the earth.

The resolution is a precarious one, and World War I was to undermine it still further. Forster spent three war-time years in Alexandria, doing civilian war work, and visited India twice, in 1912–13 and 1921. When he returned to former themes in his postwar novel *A Passage to India* (1924), they presented themselves in a negative form: against the vaster scale of India, in which the earth itself seems alien, a resolution between it and the imagination could appear as almost impossible to achieve. Only Adela Quested, the young girl who is most open to experience, can glimpse their possible concord, and then only momentarily, in the courtroom during the trial at which she is the central witness. Much of the novel is devoted to less spectacular values: those of seriousness and truthfulness (represented here by the administrator Fielding) and of an outgoing and benevolent sensibility (embodied in the English visitor Mrs. Moore). Neither Fielding nor Mrs. Moore is totally successful; neither totally fails. The novel ends in an uneasy equilibrium. Immediate reconciliation between Indians and British is ruled out, but the further possibilities inherent in Adela's experience, along with the surrounding uncertainties, are echoed in the ritual birth of the God of Love amid scenes of confusion at a Hindu festival.

The values of truthfulness and kindness dominate Forster's later thinking. A reconciliation of humanity to the earth and its own imagination may be the ultimate ideal, but Forster sees it receding in a civilization devoting itself more and more to technological progress. The values of common sense, goodwill, and regard for the individual, on the other hand, can still be cultivated, and these underlie Forster's later pleas for more liberal attitudes. During World War II he acquired a position of particular respect as a man who had never been seduced by totalitarianisms of any kind and whose belief in personal relationships and the simple decencies seemed to embody some of the common values behind the fight against Nazism and Fascism. In 1946 his old college gave him an honorary fellowship, which enabled him to make his home in Cambridge and to keep in communication with both old and young until his death in 1970.

FORD MADOX FORD

Ford Madox Ford was born Ford Hermann Hueffer in 1873. The son of a German music critic, Francis Hueffer, and a grandson of Ford Madox Brown, one of the Pre-Raphaelite painters, he grew up in a cultured, artistic environment. At 18 he wrote his first novel, *The Shifting of Fire* (1892). His acquaintance with Joseph Conrad in 1897 led to their collaboration in *The Inheritors* (1901) and *Romance* (1903). In 1908 he founded the *English Review,* publishing pieces by the foremost contemporary British authors and also by the then-unknown D.H. Lawrence, Wyndham Lewis, Ezra Pound, and H.M. Tomlinson. At the same time, Ford produced works of his own: a trilogy of historical novels about the ill-fated Catherine Howard and novels of contemporary life in which he experimented with technique and style. It was not until *The Good Soldier* (1915), considered by many to be his best work, that he matched an assured, controlled technique with powerful content. This work skillfully reveals the destructive effects of contradictory sexual and religious impulses upon a quartet of upper-middle-class characters.

Ford took part in World War I, in which he was gassed and shell-shocked. Afterward he changed his name from Hueffer to Ford and tried farming in Sussex and Left Bank life in Paris. While in Paris he edited the *Transatlantic Review* (January 1924–January 1925), which published works by James Joyce and Ernest Hemingway.

In his long literary career Ford had fruitful contacts with most of the important writers of the day and is remembered for his generous encouragement of younger writers. Of more than 70 published works, those on which his reputation rests are *The Good Soldier* and the tetralogy *Parade's End* (1950; comprising *Some Do Not* [1924], *No More Parades* [1925], *A Man Could Stand Up* [1926], and *Last Post* [1928]). During his last years, which he spent in France and the United States, Ford produced important works of criticism, reminiscences, and a major novel, *The Rash Act* (1933), in which he continued his lifelong exploration of questions of identity and inheritance.

VIRGINIA WOOLF

In the fiction of Virginia Woolf the rewards of an outlook like that of Strachey, Forster, and her fellow members of the Bloomsbury group—a confidence that could shade into cynicism, a skepticism bound tightly with an enthusiasm that marked all members of this generational new guard—were both profound and moving. In short stories and novels of great delicacy and lyrical power, she set out to portray the limitations of the self, caught as it is in time, and suggested that these could be transcended, if only momentarily, by engagement with another self, a place, or a work of art. This preoccupation not only charged the act of reading and writing with unusual significance but also produced, in *To the Lighthouse*, *The Waves*—perhaps her most inventive and complex novel—and *Between the Acts*, her most sombre and moving work, some of the most daring fiction produced in the 20th century.

EARLY LIFE AND INFLUENCES

Born Virginia Stephen, she was the child of ideal Victorian parents. Her father, Leslie Stephen, was an eminent literary figure and the first editor (1882–91) of the *Dictionary of National Biography*. Her mother, Julia Jackson, possessed

Bloomsbury Group

The Bloomsbury group is the name given to a coterie of English writers, philosophers, and artists who frequently met between about 1907 and 1930 at the houses of Clive and Vanessa Bell and of Vanessa's brother and sister Adrian and Virginia Stephen (later Virginia Woolf) in the Bloomsbury district of London, the area around the British Museum. They discussed aesthetic and philosophical questions in a spirit of agnosticism and were strongly influenced by G.E. Moore's *Principia Ethica* (1903) and by A.N. Whitehead's and Bertrand Russell's *Principia Mathematica* (1910–13), in the light of which they searched for definitions of the good, the true, and the beautiful and questioned accepted ideas with a "comprehensive irreverence" for all kinds of sham.

Nearly all the male members of the group had been at Trinity or King's College, Cambridge, with Leslie Stephen's son Thoby, who had introduced them to his sisters Vanessa and Virginia. Most of them had been "Apostles"; i.e., members of the "society," a select, semisecret university club for the discussion of serious questions, founded at Cambridge in the late 1820s by J.F.D. Maurice and John Sterling. Tennyson, Arthur Hallam, Edward Fitzgerald, and Leslie Stephen had all been Apostles. In the early 1900s, when those who later formed the core of the Bloomsbury group were elected to the society, the literary critic Lowes Dickinson, the philosophers Henry Sidgwick, J.M.E. McTaggart, A.N. Whitehead, G.E. Moore, and the art critic Roger Fry, who became one of the Bloomsbury group himself, were members.

The Bloomsbury group included the novelist E.M. Forster, the biographer Lytton Strachey, the art critic Clive Bell, the painters Vanessa Bell and Duncan Grant, the economist John Maynard Keynes, the Fabian writer Leonard Woolf, and the novelist and critic Virginia Woolf. Other members were Desmond Macarthy, Arthur Waley, Saxon Sidney-Turner, Robert Trevelyan, Francis Birrell, J.T. Sheppard (later provost of King's College), and the critic Raymond Mortimer and the sculptor Stephen Tomlin, both Oxford men. Bertrand Russell, Aldous Huxley, and T.S. Eliot were sometimes associated with the group, as was the economist Gerald Shove. The group survived World War I but by the early 1930s had ceased to exist in its original form, having by that time merged with the general intellectual life of London, Oxford, and Cambridge. Although its members shared certain ideas and values, the Bloomsbury group did not constitute a school. Its significance lies in the extraordinary number of talented persons associated with it.

great beauty and a reputation for saintly self-sacrifice; she also had prominent social and artistic connections, which included Julia Margaret Cameron, her aunt and one of the greatest portrait photographers of the 19th century. Both Julia Jackson's first husband, Herbert Duckworth, and Leslie's first wife, a daughter of the novelist William Makepeace Thackeray, had died unexpectedly, leaving her three children and him one. Julia Jackson Duckworth and Leslie Stephen married in 1878, and four children followed: Vanessa (born 1879), Thoby (born 1880), Virginia (born 1882), and Adrian (born 1883). While these four children banded together against their older half siblings, loyalties shifted among them. Virginia was jealous of Adrian for being their mother's favourite. At age nine, she was the genius behind a family newspaper, the *Hyde Park Gate News*, that often teased Vanessa and Adrian. Vanessa mothered the others, especially Virginia, but the dynamic between need (Virginia's) and aloofness (Vanessa's) sometimes expressed itself as rivalry between Virginia's art of writing and Vanessa's of painting.

The Stephen family made summer migrations from their London town house near Kensington Gardens to the rather disheveled Talland House on the rugged Cornwall coast. That annual relocation structured Virginia's childhood world in terms of opposites: city and country, winter and summer, repression and freedom, fragmentation and wholeness. Her neatly divided, predictable world ended, however, when her mother died in 1895 at age 49. Virginia, at 13, ceased writing amusing accounts of family news. Almost a year passed before she wrote a cheerful letter to her brother Thoby. She was just emerging from depression when, in 1897, her half sister Stella Duckworth died at age 28, an event Virginia noted in her diary as "impossible to write of." Then in 1904, after her father died, Virginia had a nervous breakdown.

While Virginia was recovering, Vanessa supervised the Stephen children's move to the bohemian Bloomsbury section of London. There the siblings lived independent of their Duckworth half brothers, free to pursue studies, to paint or write, and to entertain. Leonard Woolf dined with them in November 1904, just before sailing to Ceylon (now Sri Lanka) to become a colonial administrator. Soon the Stephens hosted weekly gatherings of radical young people, including Clive Bell, Lytton Strachey, and John Maynard Keynes, all later to achieve fame as, respectively, an art critic, a biographer, and an economist. Then, after a family excursion to Greece in 1906, Thoby died of typhoid fever. He was 26. Virginia grieved but did not slip into depression. She overcame the loss of Thoby and the "loss" of Vanessa, who became engaged to Bell just after Thoby's death, through writing. Vanessa's marriage (and perhaps Thoby's absence) helped transform conversation at the avant-garde gatherings of what came to be known as the Bloomsbury group into irreverent, sometimes bawdy repartee that inspired Virginia to exercise her wit publicly, even while privately she was writing her poignant "Reminiscences"—about her childhood and her lost mother—which was published in 1908. Viewing Italian art that summer, she committed herself to creating in language "some kind of whole made of shivering fragments," to capturing "the flight of the mind."

EARLY FICTION

Virginia Stephen determined in 1908 to "re-form" the novel by creating a holistic form embracing aspects of life that were "fugitive" from the Victorian novel. While writing anonymous reviews for the *Times Literary Supplement* and other journals, she experimented with such a novel, which she called *Melymbrosia*. In November 1910, Roger Fry, a new friend of the Bells, launched the exhibit "Manet and the Post-Impressionists," which introduced radical European art to the London bourgeoisie. Virginia was at once outraged over the attention that painting garnered and intrigued by the possibility of borrowing from the likes of artists Paul Cézanne and Pablo Picasso. As Clive Bell was unfaithful, Vanessa began an affair with Fry, and Fry began a lifelong debate with Virginia about the visual and verbal arts. In the summer of 1911, Leonard Woolf returned from the East. After he resigned from the colonial service, Leonard and Virginia married in August 1912. She continued to work on her first novel; he wrote the anticolonialist novel *The Village in the Jungle* (1913) and *The Wise Virgins* (1914), a Bloomsbury exposé. Then he became a political writer and an advocate for peace and justice.

Between 1910 and 1915, Virginia's mental health was precarious. Nevertheless, she completely recast *Melymbrosia* as *The Voyage Out* in 1913. She based many of her novel's characters on real-life prototypes: Lytton Strachey, Leslie Stephen, her half brother George Duckworth, Clive and Vanessa Bell, and herself. Rachel Vinrace, the novel's central character, is a sheltered young woman who, on an excursion to South America, is

Virginia Woolf created complex, daring fiction while fighting mania and depression wrought by a series of unfortunate events in her personal life. Hulton Archive/Getty Images

introduced to freedom and sexuality (though from the novel's inception she was to die before marrying). Woolf first made Terence, Rachel's suitor, rather Clive-like; as she revised, Terence became a more sensitive, Leonard-like character. After an excursion up the Amazon, Rachel contracts a terrible illness that plunges her into delirium and then death. As possible causes for this disaster, Woolf's characters suggest everything from poorly washed vegetables to jungle disease to a malevolent universe, but the book endorses no explanation. That indeterminacy, at odds with the certainties of the Victorian era, is echoed in descriptions that distort perception: while the narrative often describes people, buildings, and natural objects as featureless forms, Rachel, in dreams and then delirium, journeys into surrealistic worlds. Rachel's voyage into the unknown began Woolf's voyage beyond the conventions of realism.

Woolf's manic-depressive worries (that she was a failure as a writer and a woman, that she was despised by Vanessa and unloved by Leonard) provoked a suicide attempt in September 1913. Publication of *The Voyage Out* was delayed until early 1915; then, that April, she sank into a distressed state in which she was often delirious. Later that year she overcame the "vile imaginations" that had threatened her sanity. She kept the demons of mania and depression mostly at bay for the rest of her life.

In 1917 the Woolfs bought a printing press and founded the Hogarth Press, named for Hogarth House, their home in the London suburbs. The Woolfs themselves (she was the compositor while he worked the press) published their own *Two Stories* in the summer of 1917. It consisted of Leonard's *Three Jews* and Virginia's *The Mark on the Wall,* the latter about contemplation itself.

Since 1910, Virginia had kept (sometimes with Vanessa) a country house in Sussex, and in 1916 Vanessa settled into a Sussex farmhouse called Charleston. She had ended her affair with Fry to take up with the painter Duncan Grant, who moved to Charleston with Vanessa and her children, Julian and Quentin Bell; a daughter, Angelica, would be born to Vanessa and Grant at the end of 1918. Charleston soon became an extravagantly decorated, unorthodox retreat for artists and writers, especially Clive Bell, who continued on friendly terms with Vanessa, and Fry, Vanessa's lifelong devotee.

Virginia had kept a diary, off and on, since 1897. In 1919 she envisioned "the shadow of some kind of form which a diary might attain to," organized not by a mechanical recording of events but by the interplay between the objective and the subjective. Her diary, as she wrote in 1924, would reveal people as "splinters & mosaics; not, as they used to hold, immaculate, monolithic, consistent wholes." Such terms later inspired critical distinctions, based on anatomy and culture, between the feminine and the masculine, the feminine being a varied but all-embracing way of experiencing the world and the masculine a monolithic or linear way. Critics using these distinctions have credited Woolf with evolving a distinctly feminine diary form, one that explores, with perception, honesty, and humour, her own ever-changing, mosaic self.

Proving that she could master the traditional form of the novel before breaking it, she plotted her next novel in two romantic triangles, with its protagonist Katharine in both. *Night and Day* (1919) answers Leonard's *The Wise Virgins*, in which he had his Leonard-like protagonist lose the Virginia-like beloved and end up in a conventional marriage. In *Night and Day*, the Leonard-like Ralph learns to value Katharine for herself, not as some superior being. And Katharine overcomes (as Virginia had) class and familial prejudices to marry the good and intelligent

Ralph. This novel focuses on the very sort of details that Woolf had deleted from *The Voyage Out*: credible dialogue, realistic descriptions of early 20th-century settings, and investigations of issues such as class, politics, and suffrage.

Woolf was writing nearly a review a week for the *Times Literary Supplement* in 1918. Her essay "Modern Novels" (1919; revised in 1925 as "Modern Fiction") attacked the "materialists" who wrote about superficial rather than spiritual or "luminous" experiences. The Woolfs also printed by hand, with Vanessa Bell's illustrations, Virginia's *Kew Gardens* (1919), a story organized, like a Post-Impressionistic painting, by pattern. With the Hogarth Press's emergence as a major publishing house, the Woolfs gradually ceased being their own printers.

In 1919 they bought a cottage in Rodmell village called Monk's House, which looked out over the Sussex Downs and the meadows where the River Ouse wound down to the English Channel. Virginia could walk or bicycle to visit Vanessa, her children, and a changing cast of guests at the bohemian Charleston and then retreat to Monk's House to write. She envisioned a new book that would apply the theories of "Modern Novels" and the achievements of her short stories to the novel form. In early 1920 a group of friends, evolved from the early Bloomsbury group, began a "Memoir Club," which met to read irreverent passages from their autobiographies. Her second presentation was an exposé of Victorian hypocrisy, especially that of George Duckworth, who masked inappropriate, unwanted caresses as affection honouring their mother's memory.

In 1921 Woolf's minimally plotted short fictions were gathered in *Monday or Tuesday*. Meanwhile, typesetting having heightened her sense of visual layout, she began a new novel written in blocks to be surrounded by white spaces. In "On Re-Reading Novels" (1922), Woolf argued that the novel was not so much a form but an "emotion which you feel." In *Jacob's Room* (1922) she achieved such emotion, transforming personal grief over the death of Thoby Stephen into a "spiritual shape." Though she takes Jacob from childhood to his early death in war, she leaves out plot, conflict, even character. The emptiness of Jacob's room and the irrelevance of his belongings convey in their minimalism the profound emptiness of loss. Though *Jacob's Room* is an antiwar novel, Woolf feared that she had ventured too far beyond representation. She vowed to "push on," as she wrote Clive Bell, to graft such experimental techniques onto more-substantial characters.

Major Period

At the beginning of 1924, the Woolfs moved their city residence from the suburbs back to Bloomsbury, where they were less isolated from London society. Soon the aristocratic Vita Sackville-West began to court Virginia, a relationship that would blossom into a lesbian affair. Having already written a story about a Mrs. Dalloway, Woolf thought of a foiling device that would pair that highly sensitive woman with a shell-shocked war victim, a Mr. Smith, so that "the sane and the insane" would exist "side by side." Her aim was to "tunnel" into these two characters until Clarissa Dalloway's affirmations meet Septimus Smith's negations. Also in 1924 Woolf gave a talk at Cambridge called "Character in Fiction," revised later that year as the Hogarth Press pamphlet *Mr. Bennett and Mrs. Brown.* In it she celebrated the breakdown in patriarchal values that had occurred "in or about December, 1910"—during Fry's exhibit "Manet and the Post-Impressionists"—and she attacked "materialist" novelists for omitting the essence of character.

In *Mrs. Dalloway* (1925), the boorish doctors presume to understand personality, but its essence evades them.

Dust jacket designed by Vanessa Bell for the first edition of Virginia Woolf's To the Lighthouse, *published by the Hogarth Press in 1927.* Between the Covers Rare Books, Merchantville, NJ

This novel is as patterned as a Post-Impressionist paint-ing but is also so accurately representational that the reader can trace Clarissa's and Septimus's movements through the streets of London on a single day in June 1923. At the end of the day, Clarissa gives a grand party and Septimus commits suicide. Their lives come together when the doctor who was treating (or, rather, mistreating) Septimus arrives at Clarissa's party with news of the death. The main characters are connected by motifs and, finally, by Clarissa's intuiting why Septimus threw his life away.

Woolf wished to build on her achievement in *Mrs. Dalloway* by merging the novelistic and elegiac forms. As an elegy, *To the Lighthouse*—published on May 5, 1927, the 32nd anniversary of Julia Stephen's death—evoked child-hood summers at Talland House. As a novel, it broke narrative continuity into a tripartite structure. The first section, "The Window," begins as Mrs. Ramsay and James, her youngest son—like Julia and Adrian Stephen—sit in the French window of the Ramsays' summer home while a houseguest named Lily Briscoe paints them and James begs to go to a nearby lighthouse. Mr. Ramsay, like Leslie Stephen, sees poetry as didacticism, conversation as win-ning points, and life as a tally of accomplishments. He uses logic to deflate hopes for a trip to the lighthouse, but he needs sympathy from his wife. She is more attuned to emotions than reason. In the climactic dinner-party scene, she inspires such harmony and composure that the moment "partook, she felt,...of eternity." The novel's middle "Time Passes" section focuses on the empty house during a 10-year hiatus and the last-minute housecleaning for the returning Ramsays. Woolf describes the progress of weeds, mold, dust, and gusts of wind, but she merely announces such major events as the deaths of Mrs. Ramsay and a son and daughter. In the novel's third section, "The

Lighthouse," Woolf brings Mr. Ramsay, his youngest children (James and Cam), Lily Briscoe, and others from "The Window" back to the house. As Mr. Ramsay and the now-teenage children reach the lighthouse and achieve a moment of reconciliation, Lily completes her painting. *To the Lighthouse* melds into its structure questions about creativity and the nature and function of art. Lily argues effectively for nonrepresentational but emotive art, and her painting (in which mother and child are reduced to two shapes with a line between them) echoes the abstract structure of Woolf's profoundly elegiac novel.

In two 1927 essays, "The Art of Fiction" and "The New Biography," she wrote that fiction writers should be less concerned with naive notions of reality and more with language and design. However restricted by fact, she argued, biographers should yoke truth with imagination, "granite-like solidity" with "rainbow-like intangibility." Their relationship having cooled by 1927, Woolf sought to reclaim Sackville-West through a "biography" that would include Sackville family history. Woolf solved biographical, historical, and personal dilemmas with the story of Orlando, who lives from Elizabethan times through the entire 18th century; he then becomes female, experiences debilitating gender constraints, and lives into the 20th century. Orlando begins writing poetry during the Renaissance, using history and mythology as models, and over the ensuing centuries returns to the poem "The Oak Tree," revising it according to shifting poetic conventions. Woolf herself writes in mock-heroic imitation of biographical styles that change over the same period of time. Thus, *Orlando: A Biography* (1928) exposes the artificiality of both gender and genre prescriptions. However fantastic, *Orlando* also argues for a novelistic approach to biography.

Dust jacket designed by Vanessa Bell for the first edition of Virginia Woolf's
The Waves, *published by the Hogarth Press in 1931.* Between the Covers
Rare Books, Merchantville, NJ

In 1921 John Maynard Keynes had told Woolf that her memoir "on George," presented to the Memoir Club that year or a year earlier, represented her best writing. Afterward she was increasingly angered by masculine condescension to female talent. In *A Room of One's Own* (1929), Woolf blamed women's absence from history not on their lack of brains and talent but on their poverty. For her 1931 talk "Professions for Women," Woolf studied the history of women's education and employment and argued that unequal opportunities for women negatively affect all of society. She urged women to destroy the "angel in the house," a reference to Coventry Patmore's poem of that title, the quintessential Victorian paean to women who sacrifice themselves to men.

Having praised a 1930 exhibit of Vanessa Bell's paintings for their wordlessness, Woolf planned a mystical novel that would be similarly impersonal and abstract. In *The Waves* (1931), poetic interludes describe the sea and sky from dawn to dusk. Between the interludes, the voices of six named characters appear in sections that move from their childhood to old age. In the middle section, when the six friends meet at a farewell dinner for another friend leaving for India, the single flower at the centre of the dinner table becomes a "seven-sided flower . . . a whole flower to which every eye brings its own contribution." *The Waves* offers a six-sided shape that illustrates how each individual experiences events—including their friend's death—uniquely. Bernard, the writer in the group, narrates the final section, defying death and a world "without a self." Unique though they are (and their prototypes can be identified in the Bloomsbury group), the characters become one, just as the sea and sky become indistinguishable in the interludes. This oneness with all creation was the primal experience Woolf had felt as a child in Cornwall. In this her most experimental novel, she achieved its poetic equivalent. Through *To the Lighthouse* and *The Waves*, Woolf became, with James Joyce and William Faulkner, one of the three major English-language Modernist experimenters in stream-of-consciousness writing.

LATE WORK

From her earliest days, Woolf had framed experience in terms of oppositions, even while she longed for a holistic state beyond binary divisions. The "perpetual marriage of granite and rainbow" Woolf described in her essay "The New Biography" typified her approach during the 1930s to individual works and to a balance between writing works of fact and of imagination. Even before finishing *The Waves*, she began compiling a scrapbook of clippings illustrating the horrors of war, the threat of fascism, and the oppression of women. The discrimination against women that Woolf had discussed in *A Room of One's Own* and "Professions for Women" inspired her to plan a book that would trace the story of a fictional family named Pargiter and explain the social conditions affecting family members over a period of time. In *The Pargiters: A Novel-Essay* she would alternate between sections of fiction and of fact. For the fictional historical narrative, she relied upon experiences of friends and family from the Victorian Age to the 1930s. For the essays, she researched that 50-year span of history. The task, however, of moving between fiction and fact was daunting.

Woolf took a holiday from *The Pargiters* to write a mock biography of Flush, the dog of poet Elizabeth Barrett Browning. Lytton Strachey having recently died, Woolf muted her spoof of his biographical method; nevertheless, *Flush* (1933) remains both a biographical satire and a lighthearted exploration of perception, in this case a dog's. In 1935 Woolf completed *Freshwater*, an absurdist drama based on the life of her great-aunt Julia Margaret Cameron. Featuring such other eminences as the poet Alfred, Lord Tennyson, and the painter George Frederick Watts, this riotous play satirizes high-minded Victorian notions of art.

Meanwhile, Woolf feared she would never finish *The Pargiters*. Alternating between types of prose was proving cumbersome, and the book was becoming too long. She solved this dilemma by jettisoning the essay sections, keeping the family narrative, and renaming her book *The Years*. She narrated 50 years of family history through the decline of class and patriarchal systems, the rise of feminism, and the threat of another war. Desperate to finish, Woolf lightened the book with poetic echoes of gestures, objects, colours, and sounds and with wholesale deletions, cutting epiphanies for Eleanor Pargiter and explicit references to women's bodies. The novel illustrates the damage done to women and society over the years by sexual repression, ignorance, and discrimination. Though (or perhaps because) Woolf's trimming muted the book's radicalism, *The Years* (1937) became a best seller.

When Fry died in 1934, Virginia was distressed; Vanessa was devastated. Then in July 1937 Vanessa's elder son, Julian Bell, was killed in the Spanish Civil War while driving an ambulance for the Republican army. Vanessa was so disconsolate that Virginia put aside her writing for a time to try to comfort her sister. Privately a lament over Julian's death and publicly a diatribe against war, *Three Guineas* (1938) proposes answers to the question of how to prevent war. Woolf connected masculine symbols of authority with militarism and misogyny, an argument buttressed by notes from her clippings about aggression, fascism, and war.

Still distressed by the deaths of Roger Fry and Julian Bell, she determined to test her theories about experimental, novelistic biography in a life of Fry. As she acknowledged in "The Art of Biography" (1939), the recalcitrance of evidence brought her near despair over the possibility of writing an imaginative biography. Against the "grind" of finishing the Fry biography, Woolf wrote a verse play about the history of English literature. Her next novel, *Pointz Hall* (later retitled *Between the Acts*), would include the play as a pageant performed by villagers and would convey the gentry's varied reactions to it. As another holiday from Fry's biography, Woolf returned to her own childhood with "A Sketch of the Past," a memoir about her mixed feelings toward her parents and her past and about memoir writing itself. (Here surfaced for the first time in writing a memory of the teenage Gerald Duckworth, her other half brother, touching her inappropriately when she was a girl of perhaps four or five.) Through last-minute borrowing from the letters between Fry and Vanessa, Woolf finished her biography. Though convinced that *Roger Fry* (1940) was more granite than rainbow, Virginia congratulated herself on at least giving back to Vanessa "her Roger."

Woolf's chief anodyne against Adolf Hitler, World War II, and her own despair was writing. During the bombing of London in 1940 and 1941, she worked on her memoir and *Between the Acts*. In her novel, war threatens art and humanity itself, and, in the interplay between the pageant—performed on a June day in 1939—and the audience, Woolf raises questions about perception and response. Despite *Between the Acts*'s affirmation of the value of art, Woolf worried that this novel was "too slight" and indeed that all writing was irrelevant when England seemed on the verge of invasion and civilization about to slide over a precipice. Facing such horrors, a depressed

Woolf found herself unable to write. The demons of self-doubt that she had kept at bay for so long returned to haunt her. On March 28, 1941, fearing that she now lacked the resilience to battle them, she walked behind Monk's House and down to the River Ouse, put stones in her pockets, and drowned herself. *Between the Acts* was published posthumously later that year.

PERSPECTIVE AND IMPACT

Woolf believed that her viewpoint offered an alternative to the destructive egotism of the masculine mind, an egotism that had found its outlet in World War I, but, as she made clear in her long essay *A Room of One's Own*, she did not consider this viewpoint to be the unique possession of women. In her fiction she presented men who possessed what she held to be feminine characteristics, a regard for others and an awareness of the multiplicity of experience; but she remained pessimistic about women gaining positions of influence, even though she set out the desirability of this in *Three Guineas*. Together with Joyce, who greatly influenced her *Mrs. Dalloway*, Woolf transformed the treatment of subjectivity, time, and history in fiction and helped create a feeling among her contemporaries that traditional forms of fiction—with their frequent indifference to the mysterious and inchoate inner life of characters—were no longer adequate. Her eminence as a literary critic and essayist did much to foster an interest in the work of other female Modernist writers of the period, such as Katherine Mansfield (born in New Zealand) and Dorothy Richardson.

Woolf's experiments with point of view confirm that, as Bernard thinks in *The Waves*, "we are not single." Being neither single nor fixed, perception in her novels is fluid, as is the world she presents. While Joyce and Faulkner separate one character's interior monologues from another's, Woolf's narratives move between inner and outer and between characters without clear demarcations. Furthermore, she avoids the self-absorption of many of her contemporaries and implies a brutal society without the explicit details some of her contemporaries felt obligatory. Her nonlinear forms invite reading not for neat solutions but for an aesthetic resolution of "shivering fragments," as she wrote in 1908. While Woolf's fragmented style is distinctly Modernist, her indeterminacy anticipates a postmodern awareness of the evanescence of boundaries and categories.

Woolf's many essays about the art of writing and about reading itself today retain their appeal to a range of, in Samuel Johnson's words, "common" (unspecialized) readers. Woolf's collection of essays *The Common Reader* (1925) was followed by *The Common Reader: Second Series* (1932; also published as *The Second Common Reader*). She continued writing essays on reading and writing, women and history, and class and politics for the rest of her life. Many were collected after her death in volumes edited by Leonard Woolf.

Virginia Woolf wrote far more fiction than Joyce and far more nonfiction than either Joyce or Faulkner. Six volumes of diaries (including her early journals), six volumes of letters, and numerous volumes of collected essays show her deep engagement with major 20th-century issues. Though many of her essays began as reviews, written anonymously to deadlines for money, and many include imaginative settings and whimsical speculations, they are serious inquiries into reading and writing, the novel and the arts, perception and essence, war and peace, class and politics, privilege and discrimination, and the need to reform society.

Woolf's haunting language, her prescient insights into wide-ranging historical, political, feminist, and artistic issues, and her revisionist experiments with novelistic form during a remarkably productive career altered the course of Modernist and postmodernist letters.

WOMEN AND MODERNISM

As a result of late 20th-century rereadings of Modernism, scholars now recognize the central importance of women writers to British Modernism, particularly as manifested in the works of Mansfield, Richardson, May Sinclair, Mary Butts, Rebecca West (pseudonym of Cicily Isabel Andrews), Jean Rhys (born in the West Indies), and the American poet Hilda Doolittle (who spent her adult life mainly in England and Switzerland). Sinclair, who produced 24 novels in the course of a prolific literary career, was an active feminist and an advocate of psychical research, including psychoanalysis. These concerns were evident in her most accomplished novels, *Mary Olivier: A Life* (1919) and *Life and Death of Harriett Frean* (1922), which explored the ways in which her female characters contributed to their own social and psychological repression. West, whose pen name was based on one of Norwegian playwright Henrik Ibsen's female characters, was similarly interested in female self-negation. From her first and greatly underrated novel, *The Return of the Soldier* (1918), to later novels such as *Harriet Hume* (1929), she explored how and why middle-class women so tenaciously upheld the division between private and public spheres and helped to sustain the traditional values of the masculine world. West became a highly successful writer on social and political issues—she wrote memorably on the Balkans and on the Nürnberg trials at the end of World War II—but her public acclaim as a journalist obscured during her lifetime her greater achievements as a novelist.

In her 13-volume *Pilgrimage* (the first volume, *Pointed Roofs*, appeared in 1915; the last, *March Moonlight*, in 1967),

Richardson was far more positive about the capacity of women to realize themselves. She presented events through the mind of her autobiographical persona, Miriam Henderson, describing both the social and economic limitations and the psychological and intellectual possibilities of a young woman without means coming of age with the new century. Other women writers of the period also made major contributions to new kinds of psychological realism. In *Bliss and Other Stories* (1920) and *The Garden Party and Other Stories* (1922), Mansfield (who went to England at age 19) revolutionized the short story by rejecting the mechanisms of plot in favour of an impressionistic sense of the flow of experience, punctuated by an arresting moment of insight. In *Postures* (1928, reprinted as *Quartet* in 1969), *Voyage in the Dark* (1934), and *Good Morning, Midnight* (1939), Rhys depicted the lives of vulnerable women adrift in London and Paris, vulnerable because they were poor and because the words in which they innocently believed—honesty in relationships, fidelity in marriage—proved in practice to be empty.

Creating heavily symbolic novels based on the quest-romance, such as *Ashe of Rings* (1925) and *Armed with Madness* (1928), Butts explored a more general loss of value in the contemporary wasteland (T.S. Eliot was an obvious influence on her work), while Doolittle (whose reputation rested upon her contribution to the Imagist movement in poetry) used the quest-romance in a series of autobiographical novels—including *Paint It Today* (written in 1921 but first published in 1992) and *Bid Me to Live* (1960)—to chart a way through the contemporary world for female characters in search of sustaining, often same-sex relationships. Following the posthumous publication of her strikingly original prose, Doolittle's reputation was revised and enhanced.

THE 1930S

World War I created a profound sense of crisis in English culture, and this became even more intense with the worldwide economic collapse of the late 1920s and early '30s, the rise of fascism, the Spanish Civil War (1936–39), and the approach of another full-scale conflict in Europe. It is not surprising, therefore, that much of the writing of the 1930s was bleak and pessimistic: even Evelyn Waugh's sharp and amusing satire on contemporary England, *Vile Bodies* (1930), ended with another, more disastrous war.

Divisions of class and the burden of sexual repression became common and interrelated themes in the fiction of the 1930s. In his trilogy *A Scots Quair* (*Sunset Song* [1932], *Cloud Howe* [1933], and *Grey Granite* [1934]), the novelist Lewis Grassic Gibbon (pseudonym of James Leslie Mitchell) gives a panoramic account of Scottish rural and working-class life. The work resembles Lawrence's novel *The Rainbow* in its historical sweep and intensity of vision. Walter Greenwood's *Love on the Dole* (1933) is a bleak record, in the manner of Bennett, of the economic depression in a northern working-class community; and Graham Greene's *It's a Battlefield* (1934) and *Brighton Rock* (1938) are desolate studies, in the manner of Conrad, of the loneliness and guilt of men and women trapped in a contemporary England of conflict and decay. *A Clergyman's Daughter* (1935) and *Keep the Aspidistra Flying* (1936), by George Orwell, are evocations—in the manner of Wells and, in the latter case unsuccessfully, of Joyce—of contemporary lower-middle-class existence, and *The Road to Wigan Pier* (1937) is a report of northern working-class mores. Elizabeth Bowen's *Death of the Heart* (1938) is a sardonic analysis, in the manner of James, of contemporary upper-class values.

Yet the most characteristic writing of the decade grew out of the determination to supplement the diagnosis of class division and sexual repression with their cure. It was no accident that the poetry of W.H. Auden and his Oxford contemporaries C. Day-Lewis, Louis MacNeice, and Stephen Spender became quickly identified as the authentic voice of the new generation, for it matched despair with defiance. These self-styled prophets of a new world envisaged freedom from the bourgeois order being achieved in various ways. For Day-Lewis and Spender, technology held out particular promise. This, allied to Marxist precepts, would in their view bring an end to poverty and the suffering it caused. For Auden especially, sexual repression was the enemy, and here the writings of Sigmund Freud and D.H. Lawrence were valuable. Whatever their individual preoccupations, these poets produced in the very play of their poetry, with its mastery of different genres, its rapid shifts of tone and mood, and its strange juxtapositions of the colloquial and esoteric, a blend of seriousness and high spirits irresistible to their peers.

The adventurousness of the new generation was shown in part by its love of travel (as in Christopher Isherwood's novels *Mr. Norris Changes Trains* [1935] and *Goodbye to Berlin* [1939], which reflect his experiences of postwar Germany), in part by its readiness for political involvement, and in part by its openness to the writing of the avant-garde of the Continent. The verse dramas coauthored by Auden and Isherwood, of which *The Ascent of F6* (1936) is the most notable, owed much to Bertolt Brecht; the political parables of Rex Warner, of which *The Aerodrome* (1941) is the most accomplished, owed much to Franz Kafka; and the complex and often obscure poetry of David Gascoyne and Dylan Thomas owed much to the Surrealists. Even so, Yeats's mature poetry and Eliot's

Waste Land, with its parodies, its satirical edge, its multiplicity of styles, and its quest for spiritual renewal, provided the most significant models and inspiration for the young writers of the period.

The writing of the interwar period had great breadth and diversity, from Modernist experimentation to new documentary modes of realism and from art as propaganda (particularly in the theatre) to conventional fiction, drama, and poetry produced for the popular market. Two trends stand out: first, the impact of film on the writing of the decade, not least on styles of visual realization and dialogue, and, second, the ubiquitous preoccupation with questions of time, on the psychological, historical, and even cosmological levels. As the world became less stable, writers sought both to reflect this and to seek some more-fundamental grounding than that provided by contemporary circumstances.

W.H. AUDEN

In 1908, a year after Auden's birth in York, Auden's family moved to Birmingham, where his father became medical officer and professor in the university. Since the father was a distinguished physician of broad scientific interests and the mother had been a nurse, the atmosphere of the home was more scientific than literary. It was also devoutly Anglo-Catholic, and Auden's first religious memories were of "exciting magical rites." The family name, spelled Audun, appears in the Icelandic sagas, and Auden inherited from his father a fascination with Iceland.

His education followed the standard pattern for children of the middle and upper classes. At 8 he was sent away to St. Edmund's preparatory school, in Surrey, and at 13 to a public (private) school, Gresham's, at Holt, in Norfolk. Auden intended to be a mining engineer and was interested primarily in science; he specialized in biology. By 1922 he had discovered his vocation as a poet, and two years later his first poem was published in *Public School Verse*. In 1925 he entered the University of Oxford (Christ Church), where he established a formidable reputation as poet and sage, having a strong influence on such other literary intellectuals as C. Day-Lewis (named poet laureate in 1968), Louis MacNeice, and Stephen Spender, who printed by hand the first collection of Auden's poems in 1928. Though their names were often linked with his as poets of the so-called Auden generation, the notion of an "Auden Group" dedicated to revolutionary politics was largely a journalistic invention. Upon graduating from Oxford in 1928, Auden, offered a year abroad by his parents, chose Berlin rather than the Paris by which the previous literary generation had been fascinated. He fell in love with the German language and was influenced by its poetry, cabaret songs, and plays, especially those by Bertolt Brecht. He returned to become a schoolmaster in Scotland and England for the next five years.

In his *Collected Shorter Poems* Auden divides his career into four periods. The first extends from 1927, when he was still an undergraduate, through *The Orators* of 1932. The "charade" *Paid on Both Sides*, which along with *Poems* established Auden's reputation in 1930, best reveals the imperfectly fused but fascinating amalgam of material from the Icelandic sagas, Old English poetry, public-school stories, Karl Marx, Sigmund Freud and other psychologists, and schoolboy humour that enters into all these works. The poems are uneven and often obscure, pulled in contrary directions by the subjective impulse to fantasy, the mythic and unconscious, and the objective impulse to a diagnosis of the ills of society and the psychological and moral defects of the individuals who constitute it. Though the social and political implications of the

Through his poems, W.H. Auden (right), with Christopher Isherwood, challenged the sexual mores, social conventions, and political ideals of 1930s England. John F. Stephenson/Hulton Archive/Getty Images

poetry attracted most attention, the psychological aspect is primary. The notion of poetry as a kind of therapy, performing a function somehow analogous to the psycho-analytical, remains fundamental in Auden.

The second period, 1933–38, is that in which Auden was the hero of the left. Continuing the analysis of the evils of capitalist society, he also warned of the rise of totalitarianism. In *On This Island* (1937; in Britain, *Look, Stranger!*, 1936) his verse became more open in texture and accessible to a larger public. For the Group Theatre, a society that put on experimental and noncommercial plays in London, he wrote first *The Dance of Death* (a musi-cal propaganda play) and then three plays in collaboration

with Christopher Isherwood, Auden's friend since preparatory school: *The Dog Beneath the Skin* (1935), *The Ascent of
F 6* (1936), and *On the Frontier* (1938). Auden also wrote
commentaries for documentary films, including a classic
of that genre, *Night Mail* (1936); numerous essays and book
reviews; and reportage, most notably on a trip to Iceland
with MacNeice, described in *Letters from Iceland* (1937),
and a trip to China with Isherwood that was the basis of
Journey to a War (1939). Auden visited Spain briefly in 1937,
his poem *Spain* (1937) being the only immediate result; but
the visit, according to his later recollections, marked the
beginning both of his disillusion with the left and of his
return to Christianity. In 1936 he married Erika Mann, the
daughter of the German novelist Thomas Mann, in order
to provide her with a British passport. When he and
Isherwood went to China, they crossed the United States
both ways, and on the return journey they both decided to
settle there. In January 1939, both did so.

In the third period, 1939–46, Auden became an
American citizen and underwent decisive changes in his
religious and intellectual perspective. *Another Time* (1940)
contains some of his best songs and topical verse, and *The
Double Man* (containing "New Year Letter," which provided the title of the British edition; 1941) embodies his
position on the verge of commitment to Christianity. The
beliefs and attitudes that are basic to all of Auden's work
after 1940 are defined in three long poems: religious in the
Christmas oratorio *For the Time Being* (1944); aesthetic in
the same volume's *Sea and the Mirror* (a quasi-dramatic
"commentary" on William Shakespeare's *The Tempest*); and
social-psychological in *The Age of Anxiety* (1947), the
"baroque eclogue" that won Auden the Pulitzer Prize in
1948. Auden wrote no long poems after that.

The fourth period began in 1948, when Auden established the pattern of leaving New York City each year to

spend the months from April to October in Europe. From 1948 to 1957 his summer residence was the Italian island of Ischia; in the latter year he bought a farmhouse in Kirchstetten, Austria, where he then spent his summers. In *The Shield of Achilles* (1955), *Homage to Clio* (1960), *About the House* (1965), and *City Without Walls* (1969) are sequences of poems arranged according to an external pattern (canonical hours, types of landscape, rooms of a house). With Chester Kallman, an American poet and close friend who lived with him for more than 20 years, he rehabilitated the art of the opera libretto. Their best-known collaborations are *The Rake's Progress* (1951), for Igor Stravinsky; *Elegy for Young Lovers* (1961) and *The Bassarids* (1966), for Hans Werner Henze; and *Love's Labour's Lost* for Nicolas Nabokov. They also edited *An Elizabethan Song Book* (1956). In 1962 Auden published a volume of criticism, *The Dyer's Hand,* and in 1970 a commonplace book, *A Certain World.* He spent much time on editing and translating, notably *The Collected Poems of St. John Perse* (1972). In 1972 Auden transferred his winter residence from New York City to Oxford, where he was an honorary fellow at Christ Church College. Of the numerous honours conferred on Auden in this last period, the Bollingen Prize (1953), the National Book Award (1956), and the professorship of poetry at Oxford (1956–61) may be mentioned.

In the early 1930s W.H. Auden was acclaimed prematurely by some as the foremost poet then writing in English, on the disputable ground that his poetry was more relevant to contemporary social and political realities than that of T.S. Eliot and William Butler Yeats, who previously had shared the summit. By the time of Eliot's death in 1965, however, a convincing case could be made for the assertion that Auden was indeed Eliot's successor, as Eliot had inherited sole claim to supremacy when Yeats died in 1939.

Auden was, as a poet, far more copious and varied than Eliot and far more uneven. He tried to interpret the times, to diagnose the ills of society and deal with intellectual and moral problems of public concern. But the need to express the inner world of fantasy and dream was equally apparent, and, hence, the poetry is sometimes bewildering. If the poems, taken individually, are often obscure—especially the earlier ones—they create, when taken together, a meaningful poetic cosmos with symbolic landscapes and mythical characters and situations. In his later years Auden ordered the world of his poetry and made it easier of access; he collected his poems, revised them, and presented them chronologically in two volumes: *Collected Shorter Poems 1927–57* (1967) and *Collected Longer Poems* (1969).

ELIZABETH BOWEN

Bowen was born in 1899 of the Anglo-Irish gentry and spent her early childhood in Dublin, as related in her autobiographical fragment *Seven Winters* (1942), and at the family house she later inherited at Kildorrery, County Cork. The history of the house is recounted in *Bowen's Court* (1942), and it is the scene of her novel *The Last September* (1929), which takes place during the troubles that preceded Irish independence. When she was 7, her father suffered a mental illness, and she departed for England with her mother, who died when Elizabeth was 12. An only child, she lived with relatives on the Kentish coast.

With a little money that enabled her to live independently in London and to winter in Italy, Bowen began writing short stories at 20. Her first collection, *Encounters,* appeared in 1923. It was followed in 1927 by *The Hotel,* which contains a typical Bowen heroine—a girl attempting to cope with a life for which she is unprepared. *The*

Last September (1929) is an autumnal picture of the Anglo-Irish gentry. *The House in Paris* (1935), one of her highly praised novels, is a story of love and betrayal told partly through the eyes of two children. Bowen employed a finely wrought prose style in fictions frequently detailing uneasy and unfulfilling relationships among the upper-middle class. *The Death of the Heart* (1938), the title of one of her most praised novels, effectively expresses the tone and content of many of her works.

During World War II, Bowen worked for the Ministry of Information in London and served as an air raid warden. Her novel set in wartime London, *The Heat of the Day* (1949), is among her most significant works. The war also forms the basis for one of her collections of short stories, *The Demon Lover* (1945; U.S. title, *Ivy Gripped the Steps*). Her essays appear in *Collected Impressions* (1950) and *Afterthought* (1962). Bowen's last book, *Pictures and Conversations* (1975), is an introspective, partly autobiographical collection of essays and articles.

GEORGE ORWELL

Born Eric Arthur Blair, Orwell never entirely abandoned his original name, but his first book (*Down and Out in Paris and London*) appeared as the work of George Orwell (the surname he derived from the River Orwell in East Anglia). In time his nom de plume became so closely attached to him that few people but relatives knew his real name was Blair. The change in name corresponded to a profound shift in Orwell's life-style, in which he changed from a pillar of the British imperial establishment into a literary and political rebel.

He was born in Bengal in 1903, into the class of sahibs. His father was a minor British official in the Indian civil service; his mother, of French extraction, was the daughter of an unsuccessful teak merchant in Burma. Their attitudes were those of the "landless gentry," as Orwell later called lower-middle-class people whose pretensions to social status had little relation to their income. Orwell was thus brought up in an atmosphere of impoverished snobbery. After returning with his parents to England, he was sent in 1911 to a preparatory boarding school on the Sussex coast, where he was distinguished among the other boys by his poverty and his intellectual brilliance. He grew up a morose, withdrawn, eccentric boy, and he was later to tell of the miseries of those years in his posthumously published autobiographical essay, *Such, Such Were the Joys* (1953).

Orwell won scholarships to two of England's leading schools, Winchester and Eton, and chose the latter. He stayed from 1917 to 1921. Aldous Huxley was one of his masters, and it was at Eton that he published his first writing in college periodicals. Instead of accepting a scholarship to a university, Orwell decided to follow family tradition and, in 1922, went to Burma as assistant district superintendent in the Indian Imperial Police. He served in a number of country stations and at first appeared to be a model imperial servant. Yet from boyhood he had wanted to become a writer, and when he realized how much against their will the Burmese were ruled by the British, he felt increasingly ashamed of his role as a colonial police officer. Later he was to recount his experiences and his reactions to imperial rule in his novel *Burmese Days* and in two brilliant autobiographical sketches, "Shooting an Elephant" and "A Hanging," classics of expository prose.

In 1927 Orwell, on leave to England, decided not to return to Burma, and on Jan. 1, 1928, he took the decisive step of resigning from the imperial police. Already in the autumn of 1927 he had started on a course of action that was to shape his character as a writer. Having felt guilty

Early fictionalized, firsthand accounts of George Orwell's time as a starving artist in Paris and London eventually gave way to novels with themes of revolution and the threat of totalitarianism. Popperfoto/Getty Images

that the barriers of race and caste had prevented his mingling with the Burmese, he thought he could expiate some of his guilt by immersing himself in the life of the poor and outcast people of Europe. Donning ragged clothes, he went into the East End of London to live in cheap lodging houses among labourers and beggars; he spent a period in the slums of Paris and worked as a dishwasher in French hotels and restaurants; he tramped the roads of England with professional vagrants and joined the people of the London slums in their annual exodus to work in the Kentish hopfields.

These experiences gave Orwell the material for *Down and Out in Paris and London* (1933), in which actual incidents are rearranged into something like fiction. The book's publication in 1933 earned him some initial literary recognition. Orwell's first novel, *Burmese Days* (1934), established the pattern of his subsequent fiction in its portrayal of a sensitive, conscientious, and emotionally isolated individual who is at odds with an oppressive or dishonest social environment. The main character of *Burmese Days* is a minor administrator who seeks to escape from the dreary and narrow-minded chauvinism of his fellow British colonialists in Burma. His sympathies for the Burmese, however, end in an unforeseen personal tragedy. The protagonist of Orwell's next novel, *A Clergyman's Daughter* (1935), is an unhappy spinster who achieves a brief and accidental liberation in her experiences among some agricultural labourers. *Keep the Aspidistra Flying* (1936) is about a literarily inclined bookseller's assistant who despises the empty commercialism and materialism of middle-class life but who in the end is reconciled to bourgeois prosperity by his forced marriage to the girl he loves.

Orwell's revulsion against imperialism led not only to his personal rejection of the bourgeois life-style but to a political reorientation as well. Immediately after returning from Burma he called himself an anarchist and continued to do so for several years; during the 1930s, however, he began to consider himself a socialist, though he was too libertarian in his thinking ever to take the further step—so common in the period—of declaring himself a communist.

Orwell's first socialist book was an original and unorthodox political treatise entitled *The Road to Wigan Pier* (1937). It begins by describing his experiences when he went to live among the destitute and unemployed miners of northern England, sharing and observing their lives; it ends in a series of sharp criticisms of existing socialist movements. It combines mordant reporting with a tone of generous anger that was to characterize Orwell's subsequent writing.

By the time *The Road to Wigan Pier* was in print, Orwell was in Spain; he went to report on the Civil War there and stayed to join the Republican militia, serving on the Aragon and Teruel fronts and rising to the rank of second lieutenant. He was seriously wounded at Teruel, damage to his throat permanently affecting his voice and endowing his speech with a strange, compelling quietness. Later, in May 1937, after having fought in Barcelona against communists who were trying to suppress their political opponents, he was forced to flee Spain in fear of his life. The experience left him with a lifelong dread of communism, first expressed in the vivid account of his Spanish experiences, *Homage to Catalonia* (1938), which many consider one of his best books.

Returning to England, Orwell showed a paradoxically conservative strain in writing *Coming Up for Air* (1939), in which he uses the nostalgic recollections of a middle-aged man to examine the decency of a past England and express his fears about a future threatened by war and fascism. When war did come, Orwell was rejected for military service, and instead he headed the Indian service of the British Broadcasting Corporation (BBC). He left the BBC in 1943 and became literary editor of the *Tribune,* a left-wing socialist paper associated with the British Labour leader Aneurin Bevan. At this period Orwell was a prolific journalist, writing many newspaper articles and reviews, together with serious criticism, like his classic essays on Charles Dickens and on boys' weeklies and a number of books about England (notably *The Lion and the Unicorn,* 1941) that combined patriotic sentiment with the advocacy of a libertarian, decentralist socialism very much unlike that practiced by the British Labour Party.

In 1944 Orwell finished *Animal Farm,* a political fable based on the story of the Russian Revolution and its betrayal by Joseph Stalin. In this book a group of barnyard animals overthrow and chase off their exploitative human masters and set up an egalitarian society of their own. Eventually the animals' intelligent and power-loving leaders, the pigs, subvert the revolution and form a dictatorship whose bondage is even more oppressive and heartless than that of their former human masters. ("All animals are equal, but some animals are more equal than others.") At first Orwell had difficulty finding a publisher for this small masterpiece, but when it appeared in 1945 *Animal Farm* made him famous and, for the first time, prosperous.

Animal Farm was one of Orwell's finest works, full of wit and fantasy and admirably written. It has, however, been overshadowed by his last book, *Nineteen Eighty-four* (1949), a novel he wrote as a warning after years of brooding on the twin menaces of Nazism and Stalinism. The novel is set in an imaginary future in which the world is dominated by three perpetually warring totalitarian police states. The book's hero, the Englishman Winston Smith, is a minor party functionary in one of these states. His longing for truth and decency leads him to secretly rebel against the government, which perpetuates its rule by systematically distorting the truth and continuously rewriting history to suit its own purposes. Smith has a love affair with a like-minded woman, but then they are both arrested by the Thought Police. The ensuing imprisonment, torture, and reeducation of Smith are intended not merely to break him physically or make him submit but to root out his independent mental existence and his spiritual dignity until he can love only the figure he previously most hated: the apparent leader of the party, Big Brother. Smith's surrender to the monstrous brainwashing techniques of his jailers is tragic enough, but the novel gains much of its power from the comprehensive rigour with which it extends the premises of totalitarianism to their logical end: the love of power and domination over others has acquired its perfected expression in the perpetual surveillance and omnipresent dishonesty of an unassailable and irresistible police state under whose rule every human virtue is slowly being suborned and extinguished. Orwell's warning of the potential dangers of totalitarianism made a deep impression on his contemporaries and upon subsequent readers, and the book's title and many of its coined words and phrases ("Big Brother is watching you," "newspeak," "doublethink") became bywords for modern political abuses.

Orwell wrote the last pages of *Nineteen Eighty-four* in a remote house on the Hebridean island of Jura, which he had bought from the proceeds of *Animal Farm*. He worked between bouts of hospitalization for tuberculosis, of which he died in a London hospital in January 1950.

THE LITERATURE OF WORLD WAR II (1939–45)

The outbreak of war in 1939, as in 1914, brought to an end an era of great intellectual and creative exuberance. Individuals were dispersed; the rationing of paper affected the production of magazines and books; and the poem and the short story, convenient forms for men under arms, became the favoured means of literary expression. It was hardly a time for new beginnings, although the poets of the New Apocalypse movement produced three anthologies (1940–45) inspired by Neoromantic anarchism. No important new novelists or playwrights appeared. In fact, the best fiction about wartime—Evelyn Waugh's *Put Out More Flags* (1942), Henry Green's *Caught* (1943), James Hanley's *No Directions* (1943), Patrick Hamilton's *The Slaves of Solitude* (1947), and Elizabeth Bowen's *The Heat of the Day* (1949)—was produced by established writers. Only three new poets (all of whom died in active service) showed promise: Alun Lewis, Sidney Keyes, and Keith Douglas, the latter the most gifted and distinctive, whose eerily detached accounts of the battlefield revealed a poet of potential greatness. Lewis's haunting short stories about the lives of officers and enlisted men are also works of very great accomplishment.

It was a poet of an earlier generation, T.S. Eliot, who produced in his *Four Quartets* the masterpiece of the war. Reflecting upon language, time, and history, he searched, in the three quartets written during the war, for moral and religious significance in the midst of destruction and strove to counter the spirit of nationalism inevitably present in a nation at war. The creativity that had seemed to end with the tortured religious poetry and verse drama of the 1920s and '30s had a rich and extraordinary late flowering as Eliot concerned himself, on the scale of *The Waste Land* but in a very different manner and mood, with the well-being of the society in which he lived.

T.S. ELIOT

Born in 1888, Eliot was descended from a distinguished New England family that had relocated to St. Louis, Missouri. His family allowed him the widest education available in his time, with no influence from his father to be "practical" and to go into business. From Smith Academy in St. Louis he went to Milton, in Massachusetts; from Milton he entered Harvard in 1906; he received a B.A. in 1909, after three instead of the usual four years. The men who influenced him at Harvard were George Santayana, the philosopher and poet, and the critic Irving Babbitt. From Babbitt he derived an anti-Romantic attitude that, amplified by his later reading of British philosophers F.H. Bradley and T.E. Hulme, lasted through his life. In the academic year 1909–10 he was an assistant in philosophy at Harvard.

He spent the year 1910–11 in France, attending Henri Bergson's lectures in philosophy at the Sorbonne and reading poetry with Alain-Fournier. Eliot's study of the poetry of Dante, of the English writers John Webster and John Donne, and of the French Symbolist Jules Laforgue helped him to find his own style. From 1911 to 1914 he was back at Harvard reading Indian philosophy and studying Sanskrit. In 1913 he read Bradley's *Appearance and Reality*; by 1916 he had finished, in Europe, a dissertation entitled "Knowledge and Experience in the Philosophy of F.H. Bradley." But World War I had intervened, and he never returned to Harvard to take the final oral examination for the Ph.D. degree. In 1914 Eliot met and began a close association with the American poet Ezra Pound.

Against the backdrop of World War II, T.S. Eliot (right), with William Butler Yeats, published poems that left the disillusionment of previous works, like The Waste Land, *behind for themes of hope and beauty.* Hulton Archive/Getty Images

"Prufrock" and *The Waste Land*

Eliot was to pursue four careers: editor, dramatist, literary critic, and philosophical poet. He was probably the most erudite poet of his time in the English language. His undergraduate poems were "literary" and conventional. His first important publication, and the first masterpiece of "modernism" in English, was "The Love Song of J. Alfred Prufrock."

> *Let us go then, you and I,*
> *When the evening is spread out against the sky*
> *Like a patient etherized upon a table . . . .*

Although Pound had printed privately a small book, *A lume spento*, as early as 1908, "Prufrock" was the first poem by either of these literary revolutionists to go beyond experiment to achieve perfection. It represented a break with the immediate past as radical as that of Samuel Taylor Coleridge and William Wordsworth in *Lyrical Ballads* (1798). From the appearance of Eliot's first volume, *Prufrock and Other Observations*, in 1917, one may conveniently date the maturity of the 20th-century poetic revolution. The significance of the revolution is still disputed, but the striking similarity to the Romantic revolution of Coleridge and Wordsworth is obvious: Eliot and Pound, like their 18th-century counterparts, set about reforming poetic diction. Whereas Wordsworth thought he was going back to the "real language of men," Eliot struggled to create new verse rhythms based on the rhythms of contemporary speech. He sought a poetic diction that might be spoken by an educated person, being "neither pedantic nor vulgar."

For a year Eliot taught French and Latin at the Highgate School; in 1917 he began his brief career as a bank clerk in Lloyds Bank Ltd. Meanwhile he was also a prolific reviewer and essayist in both literary criticism and technical philosophy. In 1919 he published *Poems*, which contained the poem "Gerontion," a meditative interior monologue in blank verse: nothing like this poem had appeared in English.

With the publication in 1922 of his poem *The Waste Land*, Eliot won an international reputation. *The Waste Land* expresses with great power the disenchantment, disillusionment, and disgust of the period after World War I. In a series of vignettes, loosely linked by the legend of the search for the Grail, it portrays a sterile world of panicky fears and barren lusts, and of human beings waiting for some sign or promise of redemption. The poem's style is highly complex, erudite, and allusive, and the poet provided notes and references to explain the work's many quotations and allusions. This scholarly supplement distracted some readers and critics from perceiving the true originality of the poem, which lay rather in its rendering of the universal human predicament of man desiring salvation, and in its manipulation of language, than in its range of literary references. In his earlier poems Eliot had shown himself to be a master of the poetic phrase. *The Waste Land* showed him to be, in addition, a metrist of great virtuosity, capable of astonishing modulations ranging from the sublime to the conversational.

The Waste Land consists of five sections and proceeds on a principle of "rhetorical discontinuity" that reflects the fragmented experience of the 20th-century sensibility of the great modern cities of the West. Eliot expresses the hopelessness and confusion of purpose of life in the secularized city, the decay of *urbs aeterna* (the "eternal city"). This is the ultimate theme of *The Waste Land*, concretized by the poem's constant rhetorical shifts and its juxtapositions of contrasting styles. But *The Waste Land* is not a simple contrast of the heroic past with the degraded present; it is rather a timeless, simultaneous awareness of moral grandeur and moral evil. The poem's original manuscript of about 800 lines was cut down to 433 at the suggestion of Ezra Pound. *The Waste Land* is not Eliot's greatest poem, though it is his most famous.

Eliot said that the poet-critic must write "programmatic criticism"—that is, criticism that expresses the poet's own interests as a poet, quite different from historical scholarship, which stops at placing the poet in his background. Consciously intended or not, Eliot's criticism created an atmosphere in which his own poetry could be better understood and appreciated than if it had to appear in a literary milieu dominated by the standards of the preceding age. In the essay "Tradition and the Individual Talent," appearing in his first critical volume, *The Sacred Wood* (1920), Eliot asserts that tradition, as used by the poet, is not a mere repetition of the work of the immediate past ("novelty is better than repetition," he said); rather, it comprises the whole of European literature from Homer to the present. The poet writing in English may therefore make his own tradition by using materials from any past period, in any language. This point of view is "programmatic" in the sense that it disposes the reader to accept the revolutionary novelty of Eliot's polyglot quotations and serious parodies of other poets' styles in *The Waste Land*.

Also in *The Sacred Wood*, "Hamlet and His Problems" sets forth Eliot's theory of the objective correlative:

> *The only way of expressing emotion in the form of art is by finding an "objective correlative"; in other words, a set of objects, a situation, a chain of events which shall be the formula for that particular emotion; such that, when the external facts, which must terminate in sensory experience, are given, the emotion is immediately evoked.*

Eliot used the phrase "objective correlative" in the context of his own impersonal theory of poetry; it thus had an immense influence toward correcting the vagueness of late Victorian rhetoric by insisting on a correspondence of word and object. Two other essays, first published the year after *The Sacred Wood*, almost complete the Eliot critical canon: *The Metaphysical Poets* and "Andrew Marvell," published in *Selected Essays, 1917–32* (1932). In these essays he effects a new historical perspective on the hierarchy of English poetry, putting at the top Donne and other Metaphysical poets of the 17th century and lowering poets of the 18th and 19th centuries. Eliot's second famous phrase appears here—"dissociation of sensibility," invented to explain the change that came over English poetry after Donne and Andrew Marvell. This change seems to him to consist in a loss of the union of thought and feeling. The phrase has been attacked, yet the historical fact that gave rise to it cannot be denied, and with the poetry of Eliot and Pound it had a strong influence in reviving interest in certain 17th-century poets.

The first, or programmatic, phase of Eliot's criticism ended with *The Use of Poetry and the Use of Criticism* (1933)—his Charles Eliot Norton lectures at Harvard. Shortly before this his interests had broadened into theology and sociology; three short books, or long essays, were the result: *Thoughts After Lambeth* (1931), *The Idea of a Christian Society* (1939), and *Notes Towards the Definition of Culture* (1948). These book-essays, along with his *Dante* (1929), an indubitable masterpiece, broadened the base of literature into theology and philosophy: whether a work is poetry must be decided by literary standards; whether it is great poetry must be decided by standards higher than the literary.

Eliot's criticism and poetry are so interwoven that it is difficult to discuss them separately. The great essay on

Dante appeared two years after Eliot was confirmed in the Church of England (1927); in that year he also became a British subject. The first long poem after his conversion was *Ash Wednesday* (1930), a religious meditation in a style entirely different from that of any of the earlier poems. *Ash Wednesday* expresses the pangs and the strain involved in the acceptance of religious belief and religious discipline. This and subsequent poems were written in a more relaxed, musical, and meditative style than his earlier works, in which the dramatic element had been stronger than the lyrical. *Ash Wednesday* was not well received in an era that held that poetry, though autonomous, is strictly secular in its outlook; it was misinterpreted by some critics as an expression of personal disillusion.

Later Poetry and Plays

Eliot's masterpiece is *Four Quartets*, which was issued as a book in 1943, though each "quartet" is a complete poem. The first of the quartets, "Burnt Norton," had appeared in the *Collected Poems* of 1936. It is a subtle meditation on the nature of time and its relation to eternity. On the model of this Eliot wrote three more poems, "East Coker" (1940), "The Dry Salvages" (1941), and "Little Gidding" (1942), in which he explored through images of great beauty and haunting power his own past, the past of the human race, and the meaning of human history. Each of the poems was self-subsistent; but when published together they were seen to make up a single work, in which themes and images recurred and were developed in a musical manner and brought to a final resolution. This work made a deep impression on the reading public, and even those who were unable to accept the poems' Christian beliefs recognized the intellectual integrity with which Eliot pursued his high theme, the originality of the form he had devised, and the technical mastery of his verse. This work led

to the award to Eliot, in 1948, of the Nobel Prize for
Literature.

From wrong to wrong the exasperated spirit
Proceeds, unless restored by that refining fire
Where you must move in measure, like a dancer.
The day was breaking. In the disfigured street
He left me, with a kind of valediction,
And faded on the blowing of the horn.

The passage is 72 lines, in modified terza rima; the diction is as near to that of Dante as is possible in English;
and it is a fine example of Eliot's belief that a poet can be
entirely original when he is closest to his models.

Eliot's plays, which begin with *Sweeney Agonistes* (published 1926; first performed in 1934) and end with *The
Elder Statesman* (first performed 1958; published 1959), are,
with the exception of *Murder in the Cathedral* (published
and performed 1935), inferior to the lyric and meditative
poetry. Eliot's belief that even secular drama attracts
people who unconsciously seek a religion led him to put
drama above all other forms of poetry. All his plays are in a
blank verse of his own invention, in which the metrical
effect is not apprehended apart from the sense; thus he
brought "poetic drama" back to the popular stage. *The
Family Reunion* (1939) and *Murder in the Cathedral* are
Christian tragedies, the former a tragedy of revenge, the
latter of the sin of pride. *Murder in the Cathedral* is a modern miracle play on the martyrdom of Thomas Becket.
The most striking feature of this, his most successful play,
was the use of a chorus in the traditional Greek manner to
make apprehensible to common humanity the meaning of
the heroic action.

After World War II, Eliot returned to writing plays
with *The Cocktail Party* in 1949, *The Confidential Clerk* in

1953, and *The Elder Statesman* in 1958. These plays are comedies in which the plots are derived from Greek drama. In them Eliot accepted current theatrical conventions at their most conventional, subduing his style to a conversational level and eschewing the lyrical passages that gave beauty to his earlier plays. Only *The Cocktail Party*, which is based upon the *Alcestis* of Euripides, achieved a popular success. In spite of their obvious theatrical defects and a failure to engage the sympathies of the audience for the characters, these plays succeed in handling moral and religious issues of some complexity while entertaining the audience with farcical plots and some shrewd social satire.

Eliot's career as editor was ancillary to his main interests, but his quarterly review, *The Criterion* (1922–39), was the most distinguished international critical journal of the period. He was a "director," or working editor, of the publishing firm of Faber & Faber Ltd. from the early 1920s until his death, and as such was a generous and discriminating patron of young poets. Eliot rigorously kept his private life in the background.

From the 1920s onward, Eliot's influence as a poet and as a critic—in both Great Britain and the United States—was immense, not least among those establishing the study of English literature as an autonomous academic discipline. He also had his detractors, ranging from avant-garde American poets who believed that he had abandoned the attempt to write about contemporary America to traditional English poets who maintained that he had broken the links between poetry and a large popular audience. During his lifetime, however, his work was the subject of much sympathetic exegesis. Since his death (and coinciding with a wider challenge to the academic study of English literature that his critical precepts did much to establish) interpreters have been markedly more critical, focusing on his complex relationship to his American origins, his elitist cultural and social views, and his exclusivist notions of tradition and of race. Nevertheless, Eliot was unequaled by any other 20th-century poet in the ways in which he commanded the attention of his audience.

Evelyn Waugh

Waugh was born in 1903 and was educated at Lancing College, Sussex, and at Hertford College, Oxford. After short periods as an art student and schoolmaster, he devoted himself to solitary observant travel and to the writing of novels, soon earning a wide reputation for sardonic wit and technical brilliance. During World War II he served in the Royal Marines and the Royal Horse Guards; in 1944 he joined the British military mission to the Yugoslav Partisans. After the war he led a retired life in the west of England.

Waugh's novels are unusually highly wrought and precisely written, and their material is nearly always derived from firsthand experience. Those written before 1939 may be described as satirical. The most noteworthy are *Decline and Fall* (1928), *Vile Bodies* (1930), *Black Mischief* (1932), *A Handful of Dust* (1934), and *Scoop* (1938). A later work in that vein is *The Loved One* (1948), a satire on the morticians' industry in California.

During the war Waugh's writing took a more serious and ambitious turn. In *Brideshead Revisited* (1945) he studied the workings of providence and the recovery of faith among the members of a Roman Catholic landed family. (Waugh was received into the Roman Catholic Church in 1930.) *Helena*, published in 1950, is a novel about the mother of Constantine the Great, in which Waugh re-created one moment in Christian history to assert a particular theological point. In a trilogy—*Men at Arms*

In his novels Evelyn Waugh cast an often satirical eye on British society, cutting the levity with weightier themes as his career progressed. Topical Press Agency/Hulton Archive/Getty Images

(1952), *Officers and Gentlemen* (1955), and *Unconditional Surrender* (1961)—he analyzed the character of World War II, in particular its relationship with the eternal struggle between good and evil and the temporal struggle between civilization and barbarism.

Waugh also wrote travel books; lives of Dante Gabriel Rossetti (1928), Edmund Campion (1935), and Ronald Knox (1959); and the first part of an autobiography, *A Little Learning* (1964). *The Diaries of Evelyn Waugh* was first published in 1976, and a selection of Waugh's letters was published in 1980.

CHAPTER 3

LITERATURE AFTER 1945

Increased attachment to religion most immediately characterized literature after World War II. This was particularly perceptible in authors who had already established themselves before the war. W.H. Auden turned from Marxist politics to Christian commitment, expressed in poems that attractively combine classical form with vernacular relaxedness. Christian belief suffused the verse plays of T.S. Eliot and Christopher Fry. While Graham Greene continued the powerful merging of thriller plots with studies of moral and psychological ambiguity that he had developed through the 1930s, his Roman Catholicism loomed especially large in novels such as *The Heart of the Matter* (1948) and *The End of the Affair* (1951). Evelyn Waugh's *Brideshead Revisited* (1945) and his *Sword of Honour* trilogy (1965; published separately as *Men at Arms* [1952], *Officers and Gentlemen* [1955], and *Unconditional Surrender* [1961]) venerate Roman Catholicism as the repository of values seen as under threat from the advance of democracy. Less-traditional spiritual solace was found in Eastern mysticism by Aldous Huxley and Christopher Isherwood and by Robert Graves, who maintained an impressive output of taut, graceful lyric poetry behind which lay the creed he expressed in *The White Goddess* (1948), a matriarchal mythology revering the female principle.

FICTION

The two most innovatory novelists to begin their careers soon after World War II were also religious believers— William Golding and Muriel Spark. In novels of poetic compactness, they frequently return to the notion of original sin—the idea that, in Golding's words, "man produces evil as a bee produces honey." Concentrating on small communities, Spark and Golding transfigure them into microcosms. Allegory and symbol set wide resonances quivering, so that short books make large statements.

In Golding's first novel, *Lord of the Flies* (1954), schoolboys cast away on a Pacific island during a nuclear war

William Golding, at home in the 1960s. Golding's novels are relatively dark meditations on the nature of evil and humankind's baser instincts. Paul Schutzer/Time & Life Pictures/Getty Images

reenact humanity's fall from grace as their relationships degenerate from innocent camaraderie to totalitarian butchery. In Spark's satiric comedy, similar assumptions and techniques are discernible. Her best-known novel, *The Prime of Miss Jean Brodie* (1961), for example, makes events in a 1930s Edinburgh classroom replicate in miniature the rise of fascism in Europe. In form and atmosphere, *Lord of the Flies* has affinities with George Orwell's examinations of totalitarian nightmare, the fable *Animal Farm* (1945) and the novel *Nineteen Eighty-four* (1949). Spark's astringent portrayal of behaviour in confined little worlds is partly indebted to Dame Ivy Compton-Burnett, who, from the 1920s to the 1970s, produced a remarkable series

Muriel Spark's inherent humour and wit may have made the serious themes and offbeat characters of her novels more palatable to readers. Evening Standard/Hulton Archive/Getty Images

of fierce but decorous novels, written almost entirely in mordantly witty dialogue, that dramatize tyranny and power struggles in secluded late-Victorian households.

The stylized novels of Henry Green, such as *Concluding* (1948) and *Nothing* (1950), also seem to be precursors of the terse, compressed fiction that Spark and Golding brought to such distinction. This kind of fiction, it was argued by Iris Murdoch, a philosopher as well as a novelist, ran antiliberal risks in its preference for allegory, pattern, and symbol over the social capaciousness and realistic rendition of character at which the great 19th-century novels excelled. Murdoch's own fiction, typically engaged with themes of goodness, authenticity, selfishness, and altruism, oscillates between these two modes of writing. *A Severed Head* (1961) is the most incisive and entertaining of her elaborately artificial works. *The Bell* (1958) best achieves the psychological and emotional complexity she found so valuable in classic 19th-century fiction.

While restricting themselves to socially limited canvases, novelists such as Elizabeth Bowen, Elizabeth Taylor, and Barbara Pym continued the tradition of depicting emotional and psychological nuance that Murdoch felt was dangerously neglected in mid-20th-century novels. In contrast to their wry comedies of sense and sensibility and to the packed parables of Golding and Spark was yet another type of fiction, produced by a group of writers who became known as the Angry Young Men. From authors such as John Braine, John Wain (also a notable poet), Alan Sillitoe, Stan Barstow, and David Storey (also a significant dramatist) came a spate of novels often ruggedly autobiographical in origin and near documentary in approach. The predominant subject of these books was social mobility, usually from the northern working class to the southern middle class. Social mobility was also inspected, from an upper-class vantage point, in Anthony Powell's 12-novel sequence *A Dance to the Music of Time* (1951–75), an attempt to apply the French novelist Marcel Proust's mix of irony, melancholy, meditativeness, and social detail to a chronicle of class and cultural shifts in England from World War I to the 1960s.

Satiric watchfulness of social change was also the specialty of Kingsley Amis, whose deriding of the reactionary and pompous in his first novel, *Lucky Jim* (1954), led to his being labeled an Angry Young Man. As Amis grew older, though, his irascibility vehemently swiveled toward left-wing and progressive targets, and he established himself as a Tory satirist in the vein of Waugh or Powell. C.P. Snow's earnest 11-novel sequence, *Strangers and Brothers* (1940–70), about a man's journey from the provincial lower classes to London's "corridors of power," had its admirers.

But the most inspired fictional cavalcade of social and cultural life in 20th-century Britain was Angus Wilson's *No Laughing Matter* (1967), a book that set a triumphant seal on his progress from a writer of acidic short stories to a major novelist whose work unites 19th-century breadth and gusto with 20th-century formal versatility and experiment. The parody and pastiche that Wilson brilliantly deploys in *No Laughing Matter* and the book's fascination with the sources and resources of creativity constitute a rich, imaginative response to what had become a mood of growing self-consciousness in fiction. Thoughtfulness about the form of the novel and relationships between past and present fiction showed itself most stimulatingly in the works—generally campus novels—of the academically based novelists Malcolm Bradbury and David Lodge.

From the late 1960s onward, the outstanding trend in fiction was enthrallment with empire. The first phase of this focused on imperial disillusion and dissolution. In his vast, detailed *Raj Quartet* (*The Jewel in the Crown* [1966],

The Day of the Scorpion [1968], *The Towers of Silence* [1971], and *A Division of the Spoils* [1975]), Paul Scott charted the last years of the British in India. He followed those works with *Staying On* (1977), a poignant comedy about those who remained after independence. Three half-satiric, half-elegiac novels by J.G. Farrell (*Troubles* [1970], *The Siege of Krishnapur* [1973], and *The Singapore Grip* [1978]) likewise spotlighted imperial discomfiture. Then, in the 1980s, postcolonial voices made themselves audible. Salman Rushdie's crowded comic saga about the generation born as Indian independence dawned, *Midnight's Children* (1981), boisterously mingles material from Eastern fable, Hindu myth, Islamic lore, Bombay cinema, cartoon strips, advertising billboards, and Latin American magic realism. (Such eclecticism, sometimes called "postmodern," also showed itself in other kinds of fiction in the 1980s. Julian Barnes's *A History of the World in 10 ½ Chapters* [1989], for example, inventively mixes fact and fantasy, reportage, art criticism, autobiography, parable, and pastiche in its working of fictional variations on the Noah's Ark myth.) For Rushdie, as *Shame* (1983), *The Satanic Verses* (1988), *The Moor's Last Sigh* (1995), and *The Ground Beneath Her Feet* (1999) further demonstrate, stylistic miscellaneousness—a way of writing that exhibits the vitalizing effects of cultural cross-fertilization—is especially suited to conveying postcolonial experience. (*The Satanic Verses* was understood differently in the Islamic world, to the extent that the Iranian leader Ayatollah Ruhollah Khomeini pronounced a fatwa, in effect a death sentence [later suspended], on Rushdie.) However, not all postcolonial authors followed Rushdie's example. Vikram Seth's massive novel about India after independence, *A Suitable Boy* (1993), is a prodigious feat of realism, resembling 19th-century masterpieces in its combination of social breadth and emotional and psychological depth. Nor was India alone in inspiring vigorous postcolonial writing. Timothy Mo's novels report on colonial predicaments in East Asia with a political acumen reminiscent of Joseph Conrad. Particularly notable is *An Insular Possession* (1986), which vividly harks back to the founding of Hong Kong. Kazuo Ishiguro's spare, refined novel *An Artist of the Floating World* (1986) records how a painter's life and work became insidiously coarsened by the imperialistic ethos of 1930s Japan. Novelists such as Buchi Emecheta and Ben Okri wrote of postcolonial Africa, as did V.S. Naipaul in his most ambitious novel, *A Bend in the River* (1979). Naipaul also chronicled aftermaths of empire around the globe and particularly in his native Caribbean. Nearer England, the strife in Northern Ireland provoked fictional response, among which the bleak, graceful novels and short stories of William Trevor and Bernard MacLaverty stand out.

Widening social divides in 1980s Britain were also registered in fiction, sometimes in works that purposefully imitate the Victorian "Condition of England" novel (the best is David Lodge's elegant, ironic *Nice Work* [1988]). The most thoroughgoing of such "Two Nations" panoramas of an England cleft by regional gulfs and gross inequities between rich and poor is Margaret Drabble's *The Radiant Way* (1987). With less documentary substantiality, Martin Amis's novels, angled somewhere between scabrous relish and satiric disgust, offer prose that has the lurid energy of a strobe light playing over vistas of urban sleaze, greed, and debasement. *Money* (1984) is the most effectively focused of his books.

Just as some postcolonial novelists used myth, magic, and fable as a stylistic throwing-off of what they considered the alien supremacy of Anglo-Saxon realistic fiction, so numerous feminist novelists took to Gothic, fairy tale, and fantasy as countereffects to the "patriarchal discourse" of rationality, logic, and linear narrative. The most gifted

Salman Rushdie, photographed while taking part in a radio interview. Rushdie's blend of allegory, melodrama, and postmodern surrealism has both delighted and angered readers. Lionel Bonaventure/AFP/Getty Images

exponent of this kind of writing, which sought immediate access to the realm of the subconscious, was Angela Carter, whose exotic and erotic imagination unrolled most eerily and resplendently in her short-story collection *The Bloody Chamber and Other Stories* (1979). Jeanette Winterson also wrote in this vein. Having distinguished herself earlier in a realistic mode, as did authors such as Drabble and Pat Barker, Doris Lessing published a sequence of science fiction novels about issues of gender and colonialism, *Canopus in Argos: Archives* (1979–83).

Typically, though, fiction in the 1980s and '90s was not futuristic but retrospective. As the end of the century approached, an urge to look back—at starting points, previous eras, fictional prototypes—was widely evident. The historical novel enjoyed an exceptional heyday. One of its outstanding practitioners was Barry Unsworth, the settings of whose works range from the Ottoman Empire (*Pascali's Island* [1980], *The Rage of the Vulture* [1982]) to Venice in its imperial prime and its decadence (*Stone Virgin* [1985]) and northern England in the 14th century (*Morality Play* [1995]). Patrick O'Brian attracted an ardent following with his series of meticulously researched novels about naval life during the Napoleonic era, a 20-book sequence starting with *Master and Commander* (1969) and ending with *Blue at the Mizzen* (1999). Beryl Bainbridge, who began her fiction career as a writer of quirky black comedies about northern provincial life, turned her attention to Victorian and Edwardian misadventures: *The Birthday Boys* (1991) retraces Captain Robert Falcon Scott's doomed expedition to the South Pole; *Every Man for Himself* (1996) accompanies the *Titanic* as it steamed toward disaster; and *Master Georgie* (1998) revisits the Crimean War.

Many novels juxtaposed a present-day narrative with one set in the past. A.S. Byatt's *Possession* (1990) did so with particular intelligence. It also made extensive use of period pastiche, another enthusiasm of novelists toward the end of the 20th century. Adam Thorpe's striking first novel, *Ulverton* (1992), records the 300-year history of a fictional village in the styles of different epochs. Golding's veteran fiction career came to a bravura conclusion with a trilogy whose story is told by an early 19th-century narrator (*To the Ends of the Earth* [1991]; published separately as *Rites of Passage* [1980], *Close Quarters* [1987], and *Fire Down Below* [1989]). In addition to the interest in remote and recent history, a concern with tracing aftereffects became dominatingly present in fiction. Most subtly and powerfully exhibiting this, Ian McEwan—who came to notice in the 1970s as an unnervingly emotionless observer of contemporary decadence—grew into imaginative maturity with novels set largely in Berlin in the 1950s (*The Innocent* [1990]) and in Europe in 1946 (*Black Dogs* [1992]). These novels' scenes set in the 1990s are haunted by what McEwan perceives as the continuing repercussions of World War II. These repercussions are also felt in *Last Orders* (1996), a masterpiece of quiet authenticity by Graham Swift, a novelist who, since his acclaimed *Waterland* (1983), showed himself to be acutely responsive to the atmosphere of retrospect and of concern with the consequences of the past that suffused English fiction as the second millennium neared.

INFLUENTIAL FICTION WRITERS OF THE PERIOD

If empire, social divisions, and history itself loomed large for writers of novels and short stories during the second half of the 20th century, the most influential writers of the period explored these vast issues with finely attuned attention to their local manifestations and their deep influence on individuals.

KINGSLEY AMIS

(b. April 16, 1922, London, Eng.—d. Oct. 22, 1995, London)

Kingsley Amis's first novel, *Lucky Jim*, presented a comic figure that became a household word in Great Britain in the 1950s.

Amis was educated at the City of London School and at St. John's College, Oxford (B.A., 1949). His education was interrupted during World War II by his service as a lieutenant in the Royal Corps of Signals. From 1949 to 1961 he taught at universities in Wales, England, and the United States.

Lucky Jim (1954, film 1957), was an immediate success and remains his most popular work. Its disgruntled antihero, a young university instructor named Jim Dixon,

Kingsley Amis, standing amid row houses in Swansea, Wales. Amis wrote some 20 novels, but none reached the critical and popular acclaim of his first, Lucky Jim. *Slim Aarons/Hulton Archive/Getty Images*

epitomized a newly important social group that had risen by dint of scholarships from lower-middle-class and working-class backgrounds only to find the more comfortable perches still occupied by the well-born. *Lucky Jim* prompted critics to group Amis with the Angry Young Men, who expressed similar social discontent. Amis's next novel, *That Uncertain Feeling* (1955), had a similar antihero. A visit to Portugal resulted in the novel *I Like It Here* (1958), while observations garnered from a teaching stint in the United States were expressed in the novel *One Fat Englishman* (1963).

Amis went on to write more than 40 books, including some 20 novels, many volumes of poetry, and several collections of essays. His apparent lack of sympathy with his characters and his sharply satirical rendering of well-turned dialogue were complemented by his own curmudgeonly public persona. Notable among his later novels were *The Green Man* (1969), *Jake's Thing* (1978), and *The Old Devils* (1986). As a poet, Amis was a representative member of a group sometimes called "The Movement," whose poems began appearing in 1956 in the anthology *New Lines*. Poets belonging to this school wrote understated and disciplined verse that avoided experimentation and grandiose themes. In 1990 Amis was knighted, and his *Memoirs* were published in 1991. His son Martin Amis also became a well-known novelist.

Angry Young Men

The label Angry Young Men is applied to various British novelists and playwrights who emerged in the 1950s and expressed scorn and disaffection with the established sociopolitical order of their country. Their impatience and resentment were especially aroused by what they perceived as the hypocrisy and mediocrity of the upper and middle classes.

The Angry Young Men were a new breed of intellectuals who were mostly of working class or of lower-middle-class origin. Some had been educated at the postwar red-brick universities at the state's expense, though a few were from Oxford. They shared an outspoken irreverence for the British class system, its traditional network of pedigreed families, and the elitist Oxford and Cambridge universities. They showed an equally uninhibited disdain for the drabness of the postwar welfare state, and their writings frequently expressed raw anger and frustration as the postwar reforms failed to meet exalted aspirations for genuine change.

The trend that was evident in John Wain's novel *Hurry on Down* (1953) and in *Lucky Jim* (1954) by Kingsley Amis was crystallized in 1956 in the play *Look Back in Anger*, which became the representative work of the movement. When the Royal Court Theatre's press agent described the play's 26-year-old author John Osborne as an "angry young man," the name was extended to all his contemporaries who expressed rage at the persistence of class distinctions, pride in their lower-class mannerisms, and dislike for anything highbrow or "phoney." When Sir Laurence Olivier played the leading role in Osborne's second play, *The Entertainer* (1957), the Angry Young Men were acknowledged as the dominant literary force of the decade.

Their novels and plays typically feature a rootless, lower-middle or working-class male protagonist who views society with scorn and sardonic humour and may have conflicts with authority but who is nevertheless preoccupied with the quest for upward mobility.

Among the other writers embraced in the term are the novelists John Braine (*Room at the Top*, 1957) and Alan Sillitoe (*Saturday Night and Sunday Morning*, 1958) and the playwrights Bernard Kops (*The Hamlet of Stepney Green*, 1956) and Arnold Wesker (*Chicken Soup with Barley*, 1958). Like that of the Beat movement in the United States, the impetus of the movement was exhausted in the early 1960s.

MARTIN AMIS

(b. Aug. 25, 1949, Oxford, Oxfordshire, Eng.)

Martin Amis is a satirist known for his virtuoso storytelling technique and his dark views of contemporary English society.

As a youth, Amis, the son of Kingsley Amis, thrived literarily on a permissive home atmosphere and a "passionate street life." He graduated from Exeter College, Oxford, in 1971 with first-class honours in English and worked for several years as an editor on such publications as the *Times Literary Supplement* and the *New Statesman.*

Amis's first novel was *The Rachel Papers* (1973), the tale of a young antihero preoccupied with his health, his sex life, and his efforts to get into Oxford. Other novels include *Other People* (1981), *London Fields* (1989), and *Night Train* (1998), as well as *Time's Arrow* (1991), which inverts traditional narrative order to describe the life of a Nazi war criminal from death to birth. In Amis's works, according to one critic, "morality is nudged toward bankruptcy by 'market forces.'" His short-story collection *Einstein's Monsters* (1987) finds stupidity and horror in a world filled with nuclear weapons. The forced-labour camps under Soviet leader Joseph Stalin are the subject of both the nonfiction *Koba the Dread* (2002) and the novel *House of Meetings* (2006). In his novel *The Pregnant Widow* (2010), Amis examined the sexual revolution of the 1970s and its repercussions on a group of friends who lived through it.

Among Amis's volumes of essays are *The Moronic Inferno and Other Visits to America* (1986) and *The War Against Cliché* (2001), both collections of journalism. *Experience* (2000), an autobiography that often focuses on his father, was acclaimed for an emotional depth and profundity that some reviewers had found lacking in his novels.

JULIAN BARNES
(b. Jan. 19, 1946, Leicester, Eng.)

Essayist and short-story writer Julian Barnes is best known for inventive and intellectual novels about obsessed characters curious about the past.

Barnes attended Magdalen College, Oxford (B.A., 1968), and began contributing reviews to the *Times Literary Supplement* in the 1970s while publishing thrillers under his pseudonym Dan Kavanagh. These books—which include *Duffy* (1980), *Fiddle City* (1981), *Putting the Boot In* (1985), and *Going to the Dogs* (1987)—feature a man named Duffy, a bisexual ex-cop turned private detective.

The first novel published under Barnes's own name was the coming-of-age story *Metroland* (1980). Jealous obsession moves the protagonist of *Before She Met Me* (1982) to scrutinize his new wife's past. *Flaubert's Parrot* (1984) is a humorous mixture of biography, fiction, and literary criticism as a scholar becomes obsessed with Flaubert and with the stuffed parrot that Flaubert used as inspiration in writing the short story "Un Coeur simple." Barnes's later novels include *A History of the World in 10 ½ Chapters* (1989), *Talking It Over* (1991), *The Porcupine* (1992), and *Cross Channel* (1996). In the satirical *England, England* (1998), Barnes skewers modern England in his portrayal of a theme park on the Isle of Wight, complete with the royal family, the Tower of London, Robin Hood, and pubs. Critics thought Barnes showed a new depth of emotion in *The Lemon Table* (2004), a collection of short stories in which most of the characters are consumed by thoughts of death. He explored why some people are remembered after their death and others are not in the historical novel *Arthur & George* (2006), in which one of the title characters is based on Sir Arthur Conan Doyle.

Barnes's nonfiction work includes a collection of essays about France and French culture, *Something to Declare* (2002), as well as *The Pedant in the Kitchen* (2003), which explores his love of food. His memoir *Nothing to Be Frightened Of* (2008) is an honest, oftentimes jarringly critical look at his relationship with his parents and older brother.

A.S. BYATT

(b. Aug. 24, 1936, Sheffield, Eng.)

A.S. Byatt is a scholar, literary critic, and novelist known for erudite works whose characters are often academics or artists commenting on the intellectual process.

Byatt is the daughter of a judge and the sister of novelist Margaret Drabble. She was educated at the University of Cambridge, Bryn Mawr College, and the University of Oxford and then taught at University College, London, from 1972 to 1983, when she left to write full-time. Among her critical works are *Degrees of Freedom* (1965), the first full-length study of the British writer Iris Murdoch.

Despite the publication of two novels, *The Shadow of a Sun* (1964) and *The Game* (1967), Byatt continued to be considered mainly a scholar and a critic until the publication of her highly acclaimed *The Virgin in the Garden* (1978). The novel is a complex story set in 1953, at the time of the coronation of Queen Elizabeth II. It was written as the first of a projected tetralogy that would chronicle the lives of three members of one family from the coronation to 1980. The second volume of the series, *Still Life* (1985), concentrates on the art of painting, and it was followed by *Babel Tower* (1995) and *A Whistling Woman* (2002). *Possession* (1990; film 2002), not part of the tetralogy, is part mystery and part romance; in it

Byatt developed two related stories, one set in the 19th and one in the 20th century. Considered a brilliant example of postmodernist fiction, it was a popular success and was awarded the Booker Prize for 1990. *The Biographer's Tale* (2000) is an erudite and occasionally esoteric literary mystery, and *The Children's Book* (2009), following the family of a beloved children's author, incorporates historical figures into a sweeping turn-of-the-20th-century tale. In addition to her novels, Byatt wrote several collections of short stories, including *Sugar and Other Stories* (1987), *The Matisse Stories* (1993), and *Elementals: Stories of Fire and Ice* (1998); *Passions of the Mind* (1991), a collection of essays; and *Angels & Insects* (1991; film 1995), a pair of novellas. She was made a Dame of the British Empire in 1999.

WILLIAM GOLDING

(b. Sept. 19, 1911, St. Columb Minor, near Newquay, Cornwall, Eng.—d. June 19, 1993, Perranarworthal, near Falmouth, Cornwall)

In 1983 William Golding won the Nobel Prize for Literature for his parables of the human condition. He attracted a cult of followers, especially among the youth of the post-World War II generation.

Educated at Marlborough Grammar School, where his father taught, and at Brasenose College, Oxford, Golding graduated in 1935. After working in a settlement house and in small theatre companies, he became a schoolmaster at Bishop Wordsworth's School, Salisbury. He joined the Royal Navy in 1940, took part in the action that saw the sinking of the German battleship *Bismarck,* and commanded a rocket-launching craft during the invasion of France in 1944. After the war he resumed teaching at Bishop Wordsworth's until 1961.

Golding's first published novel was *Lord of the Flies* (1954; film 1963 and 1990), the story of a group of school-boys isolated on a coral island who revert to savagery. Its imaginative and brutal depiction of the rapid and inevitable dissolution of social mores aroused widespread interest. *The Inheritors* (1955), set in the last days of Neanderthal man, is another story of the essential violence and depravity of human nature. The guilt-filled reflections of a naval officer, his ship torpedoed, who faces an agonizing death are the subject of *Pincher Martin* (1956). Two other novels, *Free Fall* (1959) and *The Spire* (1964), also demonstrate Golding's belief that "man produces evil as a bee produces honey." *Darkness Visible* (1979) tells the story of a boy horribly burned in the London blitz during World War II. His later works include *Rites of Passage* (1980), which won the Booker McConnell Prize, and its sequels, *Close Quarters* (1987) and *Fire Down Below* (1989). Golding was knighted in 1988.

DORIS LESSING

(b. Oct. 22, 1919, Kermānshāh, Persia [now Iran])

The novels and short stories of Doris Lessing are largely concerned with people involved in the social and political upheavals of the 20th century. She was awarded the Nobel Prize for Literature in 2007.

Her family was living in Persia at the time of her birth but moved to a farm in Southern Rhodesia (now Zimbabwe), where she lived from age five until she settled in England in 1949. In her early adult years she was an active communist. *In Pursuit of the English* (1960) tells of her initial months in England, and *Going Home* (1957) describes her reaction to Rhodesia on a return visit. In 1994 she published the first volume of an autobiography,

Under My Skin; a second volume, *Walking in the Shade*, appeared in 1997.

Her first published book, *The Grass Is Singing* (1950), is about a white farmer and his wife and their African servant in Rhodesia. Among her most substantial works is the series *Children of Violence* (1952–69), a five-novel sequence that centres on Martha Quest, who grows up in southern Africa and settles in England. *The Golden Notebook* (1962), in which a woman writer attempts to come to terms with the life of her times through her art, is one of the most complex and the most widely read of her novels. *The Memoirs of a Survivor* (1975) is a prophetic fantasy that explores psychological and social breakdown. A

Over the course of six decades, author Doris Lessing, pictured at home in London, has produced work in a number of genres: novels, science fiction, short stories, and autobiography. AFP/Getty Images

master of the short story, Lessing has published several collections, including *The Story of a Non-Marrying Man* (1972) and *Stories* (1978); her African stories are collected in *This Was the Old Chief's Country* (1951) and *The Sun Between Their Feet* (1973).

Lessing turned to science fiction in a five-novel sequence titled *Canopus in Argos: Archives* (1979–83). The novels *The Diary of a Good Neighbour* (1983) and *If the Old Could...* (1984) were published pseudonymously under the name Jane Somers to dramatize the problems of unknown writers. Subsequent novels include *The Good Terrorist* (1985), about a group of revolutionaries in London, and *The Fifth Child* (1988), a horror story, to which *Ben, in the World* (2000) is a sequel. *The Sweetest Dream* (2001) is a semiautobiographical novel set primarily in London during the 1960s, while the parable-like novel *The Cleft* (2007) considers the origins of human society. Her collection of essays *Time Bites* (2004) displays her wide-ranging interests, from women's issues and politics to Sufism.

Ian McEwan

(b. June 21, 1948, Aldershot, Eng.)

Ian McEwan's restrained, refined prose style accentuates the horror of his dark humour and often provocative subject matter.

McEwan graduated with honours from the University of Sussex (B.A., 1970) and studied under Malcolm Bradbury at the University of East Anglia (M.A., 1971). He earned notoriety for his first two short-story collections, *First Love, Last Rites* (1975; filmed 1997) and *In Between the Sheets* (1978), both of which feature a bizarre cast of grotesques in disturbing tales of sexual aberrance, black comedy, and macabre obsession. His first novel, *The Cement Garden* (1978), traces the incestuous decline of a family of orphaned children. *The Comfort of Strangers* (1981; filmed 1990) is a nightmarish novel about an English couple in Venice.

In the 1980s, when McEwan began raising a family, his novels became less insular and sensationalistic and more devoted to family dynamics and political intrigue: *The Child in Time* (1987) examines how a kidnapping affects the parents; *The Innocent* (1990; filmed 1993) concerns international espionage during the Cold War; *Black Dogs* (1992) tells the story of a husband and wife who have lived apart since a honeymoon incident made clear their essential moral antipathy; *The Daydreamer* (1994) explores the imaginary world of a young boy. The social satire *Amsterdam* (1998) won the Booker Prize in 1998. *Atonement* (2001; filmed 2007) traces over six decades the consequences of a lie told in the 1930s. *Saturday* (2005) is a vivid depiction of London on Feb. 15, 2003, a day of mass demonstrations against the incipient war in Iraq. *On Chesil Beach* (2007) describes the awkwardness felt by two virgins on their wedding night. Climate change is the subject of McEwan's satirical novel *Solar* (2010).

McEwan also wrote for television, radio, and film, including *The Imitation Game* (1980), *The Ploughman's Lunch* (1983), *Last Day of Summer* (1984), and *The Good Son* (1993). Several of his screenplays were adapted from his novels and short stories. In 2000 McEwan was awarded the C.B.E. (Commander of the British Empire).

MURIEL SPARK

(b. Feb. 1, 1918, Edinburgh, Scot.—d. April 13, 2006, Florence, Italy)

Muriel Spark is best known for the satire and wit with which the serious themes of her novels are presented.

Spark was educated in Edinburgh and later spent some years in Central Africa; the latter served as the setting for her first volume of short stories, *The Go-Away Bird and*

Other Stories (1958). She returned to Great Britain during World War II and worked for the Foreign Office, writing propaganda. She then served as general secretary of the Poetry Society and editor of *The Poetry Review* (1947–49). She later published a series of critical biographies of literary figures and editions of 19th-century letters, including *Child of Light: A Reassessment of Mary Wollstonecraft Shelley* (1951; rev. ed., *Mary Shelley*, 1987), *John Masefield* (1953), and *The Brontë Letters* (1954). Spark converted to Roman Catholicism in 1954.

Until 1957 Spark published only criticism and poetry. With the publication of *The Comforters* (1957), however, her talent as a novelist—an ability to create disturbing, compelling characters and a disquieting sense of moral ambiguity—was immediately evident. Her third novel, *Memento Mori* (1959), was adapted for the stage in 1964 and for television in 1992. Her best-known novel is probably *The Prime of Miss Jean Brodie* (1961), which centres on a domineering teacher at a girls' school. It also became popular in its stage (1966) and film (1969) versions.

Some critics found Spark's earlier novels minor; some of these works—such as *The Comforters*, *Memento Mori*, *The Ballad of Peckham Rye* (1960), and *The Girls of Slender Means* (1963)—are characterized by humorous and slightly unsettling fantasy. *The Mandelbaum Gate* (1965) marked a departure toward weightier themes, and the novels that followed—*The Driver's Seat* (1970, film 1974), *Not to Disturb* (1971), and *The Abbess of Crewe* (1974)—have a distinctly sinister tone. Among Spark's later novels are *Territorial Rights* (1979), *A Far Cry from Kensington* (1988), *Reality and Dreams* (1996), and *The Finishing School* (2004). Other works include *Collected Poems I* (1967) and *Collected Stories* (1967). *Curriculum Vitae* (1992) is an autobiography. Spark was made Dame Commander of the British Empire in 1993.

POETRY AND NOTABLE POETS

The last flickerings of New Apocalypse poetry—the flamboyant, surreal, and rhetorical style favoured by Dylan Thomas, George Barker, David Gascoyne, and Vernon Watkins—died away soon after World War II. In its place emerged what came to be known with characteristic understatement as The Movement. Poets such as D.J. Enright, Donald Davie, John Wain, Roy Fuller, Robert Conquest, and Elizabeth Jennings produced urbane, formally disciplined verse in an antiromantic vein characterized by irony, understatement, and a sardonic refusal to strike attitudes or make grand claims for the poet's role. The preeminent practitioner of this style was Philip Larkin, who had earlier displayed some of its qualities in two novels: *Jill* (1946) and *A Girl in Winter* (1947). In Larkin's poetry (*The Less Deceived* [1955], *The Whitsun Weddings* [1964], *High Windows* [1974]), a melancholy sense of life's limitations throbs through lines of elegiac elegance. Suffused with acute awareness of mortality and transience, Larkin's poetry is also finely responsive to natural beauty, vistas of which open up even in poems darkened by fear of death or sombre preoccupation with human solitude. John Betjeman, poet laureate from 1972 to 1984, shared both Larkin's intense consciousness of mortality and his gracefully versified nostalgia for 19th- and early 20th-century life.

In contrast to the rueful traditionalism of their work is the poetry of Ted Hughes, who succeeded Betjeman as poet laureate (1984–98). In extraordinarily vigorous verse, beginning with his first collection, *The Hawk in the Rain* (1957), Hughes captured the ferocity, vitality, and splendour of the natural world. In works such as *Crow* (1970), he added a mythic dimension to his fascination with savagery (a fascination also apparent in the poetry Thom Gunn produced through the late 1950s and '60s). Much of Hughes's poetry is rooted in his experiences as a farmer in Yorkshire and Devon (as in his collection *Moortown* [1979]). It also shows a deep receptivity to the way the contemporary world is underlain by strata of history. This realization, along with strong regional roots, is something Hughes had in common with a number of poets writing in the second half of the 20th century. The work of Geoffrey Hill (especially *King Log* [1968], *Mercian Hymns* [1971], *Tenebrae* [1978], and *The Triumph of Love* [1998]) treats Britain as a palimpsest whose superimposed layers of history are uncovered in poems, which are sometimes written in prose. Basil Bunting's *Briggflatts* (1966) celebrates his native Northumbria. The dour poems of R.S. Thomas commemorate a harsh rural Wales of remote hill farms where gnarled, inbred celibates scratch a subsistence from the thin soil.

Britain's industrial regions received attention in poetry too. In collections such as *Terry Street* (1969), Douglas Dunn wrote of working-class life in northeastern England. Tony Harrison, the most arresting English poet to find his voice in the later decades of the 20th century (*The Loiners* [1970], *From the School of Eloquence and Other Poems* [1978], *Continuous* [1981]), came, as he stresses, from a working-class community in industrial Yorkshire. Harrison's social and cultural journey away from that world by means of a grammar school education and a degree in classics provoked responses in him that his poetry conveys with imaginative vehemence and caustic wit: anger at the deprivations and humiliations endured by the working class; guilt over the way his talent had lifted him away from these. Trenchantly combining colloquial ruggedness with classic form, Harrison's poetry—sometimes innovatively written to accompany television films—kept up a fiercely original and socially concerned commentary on such themes as inner-city dereliction (*V* [1985]), the horrors of warfare (*The Gaze of the Gorgon* [1992] and *The Shadow of Hiroshima* [1995]), and the evils of censorship (*The Blasphemers' Banquet* [1989], a verse film partly written in reaction to the fatwa on Salman Rushdie for *The Satanic Verses*).

Also from Yorkshire was Blake Morrison, whose finest work, "The Ballad of the Yorkshire Ripper" (1987), was composed in taut, macabre stanzas thickened with dialect. Morrison's work also displayed a growing development in late 20th-century British poetry: the writing of narrative verse. Although there had been earlier instances of this verse after 1945 (Betjeman's blank-verse autobiography *Summoned by Bells* [1960] proved the most popular), it was in the 1980s and '90s that the form was given renewed prominence by poets such as the Kipling-influenced James Fenton. An especially ambitious exercise in the narrative genre was Craig Raine's *History: The Home Movie* (1994), a huge semifictionalized saga, written in three-line stanzas, chronicling several generations of his and his wife's families. Before this, three books of dazzling virtuosity (*The Onion, Memory* [1978], *A Martian Sends a Postcard Home* [1979], and *Rich* [1984]) established Raine as the founder and most inventive exemplar of what came to be called the Martian school of poetry. The defining characteristic of this school was a poetry rife with startling images, unexpected but audaciously apt similes, and rapid, imaginative tricks of transformation that set the reader looking at the world afresh.

From the late 1960s onward Northern Ireland, convulsed by sectarian violence, was particularly prolific in poetry. From a cluster of significant talents—Michael Longley, Derek Mahon, Medbh McGuckian, Paul Muldoon—Seamus Heaney soon stood out. Born into a Roman Catholic farming family in County Derry, he began by publishing verse—in his collections *Death of a Naturalist* (1966) and *Door into the Dark* (1969)—that combines a tangible, tough, sensuous response to rural and agricultural life, reminiscent of that of Ted Hughes, with meditation about the relationship between the taciturn world of his parents and his own communicative calling as a poet. Since then, in increasingly magisterial books of poetry— *Wintering Out* (1972), *North* (1975), *Field Work* (1979), *Station Island* (1984), *The Haw Lantern* (1987), *Seeing Things* (1991), *The Spirit Level* (1996)—Heaney has become arguably the greatest poet Ireland has produced, eventually winning the Nobel Prize for Literature (1995). Having spent his formative years amid the murderous divisiveness of Ulster, he wrote poetry particularly distinguished by its fruitful bringing together of opposites. Sturdy familiarity with country life goes along with delicate stylistic accomplishment and sophisticated literary allusiveness. Present and past coalesce in Heaney's verses: Iron Age sacrificial victims exhumed from peat bogs resemble tarred-and-feathered victims of the atrocities in contemporary Belfast; elegies for friends and relatives slaughtered during the outrages of the 1970s and '80s are embedded in verses whose imagery and metrical forms derive from Dante. Surveying carnage, vengeance, bigotry, and gentler disjunctions such as that between the unschooled and the cultivated, Heaney made himself the master of a poetry of reconciliations.

The closing years of the 20th century witnessed a remarkable last surge of creativity from Ted Hughes (after his death in 1998, Andrew Motion, a writer of more subdued and subfusc verses, became poet laureate). In *Birthday Letters* (1998), Hughes published a poetic chronicle of his much-speculated-upon relationship with Sylvia Plath, the American poet to whom he was married from 1956 until her suicide in 1963. With *Tales from Ovid* (1997) and his versions of Aeschylus's *Oresteia* (1999) and Euripides' *Alcestis* (1999), he looked back even further. These works—part translation, part transformation—magnificently reenergize classic texts with Hughes's own imaginative powers and preoccupations. Heaney impressively effected a similar feat in his fine translation of *Beowulf* (1999).

JOHN BETJEMAN

(b. Aug. 28, 1906, London, Eng.—d. May 19, 1984, Trebetherick, Cornwall)

John Betjeman became known for poetry that expresses a nostalgia for the near past, an exact sense of place, and a precise rendering of social nuance, which made him widely read in England at a time when much of what he wrote about was rapidly vanishing. The poet, in near-Tennysonian rhythms, satirized lightly the promoters of empty and often destructive "progress" and the foibles of his own comfortable class. As an authority on English architecture and topography, he did much to popularize Victorian and Edwardian building and to protect what remained of it from destruction.

The son of a prosperous businessman, Betjeman grew up in a London suburb, where T.S. Eliot was one of his teachers. He later studied at Marlborough College (a public school) and Magdalen College, Oxford. The years from early childhood until he left Oxford were detailed in *Summoned by Bells* (1960), blank verse interspersed with lyrics.

Betjeman's first book of verse, *Mount Zion,* and his first book on architecture, *Ghastly Good Taste,* appeared in 1933. Churches, railway stations, and other elements of a townscape figure largely in both books. Four more volumes of poetry appeared before the publication of *Collected Poems* (1958). His later collections were *High and Low* (1966), *A*

Nip in the Air (1974), *Church Poems* (1981), and *Uncollected Poems* (1982). Betjemen's celebration of the more settled Britain of yesteryear seemed to touch a responsive chord in a public that was suffering the uprootedness of World War II and its austere aftermath.

Betjeman's prose works include several guidebooks to English counties; *First and Last Loves* (1952), essays on places and buildings; *The English Town in the Last Hundred Years* (1956); and *English Churches* (1964; with Basil Clarke). He was knighted in 1969, and in 1972 he succeeded C. Day-Lewis as poet laureate of England.

SEAMUS HEANEY

(b. April 13, 1939, near Castledàwson, County Londonderry, N. Ire.)

Seamus Heaney's work is notable for its evocation of Irish rural life and events in Irish history as well as for its allusions to Irish myth. He received the Nobel Prize for Literature in 1995.

After graduating from Queen's University, Belfast (B.A., 1961), Heaney taught secondary school for a year and then lectured in colleges and universities in Belfast and Dublin. He became a member of the Field Day Theatre Company in 1980, soon after its founding by playwright Brian Friel and actor Stephen Rea. In 1982 he joined the faculty of Harvard University as visiting professor and, in 1985, became full professor—a post he retained while teaching at the University of Oxford (1989–94).

Heaney's first poetry collection was the prizewinning *Death of a Naturalist* (1966). In this book and *Door into the Dark* (1969), he wrote in a traditional style about a passing way of life—that of domestic rural life in Northern Ireland. In *Wintering Out* (1972) and *North* (1975), he began to encompass such subjects as the violence in Northern Ireland and contemporary Irish experience, though he

260

Seamus Heaney casts a light on contemporary Ireland in his poetry, depicting everything from violence in Northern Ireland to a vanishing pastoral way of life with simple yet powerful verse. Johnny Eggitt/AFP/Getty Images

continued to view his subjects through a mythic and mystical filter. Among the later volumes that reflect Heaney's honed and deceptively simple style are *Field Work* (1979), *Station Island* (1984), *The Haw Lantern* (1987), and *Seeing Things* (1991). *The Spirit Level* (1996) concerns the notion of centredness and balance in both the natural and the spiritual senses. His *Opened Ground: Selected Poems, 1966–1996* was published in 1998. In *Electric Light* (2001) and *District and Circle* (2006), he returned to the Ireland of his youth.

Heaney wrote essays on poetry and on poets such as William Wordsworth, Gerard Manley Hopkins, and Elizabeth Bishop. Some of these essays have appeared in *Preoccupations: Selected Prose, 1968–1978* (1980) and *Finders Keepers: Selected Prose, 1971–2001* (2002). A collection of his lectures at Oxford was published as *The Redress of Poetry* (1995).

Heaney also produced translations, including *The Cure at Troy* (1991), which is Heaney's version of Sophocles' *Philoctetes*, and *The Midnight Verdict* (1993), which contains selections from Ovid's *Metamorphoses* and from *Cúirt an mheán oíche* (*The Midnight Court*), a work by the 18th-century Irish writer Brian Merriman. Heaney's translation of the Old English epic poem *Beowulf* (1999) became an unexpected international best seller, while his *The Burial at Thebes* (2004) gave Sophocles' *Antigone* contemporary relevance.

TED HUGHES

(b. Aug. 16, 1930, Mytholmroyd, Yorkshire, Eng.—d. Oct. 28, 1998, London)

The most characteristic verse of Ted Hughes is without sentimentality, emphasizing the cunning and savagery of animal life in harsh, sometimes disjunctive lines.

At Pembroke College, Cambridge, he found folklore and anthropology of particular interest, a concern that was reflected in a number of his poems. In 1956 he married the American poet Sylvia Plath. The couple moved to the United States in 1957, the year that his first volume of verse, *The Hawk in the Rain,* was published. Other works soon followed, including the highly praised *Lupercal* (1960) and *Selected Poems* (1962, with Thom Gunn, a poet whose work is frequently associated with Hughes's as marking a new turn in English verse).

Hughes stopped writing poetry almost completely for nearly three years following Plath's suicide in 1963 (the couple had separated earlier), but thereafter he published

Britain's former poet laureate Ted Hughes also wrote children's books and made numerous translations. Yet his body of work at times is overshadowed by the suicide of his wife, Sylvia Plath. Evening Standard/Hulton Archive/ Getty Images

prolifically, with volumes of poetry such as *Wodwo* (1967), *Crow* (1970), *Wolfwatching* (1989), and *New Selected Poems, 1957–1994* (1995). In his *Birthday Letters* (1998), he addressed his relationship with Plath after decades of silence.

Hughes wrote many books for children, notably *The Iron Man* (1968; also published as *The Iron Giant*; film 1999). *Remains of Elmet* (1979), in which he recalled the world of his childhood, is one of many publications he created in collaboration with photographers and artists. He translated Georges Schehadé's play *The Story of Vasco* from the original French and shaped it into a libretto. The resulting opera, from which significant portions of his text were cut, premiered in 1974. A play based on Hughes's original libretto was staged in 2009. His works also include an adaptation of Seneca's *Oedipus* (1968), nonfiction (*Winter Pollen*, 1994), and translations. He edited many collections of poetry, such as *The Rattle Bag* (1982, with Seamus Heaney). A collection of his correspondence, edited by Christopher Reid, was released in 2007 as *Letters of Ted Hughes*. In 1984 Hughes was appointed Britain's poet laureate.

Philip Larkin

(b. Aug. 9, 1922, Coventry, Warwickshire, Eng.—d. Dec. 2, 1985, Kingston upon Hull)

Philip Larkin is the most representative and highly regarded of the poets who gave expression to a clipped, antiromantic sensibility prevalent in English verse in the 1950s.

Larkin was educated at the University of Oxford on a scholarship, an experience that provided material for his first novel, *Jill* (1946; rev. ed. 1964). (His first book of poetry, *The North Ship*, was published at his own expense in 1945.) Another novel, *A Girl in Winter*, followed in 1947.

He became well known with *The Less Deceived* (1955), a volume of verse the title of which suggests Larkin's reaction and that of other British writers who then came into notice (e.g., Kingsley Amis and John Wain) against the political enthusiasms of the 1930s and what they saw as the emotional excesses of the poetry of the '40s. His own verse is not without emotion, but it tends to be understated.

Larkin became librarian at the University of Hull in Yorkshire in 1955 and was jazz critic for *The Daily Telegraph* (1961–71), from which occupation were gleaned the essays in *All What Jazz: A Record Diary 1961–68* (1970). *The Whitsun Weddings* (1964) and *High Windows* (1974) are his later volumes of poetry. He edited the *Oxford Book of Twentieth-Century English Verse* (1973). *Required Writing* (1982) is a collection of miscellaneous essays.

DRAMA

Apart from the short-lived attempt by T.S. Eliot and Christopher Fry to bring about a renaissance of verse drama, theatre in the late 1940s and early 1950s was most notable for the continuing supremacy of the well-made play, which focused upon, and mainly attracted as its audience, the comfortable middle class. The most accomplished playwright working within this mode was Terence Rattigan, whose carefully crafted, conventional-looking plays—in particular, *The Winslow Boy* (1946), *The Browning Version* (1948), *The Deep Blue Sea* (1952), and *Separate Tables* (1954)—affectingly disclose desperations, terrors, and emotional forlornness concealed behind reticence and gentility. In 1956 John Osborne's *Look Back in Anger* forcefully signaled the start of a very different dramatic tradition. Taking as its hero a furiously voluble working-class man and replacing staid mannerliness on stage with emotional rawness, sexual candour, and social rancour, *Look Back in Anger* initiated a move toward what critics called "kitchen-sink" drama. Shelagh Delaney (with her one influential play, *A Taste of Honey* [1958]) and Arnold Wesker (especially in his politically and socially engaged trilogy, *Chicken Soup with Barley* [1958], *Roots* [1959], and *I'm Talking About Jerusalem* [1960]) gave further impetus to this movement, as did Osborne in subsequent plays such as *The Entertainer* (1957), his attack on what he saw as the tawdriness of postwar Britain. Also working within this tradition was John Arden, whose dramas employ some of Bertold Brecht's theatrical devices. Arden wrote historical plays (*Serjeant Musgrave's Dance* [1959], *Armstrong's Last Goodnight* [1964]) to advance radical social and political views and in doing so provided a model that several later left-wing dramatists followed.

An alternative reaction against drawing-room naturalism came from the Theatre of the Absurd. Through increasingly minimalist plays—from *Waiting for Godot* (1953) to such stark brevities as his 30-second-long drama, *Breath* (1969)—Samuel Beckett used character pared down to basic existential elements and symbol to reiterate his Stygian view of the human condition (something he also conveyed in similarly gaunt and allegorical novels such as *Molloy* [1951], *Malone Dies* [1958], and *The Unnamable* [1960], all originally written in French). Some of Beckett's themes and techniques are discernible in the drama of Harold Pinter. Characteristically concentrating on two or three people maneuvering for sexual or social superiority in a claustrophobic room, works such as *The Birthday Party* (1958), *The Caretaker* (1960), *The Homecoming* (1965), *No Man's Land* (1975), and *Moonlight* (1993) are potent dramas of menace in which a slightly surreal atmosphere contrasts with and undermines dialogue of tape-recorder authenticity. Joe Orton's anarchic black comedies—*Entertaining Mr.*

Sloane (1964), *Loot* (1967), and *What the Butler Saw* (1969)—put theatrical procedures pioneered by Pinter at the service of outrageous sexual farce (something for which Pinter himself also showed a flair in television plays such as *The Lover* [1963] and later stage works such as *Celebration* [2000]). Orton's taste for dialogue in the epigrammatic style of Oscar Wilde was shared by one of the wittiest dramatists to emerge in the 1960s, Tom Stoppard. In plays from *Rosencrantz and Guildenstern Are Dead* (1966) to later triumphs such as *Arcadia* (1993) and *The Invention of Love* (1997), Stoppard set intellectually challenging concepts ricocheting in scenes glinting with the to-and-fro of polished repartee. The most prolific comic playwright from the 1960s onward was Alan Ayckbourn, whose often virtuoso feats of stagecraft and theatrical ingenuity made him one of Britain's most popular dramatists. Ayckbourn's plays showed an increasing tendency to broach darker themes and were especially scathing (for instance, in *A Small Family Business* [1987]) on the topics of the greed and selfishness that he considered to have been promoted by Thatcherism, the prevailing political philosophy in 1980s Britain.

Irish dramatists other than Beckett also exhibited a propensity for combining comedy with something more sombre. Their most recurrent subject matter during the last decades of the 20th century was small-town provincial life. Brian Friel (*Dancing at Lughnasa* [1990]), Tom Murphy (*Conversations on a Homecoming* [1985]), Billy Roche (*Poor Beast in the Rain* [1990]), Martin McDonagh (*The Beauty Queen of Leenane* [1996]), and Conor McPherson (*The Weir* [1997]) all wrote effectively on this theme.

Playwrights who had much in common with Arden's ideological beliefs and his admiration for Brechtian theatre—Edward Bond, Howard Barker, Howard Brenton—maintained a steady output of parable-like plays dramatizing radical left-wing doctrine. Their scenarios were remarkable for an uncompromising insistence on human cruelty and the oppressiveness and exploitativeness of capitalist class and social structures. In the 1980s agitprop theatre—antiestablishment, feminist, black, and gay—thrived. One of the more-durable talents to emerge from it was Caryl Churchill, whose *Serious Money* (1987) savagely encapsulated the finance frenzy of the 1980s. David Edgar developed into a dramatist of impressive span and depth with plays such as *Destiny* (1976) and *Pentecost* (1994), his masterly response to the collapse of communism and rise of nationalism in eastern Europe. David Hare similarly widened his range with confident accomplishment; in the 1990s he completed a panoramic trilogy surveying the contemporary state of British institutions—the Anglican church (*Racing Demon* [1990]), the police and the judiciary (*Murmuring Judges* [1991]), and the Labour Party (*The Absence of War* [1993]).

Hare also wrote political plays for television, such as *Licking Hitler* (1978) and *Saigon: Year of the Cat* (1983). Trevor Griffiths, author of dialectical stage plays clamorous with debate, put television drama to the same use (*Comedians* [1975] had particular impact). Dennis Potter, best known for his teleplay *The Singing Detective* (1986), deployed a wide battery of the medium's resources, including extravagant fantasy and sequences that sarcastically counterpoint popular music with scenes of brutality, class-based callousness, and sexual rapacity. Potter's works transmit his revulsion, semireligious in nature, at what he saw as widespread hypocrisy, sadism, and injustice in British society. Alan Bennett excelled in both stage and television drama. Bennett's first work for the theatre, *Forty Years On* (1968), was an expansive, mocking, and nostalgic cabaret of cultural and social change in England between and during the two World Wars. His masterpieces, though, are dramatic monologues written for television—*A Woman of No Importance* (1982) and 12 works he called *Talking Heads* (1987) and *Talking Heads 2* (1998). In these television plays, Bennett's comic genius for capturing the rich wayward-ness of everyday speech combines with psychological acuteness, emotional delicacy, and a melancholy con-sciousness of life's transience. The result is a drama, simultaneously hilarious and sad, of exceptional distinc-tion. Bennett's 1991 play, *The Madness of George III*, took his fascination with England's past back to the 1780s and in doing so matched the widespread mood of retrospec-tion with which British literature approached the end of the 20th century.

Theatre of the Absurd

The term Theatre of the Absurd is used to describe dramatic works of certain European and American dramatists of the 1950s and early '60s who agreed with the Existentialist philosopher Albert Camus's assessment, in his essay "The Myth of Sisyphus" (1942), that the human situation is essentially absurd, devoid of purpose. The term is also loosely applied to those dramatists and the production of those works. Though no formal Absurdist movement existed as such, dramatists as diverse as Samuel Beckett, Eugène Ionesco, Jean Genet, Arthur Adamov, Harold Pinter, and a few others shared a pessimistic vision of humanity struggling vainly to find a purpose and to control its fate. Humankind in this view is left feeling hopeless, bewildered, and anxious.

The ideas that inform the plays also dictate their structure. Absurdist playwrights, therefore, did away with most of the logi-cal structures of traditional theatre. There is little dramatic action as conventionally understood; however frantically the characters perform, their busyness serves to underscore the fact that nothing happens to change their existence. In Beckett's

Waiting for Godot (1952), plot is eliminated, and a timeless, circular quality emerges as two lost creatures, usually played as tramps, spend their days waiting—but without any certainty of whom they are waiting for or of whether he, or it, will ever come.

Language in an Absurdist play is often dislocated, full of cliches, puns, repetitions, and non sequiturs. The characters in Ionesco's *The Bald Soprano* (1950) sit and talk, repeating the obvious until it sounds like nonsense, thus revealing the inadequacies of verbal communication. The ridiculous, purposeless behaviour and talk give the plays a sometimes dazzling comic surface, but there is an underlying serious message of metaphysical distress. This reflects the influence of comic tradition drawn from such sources as commedia dell'arte, vaudeville, and music hall combined with such theatre arts as mime and acrobatics. At the same time, the impact of ideas as expressed by the Surrealist, Existentialist, and Expressionist schools and the writings of Franz Kafka is evident.

Originally shocking in its flouting of theatrical convention while popular for its apt expression of the preoccupations of the mid-20th century, the Theatre of the Absurd declined somewhat by the mid-1960s; some of its innovations had been absorbed into the mainstream of theatre even while serving to inspire further experiments. Some of the chief authors of the Absurd have sought new directions in their art, while others continue to work in the same vein.

HAROLD PINTER

(b. Oct. 10, 1930, London, Eng.—d. Dec. 24, 2008, London)

Harold Pinter achieved international renown as one of the most complex and challenging post-World War II dramatists. His plays are noted for their use of understatement, small talk, reticence—and even silence—to convey the substance of a character's thought, which often lies several layers beneath, and contradicts, his speech. In 2005 he won the Nobel Prize for Literature.

The son of a Jewish tailor, Pinter grew up in London's East End in a working-class area. He studied acting at the Royal Academy of Dramatic Art in 1948 but left after two terms to join a repertory company as a professional actor. Pinter toured Ireland and England with various acting companies, appearing under the name David Baron in provincial repertory theatres until 1959. After 1956 he began to write for the stage. *The Room* (first produced 1957) and *The Dumb Waiter* (first produced 1959), his first two plays, are one-act dramas that established the mood of comic menace that was to figure largely in his later works. His first full-length play, *The Birthday Party* (first produced 1958; filmed 1968), puzzled the London audiences and

An economy of dialogue and action, meant to focus attention on a character's ambivalence or alienation, are the hallmarks of plays by Harold Pinter. Jones/Hulton Archive/Getty Images

lasted only a week, but later it was televised and revived successfully on the stage.

After Pinter's radio play *A Slight Ache* (first produced 1959) was adapted for the stage (1961), his reputation was secured by his second full-length play, *The Caretaker* (first produced 1960; filmed 1963), which established him as more than just another practitioner of the then-popular Theatre of the Absurd. His next major play, *The Homecoming* (first produced 1965), helped establish him as the originator of a unique dramatic idiom. Such plays as *Landscape* (first produced 1969), *Silence* (first produced 1969), *Night* (first produced 1969), and *Old Times* (first produced 1971) virtually did away with physical activity on the stage. Pinter's later successes included *No Man's Land* (first produced 1975), *Betrayal* (first produced 1978), *Moonlight* (first produced 1993), and *Celebration* (first produced 2000). From the 1970s on, Pinter did much directing of both his own and others' works.

Pinter's plays are ambivalent in their plots, presentation of characters, and endings, but they are works of undeniable power and originality. They typically begin with a pair of characters whose stereotyped relations and role-playing are disrupted by the entrance of a stranger; the audience sees the psychic stability of the couple break down as their fears, jealousies, hatreds, sexual preoccupations, and loneliness emerge from beneath a screen of bizarre yet commonplace conversation. In *The Caretaker*, for instance, a wheedling, garrulous old tramp comes to live with two neurotic brothers, one of whom underwent electroshock therapy as a mental patient. The tramp's attempts to establish himself in the household upset the precarious balance of the brothers' lives, and they end up evicting him. *The Homecoming* focuses on the return to his London home of a university professor who brings his wife to meet his brothers and father. The woman's presence exposes a tangle of rage and confused sexuality in this all-male household, but in the end she decides to stay with the father and his two sons after having accepted their sexual overtures without protest from her overly detached husband.

Dialogue is of central importance in Pinter's plays and is perhaps the key to his originality. His characters' colloquial ("Pinteresque") speech consists of disjointed and oddly ambivalent conversation that is punctuated by resonant silences. The characters' speech, hesitations, and pauses reveal not only their own alienation and the difficulties they have in communicating but also the many layers of meaning that can be contained in even the most innocuous statements.

In addition to works for the stage, Pinter wrote radio and television dramas and a number of successful motion-picture screenplays. Among the latter are those for three films directed by Joseph Losey, *The Servant* (1963), *Accident* (1967), and *The Go-Between* (1970). He also wrote the screenplays for *The Last Tycoon* (1976), *The French Lieutenant's Woman* (1981), the screen version of his own play *Betrayal* (1983), *The Handmaid's Tale* (1990), and *Sleuth* (2007). Pinter was also a noted poet, and his verse—such as that collected in *War* (2003)—often reflected his political views and involvement in numerous causes. In 2007 Pinter was named a chevalier of the French Legion of Honour.

TERENCE RATTIGAN
(b. June 10, 1911, London, Eng.—d. Nov. 30, 1977, Hamilton, Bermuda)

Terence Rattigan was a master of the well-made play. Educated at Harrow and Trinity College, Oxford, Rattigan had early success with two farces, *French Without Tears* (performed 1936) and *While the Sun Shines* (performed 1943). *The Winslow Boy* (performed 1946), a drama based on a real-life case in which a young boy at the Royal Naval College was unjustly accused of theft, won a New York Critics award. *Separate Tables* (performed 1945), perhaps his best known work, took as its theme the isolation and frustration that result from rigidly imposed social conventions. *Ross* (performed 1960) explored the life of T.E. Lawrence (of Arabia) and was less traditional in its structure. *A Bequest to the Nation* (performed 1970) reviewed the intimate, personal aspects of Lord Nelson's life. The radio play *Cause Célèbre* was his final work; first broadcast in 1975, it was performed onstage in 1977.

Rattigan's works were treated coldly by some critics who saw them as unadventurous and catering to undemanding, middle-class taste. Several of his plays do seriously explore social or psychological themes, however, and his plays consistently demonstrate solid craftsmanship. Rattigan was knighted in 1971 for his services to the theatre. He had many screenplays to his credit, including film versions of *The Winslow Boy* (1948) and *Separate Tables* (1958), among others, and *The Yellow Rolls Royce* (1965) and *Goodbye Mr. Chips* (1968).

TOM STOPPARD

(b. July 3, 1937, Zlín, Czech. [now in Czech Republic])

Tom Stoppard's wide-ranging work is marked by verbal brilliance, ingenious action, and structural dexterity.

Stoppard was born Tomas Straussler. Soon after his birth, he and his family moved to Singapore, where his father had a job. After the Japanese invasion in 1942, his father stayed on (and was killed), but Stoppard's mother and her two sons escaped to India, where in 1946 she married a British officer, Kenneth Stoppard. Soon afterward the family went to live in England. Tom Stoppard (he had assumed his stepfather's surname) quit school and started his career as a journalist in Bristol in 1954. He began to write plays in 1960 after moving to London.

His first play, *A Walk on the Water* (1960), was televised in 1963; the stage version, with some additions and the new title *Enter a Free Man*, reached London in 1968. His play *Rosencrantz and Guildenstern Are Dead* (1964–65) was performed at the Edinburgh Festival in 1966. That same year his only novel, *Lord Malquist & Mr. Moon*, was published. His play was the greater success: it entered the repertory of Britain's National Theatre in 1967 and rapidly became internationally renowned. The irony and brilliance of this work derive from Stoppard's placing two minor characters of Shakespeare's *Hamlet* into the centre of the dramatic action.

A number of successes followed. Among the most notable stage plays were *The Real Inspector Hound* (1968), *Jumpers* (1972), *Travesties* (1974), *Every Good Boy Deserves Favour* (1978), *Night and Day* (1978), *Undiscovered Country* (1980, adapted from a play by Arthur Schnitzler), and *On the Razzle* (1981, adapted from a play by Johann Nestroy). *The Real Thing* (1982), Stoppard's first romantic comedy, deals with art and reality and features a playwright as a protagonist. *Arcadia*, which juxtaposes 19th-century Romanticism and 20th-century chaos theory and is set in a Derbyshire country house, premiered in 1993, and *The Invention of Love*, about A.E. Housman, was first staged in 1997. The trilogy *The Coast of Utopia* (*Voyage*, *Shipwreck*, and *Salvage*), first performed in 2002, explores the lives and debates of a circle of 19th-century Russian émigré intellectuals. *Rock 'n' Roll* (2006) jumps between England and Czechoslovakia during the period 1968–90.

Stoppard wrote a number of radio plays, including *In the Native State* (1991), which was reworked as the stage play *Indian Ink* (1995). He also wrote a number of notable television plays, such as *Professional Foul* (1977). Among his screenplays are *The Romantic Englishwoman* (1975), *Despair* (1978), and *Brazil* (1985). He directed the film version of *Rosencrantz and Guildenstern Are Dead* (1991), for which he also wrote the screenplay. In 1998 the screenplay for *Shakespeare in Love*, cowritten by Stoppard and Marc Norman, won an Academy Award. His numerous other honours include the Japan Art Association's Praemium Imperiale prize for theatre/film (2009). Stoppard was knighted in 1997.

Well-Made Play

A well-made play—called in French *pièce bien faite*—is a type of play, constructed according to certain strict technical principles, that dominated the stages of Europe and the United States for most of the 19th century and continued to exert influence into the 20th.

The technical formula of the well-made play, developed around 1825 by the French playwright Eugène Scribe, called for complex and highly artificial plotting, a build-up of suspense, a climactic scene in which all problems are resolved, and a happy ending. Conventional romantic conflicts were a staple subject of such plays (for example, the problem of a pretty girl who must choose between a wealthy, unscrupulous suitor and a poor but honest young man). Suspense was created by misunderstandings between characters, mistaken identities, secret information (the poor young man is really of noble birth), lost or stolen documents, and similar contrivances. Later critics, such as Émile Zola and George Bernard Shaw, denounced Scribe's work and that of his successor, Victorien Sardou, for exalting the mechanics of playmaking at the expense of honest characterizations and serious content, but both playwrights were enormously popular in their day. Scribe, with the aid of assistants, wrote literally hundreds of plays and librettos that were translated, adapted, and imitated all over Europe.

In England the well-made play was taken up by such practitioners as Wilkie Collins, who summed up the formula succinctly: "Make 'em laugh; make 'em weep; make 'em wait." Henry Arthur Jones and Arthur Pinero used the technique successfully, with somewhat improved characterizations and emotional tension, and Pinero brought it to the level of art with *The Second Mrs. Tanqueray* in 1893. The polished techniques of the well-made play were also turned to serious purposes in the plays of Émile Augier and Alexandre Dumas *fils*, which dealt with social conditions, such as prostitution and the emancipation of women, and are regarded as the precursors of the problem play.

Lillian Hellman and Terence Rattigan are among 20th-century playwrights whose works draw on the principles of the well-made play.

THE 21ST CENTURY

As the 21st century got under way, history remained the outstanding concern of English literature. Although contemporary issues such as global warming and international conflicts (especially the Second Persian Gulf War and its aftermath) received attention, writers were still more disposed to look back. Bennett's play *The History Boys* (filmed 2006) premiered in 2004; it portrayed pupils in a school in the north of England during the 1980s. Although *Cloud Atlas* (2004)—a far-reaching book by David Mitchell, one of the more ambitious novelists to emerge during this period—contained chapters that envisage future eras ravaged by malign technology and climactic and nuclear devastation, it devoted more space to scenes set in the 19th and early 20th centuries.

In doing so, it also displayed another preoccupation of the 21st century's early years: the imitation of earlier literary styles and techniques. There was a marked vogue for pastiche and revisionary Victorian novels (of which Michel Faber's *The Crimson Petal and the White* [2002] was a prominent example). McEwan's *Atonement* (2001) worked masterly variations on the 1930s fictional procedures of authors such as Elizabeth Bowen. In *Saturday* (2005), the model of Virginia Woolf's fictional presentation of a war-shadowed day in London in *Mrs. Dalloway* (1925) stood behind McEwan's vivid depiction of that city on Feb. 15, 2003, a day of mass demonstrations against the impending war in Iraq. Heaney continued to revisit the rural world of his youth in the poetry collections *Electric Light* (2001) and *District and Circle* (2006) while also reexamining and reworking classic texts, a striking instance of which was *The Burial at Thebes* (2004), which infused Sophocles' *Antigone* with contemporary resonances. Although they had entered into a new millennium, writers seemed to find greater imaginative stimulus in the past than in the present and the future.

Zadie Smith

(b. Oct. 27, 1975, London, Eng.)

Zadie Smith is best known for her treatment of race, religion, and cultural identity and for her novels' eccentric characters, savvy humour, and snappy dialogue. She became a sensation in the literary world with the publication of her first novel, *White Teeth*, in 2000.

Smith, the daughter of a Jamaican mother and an English father, changed the spelling of her first name from Sadie to Zadie at age 14. She began writing poems and stories as a child and later studied English literature at the University of Cambridge (B.A., 1998). While there, she began writing *White Teeth*, and at age 21 she submitted some 80 pages to an agent. A bidding war ensued, and the book eventually was sold to Hamish Hamilton. Smith took several more years to complete the novel, and in 2000 it received wide critical acclaim.

Set in the working-class suburb of Willesden in northwest London, *White Teeth* chronicled the lives of best friends Archie Jones, a down-on-his-luck Englishman whose failed suicide attempt opens the novel, and Samad Iqbal, a Bengali Muslim who struggles to fit into British society. Spanning some 50 years, the novel also detailed the trials and tribulations of their families. The ambitious work won numerous awards, including the Whitbread First Novel Award (2000).

Smith's second novel, *The Autograph Man*, was published in 2002. It centred on Alex-Li Tandem, a Chinese Jewish autograph trader who sets out to meet a reclusive 1950s starlet and in the process undertakes his own journey of self-discovery. *The Autograph Man*, which also addressed the public's obsession with celebrity and pop culture, received mostly positive reviews. Soon after the novel's publication, Smith became a fellow at Harvard University's Radcliffe Institute for Advanced Study.

On Beauty, published in 2005, further established Smith as one of the foremost British novelists of her day. The novel, heavily modeled on E.M. Forster's *Howards End*, chronicled the lives of two families in the fictional town of Wellington, Mass., just outside Boston. A comic work studying the culture wars and racial and ethnic overlap in a liberal college town, *On Beauty* was praised for its acumen and scathing satire. The novel won the 2006 Orange Prize for fiction.

Smith also edited and contributed to the short-story collection *The Book of Other People* (2007) and published a collection of essays, *Changing My Mind* (2009).

The Middle Ages witnessed the first emergence of English literature as a vital, dynamic body of poetry and prose that was bound together by common concerns and a slowly coalescing sense of what it meant to be English—or, perhaps, something like "English" during an era when national identity itself was an inchoate, squishy thing. Its earliest practitioners—with Geoffrey Chaucer foremost—began to stake out the boundaries of this new literature, which drew on Latin and Anglo-Norman writings but generated something wholly new. As English literature advanced through the Renaissance, it experienced a luxuriant flowering in the playhouses of London that was most vividly displayed in the plays of William Shakespeare—the most towering figure in English literature, if not all world literatures.

The England of Shakespeare's day was often a jingoistic one, in which national identity—which Shakespeare himself did much to shape—was a vigorous, sometimes destructive force. And yet it was not until the 19th century that England—or, rather, the United Kingdom, that binding together of England, Scotland, and Ireland by way of the Act of Union that took effect in 1801—achieved global dominion via an empire that stretched around the world. English literature of the Victorian era often achieved a similar expansiveness. The sprawling novels of Charles Dickens and George Eliot and the long narrative poems of Robert Browning and Elizabeth Barrett Browning embraced multiple generations and swept across wide swathes of geography.

With the end of the Victorian era, however, came a seeping anxiety that both prepared the ground for and brought about the dissolution of the British Empire. That dissolution was, in some places, achieved peacefully, but in others arrived amidst shattering violence. English literature of the 20th century was itself a literature of pieces, best epitomized by the fragments that are T.S. Eliot's *The Waste Land*. But Eliot himself also epitomized what became an increasingly typical creator of English literature over the course of the century: as an expatriate American, Eliot was a man of multiple identities. His piecework embodiment of nationality would come to be reflected in many other "English" authors.

By the turn of the 21st century, the fragmentation of the body of literary works that might be better called *literature in English*, rather than *English literature*, became its strength: its literary forms exploded and reassembled in vibrant, vivid new ways, its authors combining in themselves a wide variety of national, racial, and personal identities. The 21st century thus might be understood to represent a return to the Middle Ages. It promises to literature in English distant, unseen boundaries much like those faced by Chaucer and his peers that beckon further, intensive exploration.

allegory A symbolic fictional narrative that conveys a meaning not explicitly set forth in the narrative, such as a fable or parable.

Angry Young Men A group of 20th century British writers who lashed out at social and political conventions through their writings.

architectonic Having an organized and unified structure that suggests an architectural design.

black comedy A form of writing that seamlessly combines dark, morbid speech and actions with lighthearted or humorous elements.

capacious Large or flexible enough to contain a great number of items or ideas.

jejune Childish or insignificant.

laissez-faire A philosophy or practice characterized by a usually deliberate abstention from direction or interference especially with individual freedom of choice and action.

mimetic Consisting of imitation.

Modernism A literary movement of the 20th century that saw artists doing away with techniques or devices of the past and experimenting with new forms.

New Woman fiction Used to describe the work of British authors, male and female, in the late 19th century that addressed the role of women in society by showing strong female characters who defied convention and social mores.

pastiche A work of literature that adapts material or styles from a number of different sources to create a unique whole.

pathos An artistic representation that gives rise to feelings of pity or spurs compassion.

picaresque novel A genre of literature that originated in Spain featuring as its protagonist an antihero who lives by his or her wits and is concerned primarily with staying alive.

postmodernism Various literary movements that originated in the second half of the 20th century and have in common a skepticism toward universal notions of truth and meaning.

provincial Marked by narrow-mindedness or ignorance, specifically that considered to be a result of a lack of exposure to cultural or intellectual activity.

realism A 19th-century movement in the arts that sought the accurate, detailed, unembellished depiction of nature or of contemporary life.

Romanticism An artistic movement of the late 18th and early 19th centuries characterized by an emphasis on the individual, the subjective, the irrational, the imaginative, the personal, the spontaneous, the emotional, the visionary, and the transcendental.

satire A literary and dramatic device wherein human vices or shortcomings are ridiculed; sometimes satire is meant to spur social reform.

serialization Literature that is published in consecutive parts.

squib A short, humorous piece of writing that may be used as filler in a longer work.

transcendentalism A system of thought that includes a belief in the unity of all creation, as well as the supremacy of creative inspiration over logic.

BIBLIOGRAPHY

THE POST-ROMANTIC AND VICTORIAN ERAS

Studies of the period include Richard D. Altick, *The English Common Reader*, 2nd ed. (1998); Jerome Hamilton Buckley, *The Victorian Temper: A Study in Literary Culture* (1951, reissued 1981); Walter E. Houghton, *The Victorian Frame of Mind, 1830–1870* (1957, reissued 1985); Virgil Nemoianu, *The Taming of Romanticism: European Literature and the Age of Biedermeier* (1984); Basil Willey, *Nineteenth Century Studies: Coleridge to Matthew Arnold* (1949, reissued 1980); and Philip Davis, *The Victorians* (2002), the last being vol. 8 of the series *Oxford English Literary History*. Studies of special subjects are presented in Isobel Armstrong, *Victorian Poetry: Poetry, Poetics, and Politics* (1993); P.K. Garrett, *The Victorian Multiplot Novel* (1980); George P. Landow, *Elegant Jeremiahs: The Sage from Carlyle to Miller* (1986); George Levine, *The Realistic Imagination* (1981), and *Darwin and the Novelists* (1988); George Rowell, *The Victorian Theatre, 1792–1914*, 2nd ed. (1978); John Sutherland, *The Longman Companion to Victorian Fiction* (1988; also published as *The Stanford Companion to Victorian Fiction*, 1989); and Michael Wheeler, *English Fiction of the Victorian Period, 1830–1890*, 2nd ed. (1994).

THE 20TH CENTURY: FROM 1900 TO 1945

Michael H. Levenson, *A Genealogy of Modernism: A Study of English Literary Doctrine, 1908–1922* (1984), is a meticulously detailed history of the Modernist movement in England. Sandra M. Gilbert and Susan Gubar, *No Man's Land: The Place of the Woman Writer in the Twentieth Century*, 3 vol. (1988–94), a monumental study, has fundamentally altered approaches to British literature. Christopher Gillie, *Movements in English Literature, 1900–1940* (1975), is a straightforward introduction to the fiction, poetry, and drama of the period. Michael H. Levenson (ed.), *The Cambridge Companion to Modernism* (1999), is an excellent collection of lucid and well-informed essays. Vincent Sherry, *The Great War and the Language of Modernism* (2003), analyzes the verbal experiments of Modernist fiction and poetry, including the work of Virginia Woolf and T.S. Eliot. Vincent Sherry (ed.), *The Cambridge Companion to the Literature of the First World War* (2005), provides a valuable survey of the major British writing occasioned by World War I.

Literary historians have largely neglected the 1920s as a decade with a distinctive literature, but David Ayers, *English Literature of the 1920s* (1999), makes an important contribution, while John Lucas, *The Radical Twenties: Writing, Politics, and Culture* (1997), retrieves the long-forgotten radical writing of the decade. Valentine Cunningham, *British Writers of the Thirties* (1988), provides a still-unsurpassed account. Important reevaluations of the 1930s appear in Janet Montefiore, *Men and Women Writers of the 1930s* (1996); and Keith Williams and Steven Matthews (eds.), *Rewriting the Thirties: Modernism and After* (1997). The literature of the World War II period is ably discussed in Robert Hewison, *Under Siege: Literary Life in London, 1939–45*, rev. ed. (1988). Bernard Bergonzi, *Wartime and Aftermath: English Literature and the Background 1939–60* (1993), provides a detailed account of mid-century literature. Adam Piette, *Imagination at War: British Fiction and Poetry, 1939–1945* (1995), discusses a wide range of British poets and novelists with great subtlety and insight.

David Perkins, *A History of Modern Poetry*, 2 vol. (1976–87), is a broad study stressing the interplay between British and American poetry. British poetry of the 20th century has been comprehensively examined in Gary Day and Brian Docherty, *British Poetry 1900–50* (1995), and *British Poetry from the 1950s to the 1990s* (1997).

LITERATURE AFTER 1945

Informative general surveys of fiction, poetry, and drama include the following: Malcolm Bradbury, *The Modern British Novel*, rev. ed. (2001); Michael Gorra, *After Empire* (1997); Allan Massie, *The Novel Today: A Critical Guide to the British Novel, 1970–1989* (1990); D.J. Taylor, *After the War: The Novel and English Society Since 1945* (1993); Martin Booth, *British Poetry 1964 to 1984* (1985); Neil Corcoran, *English Poetry Since 1940* (1993); Sean O'Brien, *The Deregulated Muse* (1995); Anthony Thwaite, *Poetry Today: A Critical Guide to British Poetry, 1960–1992* (1996); James Acheson (ed.), *British and Irish Drama Since 1960* (1993); Susan Rusinko, *British Drama 1950 to the Present* (1989); Michelene Wandor, *Drama Today: A Critical Guide to British Drama, 1970–1990* (1993).

INDEX